The Auditor's Companion

The
Auditor's Companion

Concepts and Terms, from A to Z

David J. O'Regan

GEORGETOWN UNIVERSITY PRESS / WASHINGTON, DC

The publisher is not responsible for third-party websites or their content. URL links were active at time of publication.

Cataloging-in-Publication Data is on file with the Library of Congress.

ISBN 978-1-64712-419-9 (hardcover)
ISBN 978-1-64712-420-5 (paperback)
ISBN 978-1-64712-421-2 (ebook)

Interior Design: Matthew Williams
Jacket Design: Erin Kirk

♾ This paper meets the requirements of ANSI/NISO Z39.48-1992 (Permanence of Paper).

25 24   9 8 7 6 5 4 3 2   First printing

Printed in the United States of America

In memory of
Patrick Eamonn Joseph O'Regan
1935–2020

Ar scáth a chéile a mhaireann na daoine.
(We live in each other's shadows.)

Contents

Acknowledgments

I thank Hilary Claggett, my editor at Georgetown University Press, for her guidance and unwavering support and the Press's anonymous reviewers for their insights and constructive criticisms. I also thank Rachel McCarthy, Alfred Imhoff, and Francys Reed for seeing the book through production. I am also grateful for the comments of Dr. Mark Dooley, and Professors Phillip Ormrod and Michael Power, who read early drafts of some of the entries.

Three decades of involvement in auditing have brought me into contact with many auditors around the world—in private, public, and not-for-profit organizations, and in the academy. The contents of this book represent, in part, a synthesis of countless interactions, experiences, and discussions.

An expression of gratitude does not imply any endorsement of my viewpoints. This book is not the collective product of a committee of consensus, but rather one individual's attempt to capture auditing's evolving concepts and terminology. All opinions and any infelicities are my responsibility alone. I invite readers' comments and criticisms that I may put to constructive use for the accuracy of possible future editions.

Preface

An earlier edition of this reference work was published two decades before this revised edition (O'Regan 2004). Although the first edition broke new ground in its attempt to summarize the lexicon of auditing, it exhibited the typical flaws of a first attempt: occasional clumsiness, the handling of some topics with inadequate circumspection, one or two rash judgments, and perhaps some questionable choices of entries. I have therefore thoroughly revised all entries carried over from the first edition, to reflect developments in auditing terms over the intervening two decades. I have deleted some terms to reflect a declining currency of usage and added about one hundred new entries for emerging terms, from "assurance map" to the rich pool of terms connected to institutional risk assessment.

Two major differences from the previous edition are the elimination of entries for publications, institutions, and individuals, and the expansion of approximately one hundred entries beyond simple definitions to discursive clarifications. The latter include theoretical explications, sketches of arguments, historical developments, quotations from the relevant literature, guidance for further reading, and even humorous anecdotes. I have given an extended treatment to entries ranging from **the audit society** to **judgment** to **logic in auditing**. The addition of these conceptual explorations has altered the nature of the book. It is no longer merely a dictionary—it has become a hybrid reference work and a conceptual companion to auditing. Succinct, dictionary-like definitions of terms and expansive conceptual clarifications are a double helix that lock together into a coherent whole, with the intention of satisfying the needs of both novice and experienced auditors. The title of the book has been changed to *Companion* to reflect this revised approach and the expanded contents. The three appendixes now include landmark legislation and case law, in addition to lists of the abbreviations and non-English words that appear in the text.

Continuity with the first edition is founded on the *Companion*'s overriding aim of providing clarity for the complex and evolving terms of auditing. An authorial voice inevitably remains; the *Companion* conveys an individual's viewpoint, not a creation by committee. In seeking coherence in the large and complex subject matter of a terminology that is in permanent flux, the choice of entries has involved decisions on selectivity, compromise, and compression.

Not even the most zealous auditor or the most conscientious student always consults a reference book out of a sense of duty. When one's nose is not to the grindstone, a meandering exploration of the labyrinth of auditing terms can be a pleasurable means of transcending the stern dictates of work. My intention is for the book's entries to be read as well as consulted, satisfying the reader's curiosity through the text's dense network of cross-references. The cross-references illuminate the interplay of themes in sometimes unpredictable or surprising ways.

Any sophisticated profession should be capable of viewing itself with humor: we laugh at priests, lawyers, and doctors, so why neglect the funny side of auditing? Henri Bergson (1859–1941), the philosopher of humor, considered the moral function of the joke in society to be the overcoming of inflexibilities of character and the promotion of a greater elasticity and sociability in our lives. I have therefore included an entry on **humor in auditing**. It perhaps reflects that auditing has come of age. We should take seriously any profession that can laugh at itself.

There would be no greater pleasure for me than to see auditors treat the *Companion* as a trustworthy friend, with well-thumbed, dog-eared copies on their shelves. In this spirit, I present this book as a means of bringing clarity to the terms of auditing, and of providing a reliable guide to the concepts and language of this fascinating and engrossing activity.

David J. O'Regan
Falls Church, Virginia, January 2024

Introduction

Auditing Terms and Ambiguity

This book aims to bring clarity to the terms of auditing, with the understanding that these terms cover both concepts and the words used to describe them. Anyone familiar with auditing is likely to have encountered a degree of terminological slipperiness. In 1975, for instance, a research report identified at least nineteen synonyms for "operational auditing" (Smith 1975, 1). Although such ambiguities have diminished in recent years, ambivalences stubbornly remain. The persistence of this vagueness derives in part from the large number of disparate activities that self-describe as auditing. But it also originates from auditing's purpose as an evolving, socially constructed activity with normative implications: auditing suggests methods of guiding our actions and evaluating how one ought to behave.

Auditing is flanked on one side by questions of socioeconomic authority and power, and on the other by the universal, abstract, enduring techniques of traditional logic. Logic is discovered, not invented. In contrast, the social purposes of auditing are invented, rather than discovered. This *Companion* aims to embrace auditing's perennial methodologies of reasoning as well as its constantly evolving social purposes.

In opposition to the methods of logical reasoning, the socioeconomic purposes of auditing are not timeless objects to be discovered through abstract enquiry. An interpretation of socially constructed matters therefore inevitably differs from the types of interpretation found in logical reasoning; for social matters, the methods of inquiry, standards of proof, and criteria for effectiveness are often contested and open to differing, sometimes irreconcilable interpretations. As a consequence, there will always be a degree of ambiguity in the concepts and language of auditing, and the most we can realistically aim for is to reduce, rather than eliminate, the level of vagueness. The official narratives of auditing's professional associations seek to define a mainstream discourse (if not a doctrinal rigidity) of terminology, but to seek a univocal meaning for many terms in this book would be pointless.

Auditing terminology *in toto* is rather amorphous, with a solid center yet no discernible circumference. The inclusion of accounting terms in this book illustrates the fuzzy borderlines of the auditing lexicon. Given that financial auditing is the preeminent and most sophisticated branch of modern auditing, and that financial auditors focus on financial statements, it is appropriate that the *Companion* references financial statements. Having included financial statements as a term relevant to (financial) auditing, it also makes sense to include the main elements of financial statements, such as the balance sheet. In turn, the main ingredients of the balance sheet—assets, liabilities, and equity—merit coverage, and so on with the components of assets, liabilities, and equity. It is necessary to draw the line somewhere in the inclusion of accounting terms, especially in view of the *Companion*'s coverage of all types of auditing, but some readers might have taken a more constrained approach to accounting terms.

In addition to the fuzzy extremities of auditing's terminology as a whole, at the level of individual terms one often detects a similar pattern of vagueness, with a solid conceptual core surrounded by rather uncertain boundaries of usage. Notwithstanding such ambiguities, auditing possesses tolerably unified conceptual and semantic fields. Writing this text was by no means comparable to walking an unsafe tightrope of arbitrariness.

Just as surgeons disinfect their scalpels to ensure hygiene for what is to follow in the operating theater, the definition of auditing terms provides us with a strong foundation for what happens in undertaking and thinking about audits. Yet our verbal auditing scalpels can never offer the same precision as the meticulously beveled edges of surgical blades. In acknowledging the ineradicable ambiguity of auditing terms, we should recognize that a little looseness in concepts and language offers advantages, with the equivocality of terms serving as a vehicle for gradual changes in meaning. Ambiguity implies flexibility and a scope for development, perhaps comparable to the manner in which case law evolves over time in common law systems through the flexible use of precedents. The pliability of auditing's terms therefore opens the door to further evolution and creativity.

The Scope and Ambitions of This *Companion*

At this point, you may well ask: if auditing is a socially constructed activity with intractably ambiguous terms, is not this *Companion*'s aim for more clarity a somewhat modest ambition? And if ambiguity is valuable as a source of creativity, is not the relentless search for precision a somewhat counterproductive aim? Why chisel away at a vagueness that cannot be eliminated and whose existence may even be desirable?

Let us consider two responses to such observations. First, the *Companion* has objectives ancillary to the main purpose of reducing ambiguity: it has been designed as a reference tool and as a learning aid to complement study. Second, there are sound, logical grounds for the reduction of ambiguity in terms. The structure of traditional Aristotelian logic is based on three "acts of the intellect": (1) the apprehension of terms, (2) the judgment of propositions, and (3) the reasoning of arguments. The clarification of terms, as the first "act of the intellect," is therefore the foundational stage of traditional logic, upon which methodological thinking and systematic arguments are constructed. The clarification of terms is therefore the basis for cogent reasoning. With only a shaky grasp of terms, our arguments lack reliable premises, and the entire reasoning process is weakened.[1]

Furthermore, in Aristotelian logic the objectives in relation to (1) terms, (2) propositions, and (3) arguments are, respectively, (1) clarity, (2) truth, and (3) validity. Therefore, from the perspective of traditional logic, a dictionary of terms cannot aim for truth or validity, given that truth is found only in propositions and validity only in arguments. The searches for auditing's truth and validity are therefore to be undertaken elsewhere. In seeking clarity in the use of terms, the *Companion* covers the necessary preliminaries to such questions. The ambiguity of auditing terms may be ineradicable, but a reduction of the extent of ambiguity compatible with maintaining a scope for development is a logically defensible aim.[2]

This brief logical excursus reminds us that auditing is not merely an accumulation of wearisome testing. Auditing techniques are founded on the diagnostic skills of inferential reasoning and the detection of patterns in large quantities of often-complex information. Despite usually having no formal training in logic, auditors live and breathe logical reasoning. They feel in their bones that the principles of logic underpin the methodologies of auditing, even if they lack the wherewithal to articulate logical formalities. For this reason, **logic in auditing** is an important entry in the *Companion*; it makes explicit what lies often just below the threshold of consciousness.

Auditing is a sophisticated, fascinating encounter with applied logic. Nonetheless, auditing is far from an infallible logical machine—research has shown that auditors' judgments are often distorted by heuristics and cognitive bias (Maradona 2020), and the risk of poor judgment always hovers over auditing like a menacing cloud.

What Auditing Is

Further to our comments on the ambiguities of auditing terms, it should come as no surprise that a single, satisfactory definition of auditing is elusive. As a perceptive commentator has observed, "It is wiser to speak of a cluster of definitions [of auditing] which overlap but are not identical" (Power 1997, 4).[3] Accordingly, the *Companion*'s entries for **auditing** and **financial auditing** both contain a range of definitions, in addition to the definitions of specialist areas of auditing and related assurance activities. Amid this blizzard of definitions, it is important to search for the attributes of auditing shared by all the specialist categories. As a bare-bones starting point, we may define auditing as *an impartial, evidence-based, judgmental assessment for accountability purposes*. This minimalist definition captures four essential elements of auditing: (1) the auditor's impartiality; (2) the reliance of the audit process on evidence; (3) the judgmental, logico-inferential process at the heart of auditing that leads to opinions rather than guarantees of accuracy; and (4) auditing's role in providing assurance on measurable topics of accountability to parties with divergent interests and asymmetries of information and power.

This definition is purposefully skeletal, and the task of the *Companion* may be understood as adding flesh to this skeleton. The *Companion* therefore addresses many questions that are crucial to refining the concepts of auditing. For example, the concept of auditability is closely linked to the diagnosticity of evidence and in particular the existence of agreed-on, measurable standards for an auditable object. Auditors may audit the levels of sulfur dioxide (SO_2) in the air we breathe. They may audit the accuracy, fair presentation, and reliability of a balance sheet. But, according to our definition, they cannot legitimately audit the aesthetic qualities of a music drama by Richard Wagner. In all these cases they can offer opinions, but only for the SO_2 and the balance sheet are there agreed-on criteria for measurement. Opining on the beauty or otherwise of Wagner's music is the activity of a critic or an aesthete, but it is not the task of an auditor.

The elements of our definition often give rise to debates about their effectiveness in practice. For example, the notion of impartiality is of acute sensitivity for practicing auditors, and the purpose of auditing is a matter of almost continuous debate. The *Companion* also addresses other, related considerations: Is auditing possible under adversarial conditions, or is cooperation essential for auditability? Does intuition have a positive role in auditors' judgments? To what extent is skepticism fundamental to the auditor's critical thinking processes? How does auditing account for the impact of luck, both good and bad, in its sampling techniques? Has the financial auditing profession fully exorcized the ghost of **Enronitis** from the crises and scandals surrounding the collapse in 2002 of the audit firm **Arthur Andersen**? The *Companion* offers contributions related to these and many other considerations.

Auditing Over Time

The fundamental purpose of auditing has a long historical pedigree; some inherent aspect of human affairs seems to demand the surveillance and monitoring of accountability. Since the origins of literate civilization, verification practices recognizable as forms of auditing have existed: "According to earliest Mesopotamian records dating back to 3600 BC, scribes used to prepare summaries of financial transactions. . . . Tiny marks, dots, and circles indicated the painstaking comparison of one record with another. . . . Thus were born two control devices still used around the world: division of duties; provision for the review of another's work" (Sawyer and Vinten 1996, 23). Civil servants in the elaborate bureaucracies of ancient China, India, and Rome used auditing techniques to monitor and report on state finances, and to assess taxation revenues.

In medieval England, many of the parties involved in estate management and the valuation of agricultural production were illiterate. Manorial assessments were therefore usually presented orally to a reeve (i.e., the chief magistrate of a town or district); a verbal dialogue ensued, in which the declared value of agricultural output was queried and clarified. As a consequence, the English word "audit" came into use, derived from the Latin verb *audire* ("to hear"). In modern times, auditing tends to be rigorously documented, but the activity's name still hints back to the medieval era of "audit by ear" (Baxter 1996, 347).

The most sophisticated expression of modern auditing is financial auditing, with its focus on the evaluation of financial statements. This type of auditing first emerged as a professional discipline in the United Kingdom in the nineteenth century, and the context in which it emerged has often been interpreted in terms of agency theory. Information asymmetries arise when the owners of economic resources (the principals) delegate the control of those resources to managers (the agents). Principals seeking a mechanism to monitor agents (and agents seeking to justify their actions to principals) may seek the help of auditors who offer independent advice. Such a situation arose in nineteenth-century England and Scotland, when the large-scale creation of limited liability corporations resulted in an economic system characterized by a separation of the providers of capital from the managers who administered it. To monitor the accountability of the agent–principal problem, financial auditors offered an independent and objective opinion on financial statements, the primary record of managerial stewardship and corporate accountability. In this way the oral manorial audits of medieval England evolved during the Industrial Revolution to the formal examination of written records, the testing of supporting documentation, and the issuance of formal, written opinions. British legislation incrementally expanded the requirements for the auditing of large corporations and "public interest" organizations, such as the railways, and by 1900 virtually all British limited liability companies were required to undergo an annual financial audit.

Two important influences on the development of British financial auditing were the accounting profession and its powerful audit firms. The first institutions of public accounting (from whose ranks financial auditors were drawn) appeared in Scotland in 1854 and in England in 1870. With the establishment of the American Institute of Certified Public Accountants in 1887, financial auditing's professional center of gravity shifted to the United States, where it has since remained. In addition to the role of professional accounting organizations, a striking aspect of financial auditing has been the rise of powerful auditing firms of astonishing longevity. The audit firms of nineteenth-century London were the forerunners of most of today's international, multidisciplinary financial auditing firms. Among the names of London's auditing firms in 1886 were several that have survived, in various combinations, to the modern era—these include Cooper Brothers; Deloitte, Dever, Griffiths; and Price, Waterhouse (Matthews, Anderson, and Edwards 1998, 45).

Along with other professions that emerged during the British Industrial Revolution, financial auditing has struggled to attain the prestige of the erudite, "learned professions": divinity, medicine, and law. Financial auditors nonetheless have created, over nearly two centuries, a powerful and lucrative profession with high barriers to entry. Owing to the stability and immense resources of their professional organizations and major firms, the United States' Certified Public Accountants, British chartered accountants, and their global peers have benefited from almost two centuries of continuous evolution. Financial auditing is the category of auditing with the most established, sophisticated, and stable (albeit contested) conceptual basis and terminology. It is the model that has influenced all subsequent types of auditing.

Perhaps the most significant of the new branches of auditing is internal auditing, in which practitioners tend to be employees of (and often stockholders in) the organizations they audit, unlike financial auditors, who are external to audited organizations. The Institute of Internal Auditors (established in 1941) is the main professional organization for internal auditing; its activities have grown like the topsoil of a forest, by a gradual accumulation over the decades, and at the time of this writing it has more than 200,000 members throughout the world.

Auditing is a protean activity that continues to strive to maintain its relevance to modern society (Lenz and Hoos 2023). It has demonstrated a remarkable adaptivity: the proliferation of new specialisms bears witness to its flexibility and versatility. Among the many types of auditing to have emerged from the shadow of financial and internal auditing are Environmental, Social, and Governance (ESG) auditing; data auditing; intellectual property auditing; royalty auditing; clinical auditing; educational auditing; election auditing; misinformation and disinformation auditing; and many additional categories. Not all self-described types of auditing may satisfy our necessary definitional criteria; for example, an "audit" of alleged misinformation and disinformation in public discourse might not satisfy the criterion of impartiality if its underlying purpose is partisan political censorship. Nonetheless, although some verification and monitoring activities might skirt our definitional criteria, there is no reason to presume that many of the self-described auditing activities are not authentic expressions of modern auditing. Nor are there grounds to consider the auditing that takes place outside the remit of professional organizations to be somehow invalid. The *Companion* was written without any institutional affiliation, and it takes the view that in auditing there is no equivalent of the ecclesiastic exclusivity of *extra ecclesium non est salus* (outside of the Church there exists no salvation). Auditing and its terms are the shared property of all auditors, whether or not they work within the framework of a professional association. No institution holds a monopoly on the auditing lexicon; all auditing practitioners breathe and develop audit terms every day, making and remaking them.

The Social Value of Auditing

Over the centuries, auditing has contributed to civilized living by building bridges of trust between competing social interests and by narrowing gaps between governments and citizens. Environmental auditing reassures the public on steps taken to protect our biodiversity and to reduce pollution. The auditing of financial statements strengthens the orderly conduct of commerce and government by promoting accountability and facilitating the smooth operation of markets. Election auditing sustains public confidence in the fair conduct of democratic processes. In all these ways, auditing protects the social fabric by providing confidence in the reliability of flows of accountability in our institutional and economic arrangements.

If claims of auditing's civilizing mission seem hyperbolic, let us imagine a counterfactual world devoid of auditing, where organizations would publish whimsical financial statements, governments would obfuscate public finances, taxation offices would issue capricious demands, and elections would be conducted without scrutiny. Without the independent, corrective oversight of auditors, "chaotic" would not even begin to describe such a world.

Nonetheless, while acknowledging the role of auditing in promoting the orderly and trustworthy conduct of human affairs in finance, commerce, and government, auditing has often fallen short of its ideals. For a discipline built on the enduring rigors of logic, auditing surprisingly often goes wrong. Cognitive bias, logical fallacies, and generally sloppy thinking lead to misjudgments of evidence, while corruption has on occasion tarnished the reputation of auditors and their profession.

Financial auditing in particular has been prone to periods of intense public disquiet. The demise in 2002 of the audit firm Arthur Andersen led to the reputational nadir of modern financial auditing. It highlighted a long-standing "expectations gap" between public perceptions of fraud detection as the primary purpose of financial auditing, and the insistence of financial auditors that fraud detection is a by-product, not a main objective, of financial auditing. The financial auditor's task of providing impartial opinions on the accuracy and fair presentation of financial statements has had to satisfy an increasing audience of interested parties; the stakeholders of financial statements have grown far beyond simply the owners of capital, and public pressure to ensure the per-formance and integrity of financial auditing remains strong. And stakeholder expectations are growing for all the categories of auditing discussed in the *Companion*.

Notes

1. The importance of conceptual clarification and terminological precision is not limited to Aristotelian logic, nor even more generally to Western logical traditions. A simi-lar emphasis is found globally, such as in the Indian system of Nyāya (Matilal 1998, 120–26; Chakrabarti 1995, passim).
2. Aristotelian logic is "old school" logic. It carries metaphysical baggage and ontologi-cal commitments that we need not accept today, while we may nonetheless recognize its overall reliability for the reasoning process. For example, we have recognized that terms addressing auditing's socioeconomic purposes refer to evolving, socially con-structed concepts rather than essential, unchanging objects. The *Companion*'s entry **logic in auditing** includes a discussion and an example of Aristotelian syllogistic logic.
3. We might also identify clusters of different types of auditing activity, with subclusters of definitions for each cluster of activity. I thank Phillip Ormrod for bringing my atten-tion to this consideration.

User Guide

Entries

Each entry begins with a headword or head phrase in bold type. Many headwords and phrases are followed by additional information in parentheses, including abbreviations, acronyms, and the year of issuance for legislation and regulations. Entries are alphabetized letter by letter, according to the entry's entire heading, ignoring hyphens and gaps in compound words. Therefore, **bankruptcy** appears between **bank reconciliation** and **bank statement**. Where closely related variants of a term exist, both variants are listed in the headword, as in **segregation of duties / segregation of responsibilities**.

The first sentence within an entry provides a concise, basic definition of the term. Additional explanatory narratives provide further information, conceptual explications, and sometimes examples of usage. (The briefer entries are satisfied by a single definitional sentence.) Variants of definitions and meanings are glossed under numerical subheadings; in general, primary meanings are glossed before secondary (or archaic) meanings. Many terms and concepts are located at intersections of the particularistic demands of auditing and more universal characteristics; given the *Companion*'s purpose, terms are treated with a focus on their use in the context of auditing. Lists within entries are set out with lowercase Roman numerals, except for direct quotations that use another listing method.

Spelling Conventions

In general, the dictionary's spelling conventions follow those of American English, unless there is an explicit reference to another version of English. In quotations, spellings have on occasion been Americanized for consistency with the entry as a whole; the endings of some words, for example, have been changed from –ise to –ize. The use of uppercase letters where there are no hard-and-fast rules (e.g., for **Certified Internal Auditor** and **Chartered Accountant**) has been guided by general convention.

Grammar

All headwords are nouns or noun gerunds unless stated otherwise. Verbs and verb phrases are indicated by the word *verb*, and adjectives by the abbreviation *adj*, in square parentheses after headwords. Within an entry, grammatical functions are specified in cases where they involve different meanings. For example, the term **multinational** is glossed as both a noun and an adjective. In such cases, the two grammatical usages are stated in square brackets within the body of the entry.

Italics

Italics are used for the names of publications, legal cases, Internet addresses, and non-English words.

Acronyms

Abbreviations are not generally listed as separate headings in the main body of the text; they are stated instead after the relevant headword or head phrase and are used thereafter within the narrative of the corresponding entry. There is a separate list of abbreviations in appendix A.

Cross-References

Within an entry, bold type denotes a cross-reference to another entry. In the case of a cross-referenced phrase, the entire phrase is in bold. When a cross-reference is to an entry with several glosses, the number of the gloss is specified as **sense 1** or **sense 2**, and so on. The cross-referencing system ignores grammatical variants, so that **fraudulent** cross-references to **fraud**, **decentralized** to **decentralization**, and **risk-averse** to **risk aversion**. The bold type for cross-references appears only with the first appearance of a word within an entry.

Cross-references tend to indicate major connections and interrelations. Nonetheless, they are used relatively extensively in the text, as there are innumerable instances when it is worthwhile to prompt the reader to look elsewhere. To avoid overburdening the text with too many cross-references, some commonly occurring words and phrases are not always cross-referenced; these include **accounting, audit(ing), financial audit(ing), financial statements**, and **internal audit(ing)**, unless they form part of a compound word entry, like **audit shop** or **management accounting**.

Quotations and Examples of Usage

Quotations and examples of usage are given liberally throughout the *Companion*, especially to distinguish alternative glosses on a word. They are placed within quotation marks. An abbreviated bibliographical reference in parentheses after a quotation links to a full description of the source in the references section. Thus, "Power 1997" corresponds to the full format of "Power, Michael. 1997. *The Audit Society: Rituals of Verification*. Oxford: Oxford University Press." Where more than one text is listed for an individual author in a specific year, the publications are numbered with sequential lowercase letters; for example, 1997a and 1997b. Where no reference is given, phrases in quotation marks are illustrative examples of usage devised by the author. An edited quotation uses three points to indicate omissions, while the use of square brackets within a quotation indicates insertions to ease the grammatical flow of the text. Minor changes in spelling are sometimes used for continuity in quotations, especially to Americanize the spellings of some British words. All web addresses were accessed and confirmed as available in January 2024.

Etymologies

The *Companion* does not generally give the etymologies of words, unless they are unusual or add to an understanding of a term; examples include **acid test**, **blue chip**, and **boycott**.

Dictionary: Entries A–Z

abductive reasoning
See **logic in auditing**.

abnormal spoilage
Avoidable waste, **scrap**, or defective items arising from a manufacturing pro-cess. In contrast to **normal spoilage**, abnormal spoilage is not considered to be inherent to a manufacturing process. It is usually expensed as incurred as a cost **variance**.

absorption costing
A costing method that allocates production costs to units of **inventory** or other measures of output. Absorption costing takes account of manufacturing **over-head** costs as well as **direct** (or **variable**) manufacturing costs. Overhead costs are typically allocated to **cost centers** before being absorbed into units of inven-tory at predetermined rates. Nonmanufacturing costs (both fixed and variable) are expensed as incurred rather than absorbed into inventory valuation.

accelerated method
A cost allocation method that provides for larger amounts in earlier time peri-ods. The rationale for the accelerated method is that the economic activity of the underlying assets, liabilities, or circumstances is most intensive in the earli-est time periods. Example: under accelerated **amortization**, the cost of a **long-term** asset is expensed more heavily in the early years of its **useful economic life**, on the grounds that the asset is characterized by rapidly diminishing **effec-tiveness** or **efficiency**, or is subject to a risk of early **obsolescence**. When amor-tized costs are deductible for tax purposes, accelerated methods of depreciation offer accelerated tax benefits. Contrast the **straight-line basis**.

account

1 In accounting, an element of a **general ledger** in which **transactions** are grouped in relation to a category of assets, liabilities, income, or expenditures. Accounts are the recording mechanisms through which the transactions of **double entry bookkeeping** are effected, and they are summarized into a **trial balance** in a step to the preparation of **financial statements**. Some accounts, known as **memorandum accounts**, are maintained separately from the double entry bookkeeping process. See **chart of accounts**. **2** A summary of the financial transactions between two parties. Example: financial transactions between a bank and its customers are normally controlled through individually numbered accounts. Activity in accounts of this nature are normally summarized in formal, periodic statements between the two parties; a **bank statement** is the classic example. **3** A verbal or written report of a topic or event.

accountability

Responsibility for an action, activity, or **process (sense 1)**. Individuals with accountability are usually required to answer for their actions or decisions in their areas of responsibility. Modern **corporate governance** aims at defining organizational accountability and at establishing suitable mechanisms for reporting on its performance. Example: a **board of directors** delivers a large part of its accountability to investors and other **stakeholders** for the stewardship of a corporation through the mechanism of published **financial statements**.

Chains of accountability generally run upward through organizational structures, in contrast to **delegations** of **authority**, which tend to run downward. In the case of a collective responsibility for an activity, it may be difficult to identify the individuals responsible for an activity's outcomes. In such contexts, individuals might seek to evade responsibility by claiming that accountability is diffused among a broad pool of individuals. The practical implementation of accountability is therefore often difficult or contentious in practice, particularly in politically charged contexts. Example: in 1991, a senior French politician claimed "*Je suis responsable mais pas coupable*" ("I'm responsible but not guilty") in relation to a contaminated blood scandal that adversely affected the health of thousands of French citizens and undermined public trust in France's blood supplies in hospitals and clinics. Although the politician was later exonerated through a legal process (suggesting that she was in fact neither responsible nor guilty), the expression "responsible but not guilty" attained an almost folkloric status as a verbal talisman for wielders of power seeking to evade accountability.

Auditing is a mechanism of accountability. Auditing has been described as a means of "securing the accountability of individuals and organisations" in the context of "a duty for one party to perform, to be held accountable for their performance, and to give an account of that performance" (Flint 1988, 3, 24), and it has been claimed that "without audit, no accountability; without accountability, no control; and if there is no control, where is the seat of power? . . . great issues often come to light only because of scrupulous verification of details" (W. J. M. MacKenzie, foreword to Normanton 1966, vii). In **agency theory**, one party (the agent) is accountable to another party (the principal). The risks of an agent acting against a principal's interests are intensified by **asymmetries of information**. In nineteenth-century Britain, the rise of limited liability corporations resulted in a separation of the providers of capital (the principals) from the managers (the agents) who administered it. To monitor the appropriate control and administration of investments, **financial auditors** offered an independent opinion on the accuracy and fair presentation of financial statements, the primary record of managerial stewardship and corporate accountability. Financial auditors are also accountable for the quality of their audits, as manifested in the potential liabilities they face under both criminal and civil law for dishonesty or **negligence** (but not for reasonable errors of **judgment**).

Environmental auditing—like all auditing—is a mechanism of accountability, through its impartial assessments of the impact of an organization's activities on the environment. But environmental auditing is notable for the exceptionally broad spread of interested **stakeholders**, usually construed in the widest possible sense for matters like air pollution and climate change.

accountancy
A British term for **accounting**.

accountant
An individual who performs **accounting** duties. The accountant's responsibilities may overlap to a degree with those of the **bookkeeper**—in terms of the

identification, measurement, and recording of economic transactions—but the accountant's terms of reference tend to be wider than those of the bookkeeper. Among other things, accountants (i) prepare and analyze **financial statements**, (ii) prepare **tax returns**, and (iii) prepare and analyze **budgets**. Most accountants derive their knowledge, expertise, and **authority** from their membership in **professional organizations**, which require examination success, periods of relevant experience, or a combination of both.

accounting

A broad term that encompasses the identification, measurement, recording, and analysis of economic transactions, and their presentation in **financial statements**. Specializations of accounting include **bookkeeping**, **cost accounting**, **management accounting**, and **public accounting**. Regarding the last specialization, **financial auditors** are drawn from public accounting, suggesting a close relationship between the two spheres of activity. However, Mautz differentiates accounting from financial auditing in terms of the orientation of the two activities: "Accounting is . . . primarily constructive; it works from the raw data forward to the finished [financial] statements. Auditing, in contrast, is primarily analytical . . . [the auditor] must work back to determine whether or not the accountant's work has been satisfactory" (Mautz 1954, 2–3). It has also been suggested that financial auditing "has its primary roots in **logic**, not in accounting" and that, in terms of the asymmetrical relationship between accounting and financial auditing, only if auditors have "competence in accounting can [they] have competence as an auditor" (Mautz and Sharaf 1961, 192–93). The twelfth edition of *Montgomery's Auditing* describes this asymmetrical relationship as follows: "An accountant need not be knowledgeable about auditing, but an auditor must be knowledgeable about accounting" (O'Reilly et al. 1998, 1.6).

accounting equation, the

Assets = liabilities + capital. In **double entry bookkeeping**, every accounting transaction has at least one **debit entry** and at least one **credit entry** of equal value. At any moment, the mathematical integrity of bookkeeping can be established by reference to the accuracy of the accounting equation. In the **balance sheet**, assets are recorded through debit entries, and liabilities and capital are recorded through credit entries. While the accounting equation shows that a

trial balance or **balance sheet** balances, it does not indicate whether individual transactions have been allocated to the appropriate **accounts.**

accounting period
A common synonym for **financial reporting period.**

accounting standard
Rules and guidance on accounting practice. Along with legislation and custom, accounting standards form the basis of **Generally Accepted Accounting Principles (GAAP).** Accounting standards cover not only the **recognition (sense 1)**, measurement, and disclosure of **financial statement** items but also the **disclosure** of additional information like **earnings per share** and **executive remuneration.** In the twenty-first century, the term "accounting standard" has been largely superseded by **financial reporting standard**, though it is still in use.

accounts payable
Short-term, invoiced **liabilities** owed to **vendors** for the supply of goods or services. Accounts payable balances are classified as a **current liability** in the **balance sheet.**

accounts receivable
Short-term, invoiced amounts due from **customers** for the sale of goods or services. Accounts receivable are classified as a **current asset** in the **balance sheet.** When their recoverability becomes doubtful, an **allowance for bad debts** is created.

accruals basis / accruals principle
The matching of **income (sense 1)** and **expenditures** to the periods in which they are earned or incurred. In contrast to the **cash basis approach** of **recognizing** income and expenditures in line with the receipt or payment of cash, the accruals basis of accounting is based on the timing of the underlying **transaction.** Example: if interest payable to a bank is incurred evenly over a year, but the payment falls due only at the year end, the accruals basis of accounting requires **recognition (sense 1)** of the interest expense on a monthly basis. Most systems of **Generally Accepted Accounting Principles (GAAP)** require

the accruals basis of accounting. The accruals basis operates through the **bookkeeping** mechanisms of **accrued revenue**, unearned revenue, **accrued expenses**, and **prepaid expenses**. The intentional bending or circumvention of the accruals concept is a common **creative accounting** technique.

accrued asset
An alternative term for accrued revenue.

accrued expense
An unpaid expense incurred and **recognized** in a **financial reporting period** and recorded as a **liability** at the end of that period. In line with the **accruals basis** of accounting, accrued expenses are matched with the accounting periods to which they relate, and they are held in either **current** or **long-term liabilities** until the related cash payment is made. Example: an unpaid, long-term rental cost is expensed over the periods to which it relates, and an appropriate, accumulated balance is recorded in the **balance sheet** until the item is fully settled.

accrued liability
An alternative term for accrued expense.

accrued revenue
Income earned and **recognized** in a **financial reporting period**, for which the related cash has yet to be received. Accrued revenue is recorded as either a **current** or **long-term** asset at the end of the financial reporting period, in line with the **accruals basis** of accounting. Example: revenue on a multiyear contract is recognized in progression with the completion of the contract, and an appropriate, accumulated accrued revenue balance is recorded in the **balance sheet** until the accrued amounts are settled in cash.

acid test
1 The ratio of the most liquid **current assets** to **current liabilities**. The acid test ratio's alternative names include the "liquid ratio" and the "quick ratio." Only the most liquid of current assets are used in the ratio—normally **cash**, cash equivalents (e.g., marketable securities), and accounts receivable. **Inventory** is usually excluded from current assets, owing to the time delay typically required

to convert inventories into cash. **Prepaid expenses** are also typically excluded from liquid current assets in the ratio. **2** Any critically important test. The term "acid test" derives from the use of nitric acid to test for gold; by extension, it has come to refer to the testing of any important activity.

acquisition
1 The purchase of an asset, service, or legal right. **2** The purchase of an organization, or the obtaining of operational or legal control of an organization. In contrast to the generally voluntary nature of **mergers**, acquisitions are often made against the wishes of the **directors** of acquired organizations. Under most forms of **Generally Accepted Accounting Principles (GAAP)**, the accounting treatment of corporate acquisitions normally gives rise to **goodwill**, which is the difference between the **consideration** paid by the acquiring company and the **fair value** of the net assets acquired. Acquired entities are **consolidated** into the **financial statements** of the **parent organization**. In most jurisdictions, significant corporate acquisitions that concentrate market power and potentially reduce **competition** are liable to review by regulatory authorities.

acquisition cost
The purchase **price** of an asset, service, legal right, or organizational entity.

actuary
An individual who undertakes mathematical and statistical analysis of the **risks** and **probability** estimates that underpin **insurance** schemes and **pension plans**. Actuarial estimates are used to determine funding needs, and therefore the levels of participants' contributions and **premiums**, and **disclosure** requirements in financial statements.

added value
An increase in the **quantitative** or **qualitative** worth of an activity, item, or organization. Example of quantitative added value: the increase in the **monetary** worth of a manufactured consumer good as it passes through incremental stages of production. Example of qualitative added value: enhancements to technical procedures in a hospital's surgical theaters arising from the recommendations of a **clinical audit**.

ad hoc [*Latin*]

"Spontaneous" or "one-off." Example: "An *ad hoc* committee was created to address a specific production problem; once the matter was resolved, the committee was disbanded."

adjustment

In **accounting**, a change or modification to an **account**, **transaction**, or **financial statement**. Common reasons for adjustments to accounts are (i) the correction of **errors** and (ii) the **allocation** of revenue and expenditures in line with the **accruals basis** of accounting. Common adjustments to financial statements arise from (i) errors discovered during a financial audit and (ii) the occurrence of **events after the balance sheet date.**

ad valorem [*Latin*]

"In proportion to the value." *Ad valorem* principles are frequently often used as a basis for property **taxes** and **customs** duties.

advance

A **prepayment** toward future, expected expenditures.

adversariality

A state of affairs characterized by disputation, opposition, and even hostility. Auditing is not founded on an adversarial basis. This is reflected in the second of the **postulates of auditing**, developed in the early 1960s by Robert Kuhn Mautz and Hussein A. Sharaf, according to which there is no necessary **conflict of interest** between a **financial auditor** and an **auditee.**

It is instructive to contrast auditing and legal processes to shed light on the relationship of adversariality to both activities. In a criminal trial, in countries with a **common law** tradition, both sides are offered a fair hearing through advocates representing the prosecution and the defense. The search for truth is conducted through an adversarial process of challenge and argumentation, in which the truth is disputed and the outcome is decided by an impartial judge or jury. Under an inquisitorial or confessional system, in which individuals and their defense advocates are pitted against prosecutors who also fulfill the role of judges or magistrates, disputation and argumentation remain the methods of seeking truth. In contrast, an auditor normally works cooperatively with an auditee. An audit is closer to an **examination** than a cross-examination. And an audit is not an **investigation**.

The observations given above here do not suggest that audits are always tension-free. Example: financial auditors and auditees might differ in their opinions on matters like the contents and presentation of **financial statements**, and an auditee may be strongly advised to amend financial statements to avoid a **modified audit opinion**. Nonetheless, it is very difficult to undertake an audit in a hostile or adversarial environment, and auditors are usually acting within their rights to withdraw from an audit if they encounter an uncooperative or hostile attitude, or to report a **scope limitation** on the ability to conduct the audit. In financial auditing, a modified audit opinion may flow directly from inadequate auditee cooperation.

Cooperation between auditor and auditee is therefore central to the concept of **auditability**: "a [financial] audit without the **co-operation** of management becomes virtually an impossibility" (Mautz and Sharaf 1961, 53). The confrontational **inspection** or **verification** of a country's weapons of mass destruction is rarely if ever referred to as an audit (Blix 2004), owing to the imposition of cooperation on a reluctant party: an audit is a cooperative search for **assurance**. Contrast **zero-sum game**.

adverse opinion
A **financial auditor**'s **opinion** that **financial statements** do not conform with **Generally Accepted Accounting Principles (GAAP)** and do not offer a **fair representation** of an organization's financial position, the results of its operations, and changes in cash flows. Under most systems of **Generally Accepted Auditing Standards (GAAS)**, financial auditors are obliged to explain the reasons for an adverse opinion, which applies only to **material** items that could mislead the users of financial statements. An adverse external audit opinion can damage an institution's credibility among its stakeholders and, for this reason, adverse opinions are relatively rare. The pressures on the **directors** of a large corporation to amend financial statements to avoid an adverse opinion are powerful. Compare **disclaimer, qualified opinion**, and **unqualified opinion**.

adverse variance
An alternative term for **unfavorable variance**.

affiliate

1 An organization in which another entity holds a significant but not controlling interest. An affiliate contrasts with a **subsidiary**, as the latter is **consolidated** into the **financial statements** of a controlling **holding company** or **parent organization**. **2** An organization related to another through common control by a parent organization.

agency

1 Possessing the attributes of an **agent**. **2** An organization that performs intermediary services, such as hiring personnel or providing security services.

agency theory

The purported relationship between two parties, a **principal** and an **agent**, in which the former **delegates** authority to the latter. **Agency costs** arise if the goals of principals and agents are not congruent: an agent might be tempted to exploit **asymmetric information** to act in self-interest to the detriment of the principal. Adam Smith, in his *Inquiry into the Nature and Causes of the Wealth of Nations* of 1776, wrote that managers of other people's money will not "watch over it with the same anxious vigilance with which the partners in a private [partnership] frequently watch over their own. . . . Negligence and profusion [of waste and abuse] . . . must always prevail, more or less, in the management of the affairs of such a company" (quoted by Black 2019, 42).

The relationship between a corporation's **investors** and its managers is often described in terms of agency theory, with the investors as principals and the managers as agents. The monitoring of the **accountability** relationship between investors and managers is frequently portrayed as the main purpose of the auditing of **financial statements**; the **financial auditor**'s fee is "the cheapest form of insurance against defaults in the principal–agent relationship in corporate activity" (Lee 1993, 125). The notion of the role of the modern financial auditor as an impartial referee meeting an investor/manager agency need has been challenged by the **critical accounting** movement and some advocates of **stakeholder** theory: financial auditors may be perceived as **rent (sense 2)**— seeking "actors" in corporate governance and financial reporting activities who seek to maximize their self-interest rather than filling the role of impartial "referee" between principals and agents.

agent

An individual who, in **agency theory**, accepts responsibilities to represent or act on behalf of a **principal**.

aging of balances

The stratification of a **balance sheet** amount by either **transaction** or cash **settlement** date. Balances for which aged analyses are prepared typically include **accounts receivable**, **inventory**, and long-term **loans**. Aging is often used for management information purposes (e.g., to assist in establishing **allowances for bad debts**) as well as for financial reporting **disclosure** purposes. Example: an aged analysis of accounts receivable facilitates **credit control** procedures by identifying overdue customer balances.

aid

Assistance in the form of **money**, goods, or services. Government aid to a country's industrial sectors or geographical regions can take the form of **tax breaks**, **grants**, and technical assistance. International aid includes the transfer of resources from **developed** to **developing countries**, which may also take various forms, such as cash transfers, or technical or military assistance.

algorithm

A finite sequence of steps to be followed to solve a problem or to perform a calculation. The term is often applied to computerized problem solving.

Allied Crude Vegetable Oil Refining Corporation case (1963)

A landmark United States criminal case, sometimes referred to as the "Great Salad Oil Swindle," the "Soybean Oil Scandal," or similar variants. Allied Crude's sales exceeded $100 million annually, a significant sum for the 1960s, and the corporation's founder was indicted (along with others) on criminal charges of **fraud.** A notable aspect of the wrongdoings was the deceptive exaggeration of vegetable oil **inventories**. To deceive a bank official, who visited the corporation weekly to perform inventory **spot checks**, Allied Crude's managers undertook a series of tragicomic **misrepresentations**. Examples: (i) the pumping of oil from one tank to another as the bank official walked between the tanks for measurement tests and (ii) the filling of tanks with seawater, topping off the water with a layer of oil to give an impression that the tanks contained only oil (Miller 1965).

The swindle prompted **financial auditors** to enhance the evidential basis for their **opinions** on inventories, including the use of independent, **outside expertise** where appropriate. See the *McKesson and Robbins* **case (1939)** for another legal case that prompted financial auditors to adopt a more rigorous approach to the auditing of inventories.

allocation

The identification of costs or revenues with specific activities, assets, liabilities, or time periods. Examples: (i) the **recognition (sense 1)** of **amortization** expenses over the **useful economic life** of a **fixed asset** and (ii) the identification of production **overhead** with manufactured goods in **absorption costing** methodologies.

The term "allocation" frequently refers to the identification of entire items of expenditures or revenue with a single, discrete activity, asset, liability, or time period. In contrast, the term **apportionment** tends to refer to a dividing of costs and revenues between various items. However, the two terms are often used interchangeably.

allowance for bad debts

A reduction in the value of **accounts receivable** arising from collectability concerns. Allowances for bad debts represent the value of accounts receivable whose ultimate collection is in doubt; the allowance may be for specific accounts receivable balances, or it may be a general allowance based on a percentage of overall accounts receivable. In the latter case, an **aging of balances** allows different allowance rates to be applied on the basis of receivables' different overdue dates. The allowance for bad debts is **offset** against accounts receivable in the **balance sheet**, and movements on the allowance are reflected in the **income statement**.

The creation of the allowance suggests that the corresponding customer balance may ultimately be received. In other words, the receivable is doubtful rather than irrecoverable. Allowances for bad debts are reversed when initially doubtful balances are subsequently collected. Where a receivable is known with certainty to be irrecoverable, the balance is normally eliminated with a **write-off**.

alternative [audit] procedures

Supplementary **audit tests** undertaken when planned audit procedures have been ineffective or inconclusive. Example: financial auditors frequently **circularize** an organization's customers to obtain documentary evidence of the existence and accuracy of **accounts receivable balances**; if the responses to a circularization are disappointing, the auditor may adopt alternative tests to verify the accounts receivable balances, including (i) the tracing of transactions recorded in sales invoices to **inventory**-related documentation and (ii) the matching of receivable balances to subsequent cash **settlements**.

amortization

A cost **allocation** method used to record the reduction in value of a **fixed asset** over time. Example: the historical costs of items of **property, plant, and equipment** are usually amortized over their **useful economic lives**. Assets generally lose value as a result of **wear and tear**, damage, and **obsolescence**, and amortization methodologies are based on the matching of an asset's cost to the periods of time in which the asset generates economic benefits. Some users of the term amortization restrict it to **intangible assets**, in contrast to the use of **depreciation** to refer to **tangible assets**, but in practice many use the term "amortization" for both asset categories.

Amortization accounting can be on a **straight-line** basis, with regular fixed expenses, or on an **accelerated method** basis, in which larger amortization charges occur in earlier time periods. Accelerated amortization is often justified on the grounds of an asset's intensive use in the early years of its life: a **sum-of-the-digits** methodology is sometimes used for this purpose. There are also other, sophisticated amortization accounting methods that attempt to closely match an asset's costs to fluctuations in economic value over its life.

Amortization can be calculated on the full cost of an asset, but the costs of many assets are adjusted to reflect any resale or **residual value**. Example: an asset that costs $110,000 with a useful life of ten years and an estimated residual value of $10,000 could be amortized at a rate of $10,000 a year on a straight-line basis. In many countries, amortization rates are fixed by legislation, but **Generally Accepted Accounting Principles (GAAP)** in most English-speaking countries allow a corporation's managers to base amortization rates on reasonable estimates of assets' useful lives.

analogical reasoning

The proposition that two things displaying some similarities are likely to be similar in other respects. Reasoning by analogy is a form of inductive logic (discussed in the entry **logic in auditing**). Like other types of inductive reasoning, it never proves its conclusions but only illuminates their degree of strength or probability. The approach of analogical reasoning is to enhance knowledge of a poorly understood topic through the comparison of observed patterns associated with another, better-understood topic. It is most successful when the two topics under comparison share relevant characteristics. For example, an environmental auditor may visit a new geographical area and recognize that the symptoms of health problems occurring in local individuals resemble the symptoms among other populations previously confirmed as suffering from high levels of air pollution. The auditor may therefore infer, by analogy, and before detailed confirmatory testing, that the newly encountered individuals' symptoms probably indicate the presence of severe air pollution.

In financial auditing, a common example of analogical reasoning is the notion that an organization's level of rigor in its **internal control** arrangements over matters that lack **material** significance, like **petty cash**, might reflect the degree of rigor in the wider internal control environment. This way of reasoning equates a close attention to detail for low-level, **housekeeping** internal controls to a comparably close attention to detail for more significant topics. This line of analogical reasoning may go as follows: "If ABC Corporation can't be bothered to control its petty cash properly, its controls over more significant matters are likely to be sloppy." Connections between attention to small things and attention to more important matters can be found in traditional wisdom, expressed, for example, in the New Testament ("Whoever can be trusted with small things can also be trusted with big things, and whoever is dishonest in little things will also be dishonest in big things"; Luke 16:10) and by Plato ("All theft of public property, great or small, should attract the same punishment; for he that steals a small thing steals just like any other thief"; *Laws XII*, 941c). However, this line of reasoning is prone to error if unsupported by corroborating evidence. Compare **slippery slope reasoning**.

Analogical reasoning in auditing may offer insights and useful comparisons, in the manner (to use an analogy!) that the sketching of a map may provide a useful representation of a landscape, but in auditing it is not generally considered a reliable approach to **logic** and reasoning in the **judgment** of audit **evidence**. Nonetheless, as with **intuitive** reasoning, analogical reasoning may tap into an auditor's experience and knowledge and thereby generate valuable insights. It would therefore be unwise to dismiss analogical reasoning entirely from the auditor's intellectual tool kit.

analytical review

A financial auditing technique that focuses on the analysis of movements in individual or aggregated **account** balances over time. In assessing the **reasonableness** of financial statement items, an analytical review typically focuses on changes and trends in major balances and ratios. It also typically includes assessments of interrelationships between items in financial statements. Example: a doubling of an organization's revenues from one **financial reporting period** to the next would suggest (all other things being equal) that the level of **accounts receivable** would increase significantly between the two **balance sheet** dates. If the accounts receivable balances did not follow the trend of revenues, an analytical review might highlight this apparent inconsistency as an area for further analysis; one explanation for the discrepancy might relate to the timing of revenues in relation to the balance sheet date. The analytical review of financial statements may also comprise comparisons with the financial data of similar organizations. Example: an industry average of payroll cost per employee is a common **yardstick** for assessing the reasonableness of payroll costs.

Analytical review procedures are intended to highlight potential, **material** misstatements in financial statements or the underlying accounting records. As a high-level audit technique, an analytical review usually raises (rather than answers) questions, and therefore tends to be a means of identifying areas for further review. For this reason, an analytical review is often a key element of the **audit planning** processes, though it is considered a **substantive test** in its own right.

anchoring and adjustment bias

A cognitive shortcut or heuristic **bias** in which an interpretation of initial information unduly influences the interpretation of subsequent information.

The initial information is perceived as a metaphorical anchor that distorts judgment (Kahneman 2011, 119–28). In auditing, research has indicated that anchoring and adjustment bias is an impediment to the integrity of **evidence-based** reasoning (e.g., Henrizi, Himmelsbach, and Hunziker 2020). Anchoring and adjustment bias may be seen as a psychological heuristic that leads to fallacies in **logical** reasoning. See also **availability bias**, **recency bias**, and **intuition**.

annualization

The (re)statement of an item to reflect a twelve-month period. Annualization is common in financial planning and taxation calculations, which frequently **extrapolate** costs and revenues to cover a full **fiscal year**. Annualization calculations are normally performed on a simple, straight-line basis when costs or income are deemed to accrue evenly. Example: if an expense of $10,000 occurs in one month, it may be annualized to $120,000 simply by multiplying $10,000 by 12. Compare **calendarization**.

annuity

Periodic payments of a constant or **indexed** amount that continue until a specified date. Compare **perpetuity**.

antitrust laws

Legislation that encourages **competitive** markets. Antitrust laws are intended to combat the activities of **monopolies**, **oligopolies**, and **cartels**. Antitrust legislation originated in the United States: the *Sherman Anti-Trust Act* of 1890 made monopolies or the restraint of trade illegal. The 1890 *Act* reflected growing public opinion in the late nineteenth century that legislation could be used to control the imperfections of **free market** economies. (The term "antitrust" was adopted from the use of the term "trust" for monopoly in the nineteenth century.) Other landmark US antitrust laws include the *Clayton Act* of 1914, the *Robinson-Patman Act* of 1936, and the *Celler-Kefauver Act* of 1950. Antitrust laws have spread around the world. Example: the concept has been introduced in Italy, where the term "antitrust" has been directly adopted from English into the Italian language.

application control

A control over an aspect of a computer program. Application controls are designed to ensure the accuracy and completeness of data. They are usually programmed but they may be manual. Examples: validations of data input with the verification of batch totals. Auditors test the correct functioning of application controls through the use of representative **test data**.

apportionment

See **allocation**.

appraisal

1 The **quantitative** evaluation of an investment (or potential investment), or of an asset or liability. Appraisals are central to decision-making processes: a **due diligence** appraisal process, for example, usually proceeds a corporate **acquisition**.
2 An evaluation (**qualitative** or **quantitative**) of an activity, control, procedure, or employee. Examples: (i) many manufacturing operations have product appraisal procedures embedded in their **quality control** processes; and (ii) employee performance appraisals form part of most modern personnel practices.

appreciation

1 An increase in the value of an asset. Most systems of **Generally Accepted Accounting Principles (GAAP)** set out strict rules for the **recognition (sense 1)** in financial statements of the amounts by which assets—typically land, property, and **securities**—may appreciate. Contrast **depreciation (sense 2)**. **2** An increase in the value of a **currency** in relation to other, competing currencies.

appropriateness [of audit evidence]

Relevance and reliability.

appropriation

1 The allocation of funds to a budget. **2** The removal of an **asset** for one's own use, typically without seeking permission to do so. In this use, the term is a synonym for **misappropriation**.

approval
1 An alternative term for **authorization**. **2** Acceptance. In commerce, goods
sent to a customer "on approval" are sent for examination without an obligation
to purchase.

arbitrage
The exploitation of price differentials for an **asset** traded in two or more **markets**. A benefit often claimed of arbitrage is its role in bringing about price equilibrium. Example: the opportunities given to consumers in the European Union
to purchase goods throughout Europe have tended to narrow price differentials
for many consumer goods between individual European countries. Prices are
known with certainty in arbitrage, and it is therefore a less **risky** activity than
speculation; it may, on occasion, be entirely risk-free. Assets typically subjected
to arbitrage include **currencies** and **commodities**.

arbitration
A quasi-judicial recourse to an independent individual or organization to settle
a dispute between two or more parties. Arbitration is often used to settle commercial, labor, and political disputes, and it is an alternative to civil law proceed-
ings. Arbitration has a long history and was used extensively in classical Rome.
Arbitration decisions can be either binding or nonbinding, depending on the
terms of reference agreed on by the parties.

arithmetic progression
A sequential pattern of numbers with differences of equal size between consecutive numbers. An example is 1, 3, 5, 7, and so on. Contrast **geometric
progression**.

arm's-length transaction
A **transaction** at **market value** undertaken between unrelated parties or
undertaken as though between unrelated parties. A transaction of this nature
is conducted on the assumption that both parties seek to maximize their best
interests, without any distortion arising from favoritism or price discounting.
Example: "All **intercompany** sales between the corporation's overseas branches
are made at arm's length."

[in] arrears [*Adj.*]
The state of being overdue.

Arthur Andersen (AA)
A former member of the **Big Five** accounting and **financial audit** firms. Arthur Andersen imploded in 2002 after a notorious case of accounting fraud at one of its major clients, Enron Corporation, which was exacerbated by further scandals at some of its other clients, notably WorldCom. After its demise, Arthur Andersen's name became synonymous with corporate fraud, and it became a symbol of the collapse of public confidence in financial auditing that was central to the concept of **Enronitis.**

Arthur Andersen was founded in Chicago in 1913 as Andersen, DeLany & Company. It was the only member of the Big Five firms at the close of the twentieth century to have a purely American origin. The firm adopted the name Arthur Andersen in 1928. It enjoyed incredible growth, success, and prestige until the years immediately preceding its collapse. Ironically, given the circumstances of its demise, Arthur Andersen was noted for its principled stand on the correctness of accounting methodology, even at the risk of losing clients (Spacek 1989). The firm was also famous for the sophistication of its **consulting** and **management advisory services.** In contrast to the rather faceless character of its competitor firms, the Arthur Andersen culture was perceived as uniquely differentiated: the firm's ethos was reinforced by a strong internal training program that inculcated intense organizational loyalty and, perhaps, a large degree of conformity. Skeptical or envious outsiders referred, tongue-in-cheek, to Arthur Andersen employees as "Androids," owing to the stereotype of the earnest, brash, starched-collared product of the firm's collective culture.

After decades of phenomenal growth, the last few years of the firm were troubled ones, and its once-proud image became increasingly tarnished. First, a power struggle led to a bitter divorce between the firm's profitable consulting division and the auditing-driven remainder of the business, played out in full media glare; the result was the independence in 2000 of Andersen Consulting, later renamed as Accenture. More serious, and fatal, were allegations of a corrosion of values at the audit firm's heart. From its status as "a great and venerable American institution" and "a global symbol of strength and solidity," with over 80,000 employees worldwide, Arthur Andersen was accused of placing fee maximization ahead of **professional** integrity, to the extent that some of its auditing employees allegedly "forgot that the true purpose of their job was to protect the investing public" (Toffler and Reingold 2003, 7). In June 2002, a federal grand jury found Arthur Andersen guilty of obstructing justice in official investigations of Enron Corporation. The firm's shredding of thousands of Enron-related audit documents played a major part in the jury's decision-making process. Although the Supreme Court later overturned the firm's conviction for obstruction of justice, the destruction of audit **evidence** seriously undermined the firm's reputation, and the firm became the target of public ridicule. The president of the United States at the time is reported to have joked (in relation to weapons inspections before the second Gulf War of 2003): "The good news is that [Saddam Hussein is] willing to have his nuclear, biological, and chemical weapons counted. The bad news is he wants Arthur Andersen to do it" (quoted by Fox 2003, 294).

The questions raised over Arthur Andersen's fall from grace reflected a more general malaise in the financial auditing profession in the early twenty-first century (Gendron and Spira 2009). The Enron and Arthur Andersen scandals prompted legislators to pass the *Sarbanes-Oxley Act* **(SOX)** in 2002, in an attempt to reform **corporate governance** and thereby restore investor confidence.

articles of incorporation
Legal documents required for the establishment of a corporation. The articles form part of a corporation's charter and set out its mission and range of activities.

assertions
Explicit and implicit representations of items in **financial statements**. A **financial audit** may be understood as an assessment of the assertions underpinning financial statements, in line with **Generally Accepted Accounting Principles (GAAP)**. A common model uses six assertions of information in financial statements, summarized in the mnemonic acronym CEAVOP: completeness, existence/occurrence, accuracy, valuation, ownership (or obligation/rights), and presentation/disclosure. However, other commentators prefer to use five or seven assertions, overlapping with the CEAVOP model but with variations arising from the combination of some assertions and the inclusion of additional matters such as **cutoff** and **understandability.** Despite the coexistence of

various models for categorizing assertions, the general content of the models tends to be clear and consistent.

In addition to the assessment of the assertions relating to items recorded in financial statements, auditors also face the challenge of evaluating the possible existence and importance of items *not* included in the statements: "It is important to realize that a financial statement not only asserts the existence of those items listed in it, it also asserts the nonexistence of those items not so listed" (Mautz and Sharaf 1961, 98). The negative proposition of unknown or unidentified items is one of the largest challenges for all auditors, far beyond the specialization of financial auditing.

assessment

1 A financial **appraisal** of an **investment**, asset, or liability. **2** A nonquantitative evaluation of an activity, control, process, or procedure. **3** The calculation of a **taxation** liability.

asset

A resource expected to provide future economic benefits. **Generally Accepted Accounting Principles (GAAP)** around the world usually set strict criteria for the **recognition (sense 1)** and **valuation** of assets. An asset is recorded as a **debit entry** under the conventions of **double entry bookkeeping**. See **intangible asset** and **tangible asset**. Contrast **liability**.

asset stripping

A pejorative term for the depletion of **assets** in an organization for the purposes of **realizing** a **short-term** profit. Asset stripping may occur following an **acquisition (sense 2)**. Less commonly, the term "asset stripping" may also be a tactical (or even malicious) means of avoiding a corporate takeover: an organization that is the target of an unwelcome acquisition bid may take the extreme measure of depleting its assets to make it less attractive to a potential acquirer. See also **poison pill**.

assurance

A degree of confidence that an item exists and is accurately measured. The term is used widely in auditing, in the context of flows of **accountability** between various parties, to convey the effect of an auditor's **opinion** on confidence in an item. Assurance does not usually offer the certainty of a **guarantee**: indeed, to offer absolute assurance in an auditing context is generally unfeasible, owing to the existence of **risk.** It has been observed that auditors "can never be 100 percent certain of the information on which their opinion or report is based" (Flint 1988, 112) and, specifically for **financial auditing**, that "no audit provides complete assurance that the financial statements are free from material misstatement" (O'Reilly et al. 1998, 1.16). Auditors therefore tend to base their **judgments** on the **sample** testing of large audit **populations, compliance testing** of procedures and internal controls, and **analytical reviews** of data relations. Given that none of these approaches to audit **evidence** offers absolute assurance, auditors tend to prefer to talk in terms of "reasonable assurance."

There is some inconsistency in current usage of the term "assurance." Indeed, it is one the most slippery of terms in the auditing lexicon. The term is sometimes used to express a quality control review of an audit, intended to provide an opinion on the audit's accuracy; used in this sense, assurance follows an audit. Others refer to assurance as the verification of the accuracy of an accounting record, with an audit providing a higher-level evaluation of the overall accounting entries underpinning financial statements; this understanding considers assurance as preliminary to an audit. In financial auditing, an **assurance engagement** implies a large field of impartial, intermediary opinions on matters of accountability, of which an audit is only one, albeit an important, instance. Compare **attestation.**

assurance engagement

In **financial auditing**, a review of a matter to provide an impartial opinion on its accuracy and measurement. Financial audits are one kind of assurance engagement. The *International Framework for Assurance Engagements* of the International Auditing and Assurance Standards Board identifies five "elements" of an assurance engagement: (i) A three-party relationship involving a practitioner, a responsible party, and intended users (i.e., the existence of flows of **accountability**); (ii) defined subject matter (i.e., the purpose of the assurance activity); (iii) suitable criteria for **measurement**; (iv) sufficient, appropriate **evidence**; and (v) a written report with the assurance provider's **opinion.** See also **audit** and the **postulates of auditing.**

assurance map
A visual portrayal of the scope of (and responsibilities for) **assurance** activities in an organization.

asymmetric information
A mismatch of the depth and quality of information between two or more parties to a **transaction**, **contractual** arrangement, or activity. A classic example of asymmetric information is found in markets for preused automobiles: the purchaser of a preused car tends to be at a significant information disadvantage in comparison with the car's seller. The concept of *caveat emptor* is relevant in such circumstances.

Between a **principal** and an **agent**, **agency costs** can be exacerbated by asymmetries of information, as an agent may be tempted to exploit detailed knowledge of a transaction or organization to the disadvantage of a principal. See also **game theory** and the **prisoner's dilemma**.

attestation
1 A formal, documented declaration of proof of the existence of something. Attestation can be understood as a form of **assurance**. In financial auditing, attested assignments tend to be differentiated from audits, in that the former address topics other than opinions on **financial statements**: "Examples of attest[ed] services include testing and reporting on representations about the characteristic of computer software, investment performance statistics, internal control, prospective financial information, and historical occupancy data for hospitals. . . . [An attested engagement consists of] written assurance about an **assertion** or assertions made by another party" (O'Reilly et al. 1998, 2.5, 2.7).
2 The signing of a legal document, as witness to the genuineness of the signatures of the parties to a transaction or contract.

attorney's letter
A written communication sent by a **financial auditor** to an **auditee**'s lawyer, requesting details of litigation and other legal matters. The lawyer's response is used to gather or corroborate audit **evidence** of the existence and **materiality** of **contingent liabilities**.

attributes [*of auditors*]
Qualities or traits characteristic of (or desirable in) auditors. Lists of commonly accepted auditor attributes have changed over time, but they typically include **impartiality**, honesty, the possession of diagnostic skills and a **professional** commitment to the public interest. "Probity and strength of character" have been identified as two major auditor attributes (Flint 1988, 64). In 1987, the National Commission on Fraudulent Financial Reporting (also known more succinctly as the Treadway Commission) identified four essential attributes for **financial auditors:** "users of financial statements expect auditors to bring to the reporting process technical competence, integrity, **independence**, and objectivity" (*Report of the National Commission on Fraudulent Financial Reporting* 1987, 6). The **professional** status of auditors is often deemed to encompass or signal the possession of appropriate attributes.

attribute sampling
A **statistical** analysis of the rate of occurrence of a characteristic in a **population**. Example: an **internal auditor** decides to analyze an organization's **disbursements** to assess the rate of occurrence of non**authorized** items. The attribute in this case is the nonauthorization of individual disbursements. Occurrence rates of a characteristic in a sample may be **extrapolated** to the entire population from the sample extracted, subject to the precision errors inherent in sampling methodologies.

auction
The sale of an item through **competitive** bidding.

audit
An **impartial**, **evidence**-based, **judgmental** assessment for **accountability** purposes. There is no single, satisfactory definition of an audit; it is beyond doubt that "it is wiser to speak of a cluster of definitions which overlap but are not identical" (Power 1997, 4). This book provides a range of definitions for auditing specializations in the entries for **clinical auditing**, **data auditing**, **educational auditing**, **environmental auditing**, **election auditing**, **financial auditing**, **forensic auditing**, **intellectual property auditing**, **internal auditing**, and **royalty auditing**.

Nonetheless, the bare-bones definition of an "impartial, evidence-based, judgmental assessment for accountability purposes" covers four essential attributes of auditing common to all the categories of auditing discussed in this book: (i) the impartiality of auditing, whose practitioners should be **independent** (in the sense of free from judgment-distorting bias or **conflicts of interest**); (ii) the reliance of the audit process on appropriate **evidence**; (iii) the inferential judgment process at the heart of auditing, through which auditors provide **opinions** rather than absolute guarantees of accuracy; and (iv) the intermediary role of the auditor in providing **assurance** to third parties on a clearly defined, **measurable** topic of accountability. The next paragraphs consider these four attributes in turn.

That audits be conducted on an **arm's length** basis is fundamental to the integrity of auditing. For example, if our definition is correct, clinical auditors may not audit their own surgical operations. Nor may the auditors of financial statements legitimately audit financial statements they themselves prepared. But the concept of objectivity goes beyond not auditing one's own work; there is a spectrum of impartiality considerations. For financial auditors, family or financial connections with an auditee are normally considered unacceptable threats to the auditor's objectivity and credibility. For some categories of auditor (e.g., internal auditors, who usually are employees of the organization they audit), the requirements for objectivity may be at the more relaxed end of the spectrum. In the internal auditor's case, impartiality is more a state of mind than an adherence to formal conflict-of-interest rules.

The second and third fundamental elements of auditing cover the evidence-based, judgmental assessment process at the heart of the activity. An auditing assessment is an inferential evaluation of relevant evidence through critical thinking, logical reasoning, and the pragmatic lessons of prior experience, to provide an opinion on the object of the audit. The kinds of logic used by auditors are discussed in the entry **logic in auditing.** Although some types of auditing might engage in water-tight guarantees of accuracy, the task of most auditors is to provide opinions. It would be impractical for election auditors to recount every ballot cast in an election, so the auditors have recourse to techniques like the analysis of representative samples of votes and the interpretation of trends in aggregated data. Auditors use sample-based testing to make inferences about large populations of data. An audit is therefore not an unattainable hankering after cast-iron evidence, but rather an assessment of appropriate evidence to reach an informed opinion.

The fourth element of the definition addresses the purpose of auditing: "An audit cannot exist if it has no purpose" (Schandl 1978, 173). The reason for an audit is to provide intermediary assurance on accountability between two (or more) parties. It has been suggested that the existence of a requirement for accountability is "a primary condition of audit[ing]" (Flint 1988, 23). Objects of audits may vary widely: they may include financial statements, the performance of surgical operations, pollution levels, and the quality of university-level teaching. But the principles underlying the purposes of different categories of auditing are consistent.

Underpinning our definition of auditing as *an impartial, evidence-based, judgmental assessment for accountability purposes* is the requirement that an audit may be undertaken only for matters for which there are agreed-on, **measurable** standards. Environmental auditors may test the levels of carcinogenic particulate matter in the air we breathe. Financial auditors may review the accuracy, fair presentation, and reliability of a **balance sheet.** Electoral auditors may assess the accuracy of the votes recorded in a referendum. But, according to our definition, one cannot legitimately audit the aesthetic qualities of a music drama by Richard Wagner, for which there are no auditable, agreed-on, understandable criteria of measurement and performance. Opining on the beauty of Wagner's music is the activity of a critic, an aesthete, or a hobbyist, but it is not the task of an auditor. (The musical assessment would also fail to qualify as an audit on the grounds of there being no obvious element of accountability to serve as a purpose for the assessment.)

Much more could be said about the four core elements in our brief definition of auditing. The four attributes are necessary for auditing, but whether they are sufficient involves additional considerations. Other matters that bear on our understanding of auditing include the nature of auditing as a cooperative search for assurance, rather than an **adversarial** endeavor; the credibility of the formal bodies of **knowledge** of professional auditing institutions; and the manner in which auditing might be deemed to uphold social inequities. Here are four examples of widely held interpretations of the term "auditing": (i) "Auditing is a human evaluation process to establish the adherence to certain norms, resulting in an opinion (or judgment)" (Schandl 1978, 4). (ii) "The purpose of the audit is to investigate and review the actions (or inaction), decisions, achievements, statements or reports of specified persons with defined responsibilities, to compare these actions, etc., with some norm, and to form and express an opinion on the result of that investigation, review or comparison" (Flint 1988, 20). (iii) An auditor acts as an "arbiter" in the context of **agency theory** (Lee 1993, 23). And finally: (iv) Auditing is a "diverse and humble assemblage of routines, practices, and economic constraints," yet it "is not merely a collection of technical tasks but also a programmatic idea circulating in organizational environments, an idea which promises a certain style of control and organizational transparency" (Power 1997, 89, 122).

Auditing practices have been traced to the dawn of literate civilization: "According to earliest Mesopotamian records dating back to 3600 BC, scribes used to prepare summaries of financial transactions. These were separate from the lists of amounts handled and which others had prepared. . . . Tiny marks, dots, and circles indicated the painstaking comparison of one record with another—marks that have survived the centuries and that auditors still use to **tick** off their **verification** of records. Thus were born two control devices still used around the world: division [i.e., **segregation**] **of duties**; provision for the review of another's work" (Sawyer and Vinten 1996, 23). Civil servants in the elaborate bureaucracies of ancient China, India, and Rome used auditing techniques to monitor and report on state finances, and to assess taxation revenues. (Auditing in ancient India is discussed by Saputra and Anggiriawan 2021.) Perhaps systems of surveillance over economic and social activity reflect a fundamental human desire for accountability: "By attempting to alleviate human anxiety created by uncertainty surrounding specific phenomena, verification or auditing acts as a stabilizing factor in the management of human behavior" (Lee 1993, 20).

The modern term "audit" is a Latinism, derived from the practices of agricultural tallying in England in the Middle Ages. Many of the parties interested in the "manorial" agricultural production of large estates were illiterate, and audits were therefore usually presented orally. As a consequence, the modern English word "audit," derived from the Latin verb *audire* ("to hear"), came into use. In the present day, auditing tends to be rigorously documented, but the activity's name still hints back to the era of "audit by ear" in England (Baxter 1996, 347). Auditing continued as a formal practice throughout medieval and early modern England, focusing increasingly on bankruptcies and the recovery of assets from creditors. By Shakespeare's time, the English public was familiar with the term and practice of auditing—in *Timon of Athens*, first staged in the first decade of the seventeenth century, Shakespeare (or maybe Thomas Middleton, the presumed coauthor) puts the following words into the mouth of Flavius, Timon's faithful steward: "If you suspect my husbandry or falsehood, call me before the exactest auditors and set me on the proof" (Act 2, Scene 2; cited by Chambers 1995, 3). The development of the auditing of corporate financial reporting is covered in the entry for **financial auditing**.

Despite auditing's apparently long history of enhancing public trust in institutions and economic activities, auditing's dramatic and apparently inexorable rise since World War II has been met with disapproval by those who see its expansion as a symptom of declining public trust in institutions and in political and business leadership. The financial audit, for example, has been described as "the principal means by which accountability is attempted when trust in relationships disappears" (Lee 1998, 219). Another commentator has portrayed auditing as a quasi-parasitical activity: the "**audit society** is a symptom of the times . . . in which a gulf has opened up between poorly rewarded 'doing' and highly rewarded 'observing'" (Power 1997, 147). Criticisms of auditing's social and political impact, especially in the writings of the **critical accounting movement**, oppose the official narratives of professional auditing institutions on the contested topic of the social utility of auditing.

auditability

The feasibility of undertaking auditing. Auditability is the first of the **postulates of auditing** elaborated in the early 1960s by Robert Kuhn Mautz and Hussein A. Sharaf, and is the prerequisite to auditing. Three major requirements for auditability are **measurability** (there must be agreed-on assessment standards for a topic to be audited), **understandability** (an audit cannot be undertaken in a context of incomprehension), and the existence of reliable and verifiable audit **evidence**. Example regarding evidence: if all the records of a transaction-intensive organization were irretrievably lost in a fire, the organization would in all likelihood be unauditable. **Alternative procedures** may be undertaken by the auditor in such circumstances (including the reconstruction of **transactions** from memory, or the confirmation of transactions by third parties like banks and vendors), but it is highly unlikely that alternative procedures could lead to an **unqualified opinion** in the context of a complete destruction of records.

Questions of auditability might also arise from (i) inadequate cooperation and **adversarial** attitudes from **auditees** and (ii) inadequate systems of **internal control.** In both circumstances, the unauditability of a disorderly organization may be compared with the political ungovernability of a chaotic society. In addition, questions of auditability may also derive from gaps or deficits in an auditor's expertise, a problem usually addressed through reliance on **outside expertise.**

auditable unit
An organization, operation, individual, or other entity that can be subjected to an audit. An auditable unit forms part of an overall **audit universe.** Example: the auditor of a **multinational corporation** may define the organization's individual overseas branches as auditable units. Within each overseas branch, the auditor may proceed to define a series of further auditable units along the lines of the purchasing and revenue cycles and other operational activities.

audit agenda
1 An alternative term for **audit program.** **2** An alternative term for **audit schedule.**

audit approach
The strategy for the conduct of an audit, or the manner of conducting an audit. Deciding on a suitable audit approach is integral to the **audit planning** process, and a common decision is the balance to be struck between **compliance** and **substantive** testing. Audit approaches are often determined by, among other factors, (i) the characteristics of the **auditee,** (ii) the time available for the audit, (iii) the level of auditee cooperation, and (iv) the sophistication of the auditee's systems of **internal controls.** See also the **"black box" audit approach.**

audit assignment
A discrete, separately identifiable audit. Compare **special (audit) assignment.**

audit assumption
A presumption that underpins an audit or an **audit test**. Unlike the **postulates of auditing**, which are of general validity, an audit assumption is specific to an individual auditing assignment. Example: a judgment (based on audit **evidence** from **sample** testing) that an organization's **disbursements** include a troubling proportion of inadequately authorized transactions is a typical type of assumption underpinning an **internal auditor**'s assessment of an expenditure cycle.

audit charter
See **internal audit charter**.

audit committee
A committee of a **board of directors** (or similar governing body) that oversees an organization's auditing activities and **financial reporting**. Under most **corporate governance** systems, audit committees tend to be composed of **outside directors** to encourage **independence** and to minimize potential **conflicts of interest**. Typical activities of audit committees include the oversight of (i) financial reporting, (ii) the **internal control** environment, (iii) the work of financial and internal auditors, (iv) financial audit fees, and (v) the appropriateness of accounting policies.

audit competence
The ability, knowledge, and diagnostic skills of an individual who aspires to undertake auditing. It has been suggested that "the first requirement for the **authority** of auditors is competence. Audit competence requires both knowledge and skill, which are the products of education, training and experience" (Flint 1998, 48). The **professional** bodies of auditors typically seek to define and monitor their members' audit competencies (and to erect **barriers to entry** to the profession) through certifications and the continuing professional education of their members.

audit cycle
1 A sequence of tasks undertaken to complete an audit assignment. Example: in financial auditing, the audit cycle tends to be scheduled in discrete phases, typically (i) interim visits to perform **analytical reviews** and **compliance**

reviews, (ii) attendance at **physical inventory** counts, (iii) visits at (or shortly after) financial period ends to perform detailed **substantive testing**, and (iv) the finalization of the audit and its reporting. **2** A recurring audit or series of audits over time. Example: an internal audit function's overall agenda may envision coverage of the **audit universe** through a rolling cycle of audits, with different areas of focus in different time periods. Thus the internal auditors of an organization with twenty branches may find that annual risk assessment processes prioritize ten of the branches. To ensure coverage of the remaining ten branches, the internal auditors may decide to cover two or three branches per annum in its scope of work on a cyclical basis. Otherwise, the branches not prioritized by risk assessment may be neglected in the internal auditors' work plans.

auditee
An individual, organization, or organizational unit subject to an audit. Contrast **auditor**.

audit engagement
An alternative term for **audit assignment**.

audit evidence
See **evidence**.

audit guide
1 An alternative term for **audit program**. **2** An alternative term for advisory and interpretative audit-related literature.

auditing
The process or action of undertaking an **audit**. The noun gerund "auditing" places a greater emphasis on activity than does the simple noun "audit."

audit(ing) standard
1 Formal rules and guidance for auditing. Examples: (i) For **financial auditing**, the United States' Auditing Standards Board issues *Statements on Auditing Standards*, while the International Auditing and Assurance Standards Board of the International Federation of Accountants issues *International Standards*

on Auditing. Formal auditing standards of this nature are the main component (in addition to legislation and custom) of **Generally Accepted Auditing Standards (GAAS)**. (ii) For **internal auditors**, the *Standards for the Professional Practice of Internal Auditing* of the Institute of Internal Auditors are to be replaced in 2025 by the Global Internal Audit Standards.

audit objective
See **objective (senses 1 and 2)**.

audit opinion
See **opinion**.

auditor
1 An individual or organization that performs an audit. Contrast **auditee**.
2 In canon law, a member of the ecclesiastical judiciary with the right to hear petitions and to gather evidence. **3** A spiritual counsellor in the Church of Scientology.

Auditor General (AG)
An alternative term for **Chief Audit Executive**.

auditor independence
See **independence**.

auditor's luck
A semihumorous term that refers to the fortuitous inclusion in an auditor's **sample** test of awkward, discomforting, or unrepresentative items. Example: in a **judgmental** or **statistical** test sample, internal auditors select forty sales invoices from an **accounts receivable** ledger to assess the frequency with which sales transactions exceed customers' **credit limits** without appropriate authorization. They find that ten of the sample items fall within this category. The **auditee** may claim that the auditor has stumbled by chance across rare or unrepresentative exceptions whose occurrence should not be extrapolated to a wider pattern. On the relationships between chance and **sampling risk**, see also **Black Swan event** and **intuition**.

audit opinion
See **opinion**.

audit plan
1 An alternative term for **audit program**. **2** An alternative term for **audit schedule (sense 1)**.

audit planning
Preparatory activities for an audit. Planning is tailored to the purposes and circumstances of individual audits, but typically includes some or all of these: (i) information gathered to establish the general background context of an organization or activity to be audited; (ii) discussions with an **auditee** to ascertain **material** facts; (iii) a **risk assessment** of the topic(s) to be audited; (iv) **analytical reviews** of information; and (v) logistical arrangements for visiting an audit location. The planning process normally results in a formal **audit program** that sets out the scope of audit work.

audit program
A document that sets out **audit tests**. In practice, audit programs may vary significantly in detail and sophistication. At one extreme, an audit program may simply be a bullet-point list of audit tests. At the other extreme, an audit program may give extensive guidance on the performance of the tests, including the allocation of work to individual auditors.

audit quality
See **quality control**.

audit recommendation
See **recommendation**.

audit report
A communication that summarizes the findings of an audit. In **financial auditing**, the audit report contains a formal **opinion**; most systems of **Generally Accepted Auditing Standards (GAAS)** have standardized wording for financial auditors' reports and require explanations of any **unmodified opinion**

(e.g., an **adverse opinion**, a **disclaimer**, or a **qualified opinion**). In **internal auditing**, the contents and structure of audit reports are largely at the discretion of individual internal audit functions.

It has been suggested that all audit reports should follow the basic criteria of "clarity, precision, unambiguity, and comprehensiveness in disposal of the [audit's] terms of reference" (Flint 1988, 121). However, public **skepticism** over the use of the **boilerplate** language that is typical of audit reports (especially financial audit reports) has a long history. Anecdote: a humorous doggerel from the 1950s on the topic of the reliability of financial audit reports (quoted by Chambers 1995, 91): "We have audited the balance sheet and here is our report: The cash is overstated, the cashier being short / The customers' receivables are very much past due, If there are any good ones, they are very, very, few; The inventories are out of date and practically junk, And the method of their pricing is very largely bunk; / According to our figure the enterprise is wrecked. . . . But subject to these comments, the balance sheet's correct."

audit risk

1 In financial auditing, the risk of giving an inappropriate audit **opinion** on the adherence of financial statements to **Generally Accepted Accounting Principles (GAAP)**. The **sample** testing of transactions and the **compliance testing** of **internal controls** cannot offer cast-iron guarantees that all **irregularities** have been identified, though audit risk can be mitigated by (i) careful **audit planning**, (ii) **representation letters** from management, (iii) the auditor's conscientious performance of audit tests, (iv) logical **judgments** of the reliability of **evidence**, and (v) adequate **malpractice insurance**. Most auditors aim for a reasonable level of **assurance** rather than for absolute assurance. Overall audit risk is sometimes analyzed into three components—**inherent risk (sense 1)**, **control risk (sense 1)**, and **detection risk**. **2** In other categories of auditing, the **risk** of overlooking or misinterpreting **material** matters of concern, both quantitative and qualitative. See also **sampling risk**.

auditor rotation

In financial auditing, the periodic replacement of audit firms or individual partners from within a single audit firm. Rotation is a mechanism to encourage auditor **independence** (and perhaps also **audit quality**) by avoiding **conflicts**

of interest arising from overfamiliarization between auditors and auditees. It is generally considered that the benefits of impartiality from periodic auditor rotation outweigh any disruptive impact of changes. Example: in 2017 the South African Independent Regulatory Board for Auditors issued a rule, effective starting April 1, 2023, and applicable to listed corporations and other "public interest entities," that requires mandatory audit firm rotation after a period of tenure of ten years. A subsequent "cooling off" period of five years must pass before the same audit firm can be reappointed. (Details are available from the Independent Regulatory Board for Auditors' website: www.irba.co.za/guidelines -to-commentary.)

audit schedule
1 A work plan of audit assignments arising from a formal planning process.
2 An alternative term for **work paper.**

audit shop
An alternative term for **internal audit function.**

audit society, the
A term coined by Michael Power to denote allegedly pervasive and often neg- ative influences of auditing practices in modern life. Power, a professor at the London School of Economics and Political Science, elaborated the concept of the audit society in, among other writings, *The Audit Society: Rituals of Verification* (Power 1997) and "Auditing and the Production of Legitimacy" (Power 2003). The notion of the audit society has links to the polemics of the **critical accounting movement**, in that it provides challenges to the "official" narratives of **profes- sional** auditing associations.

The concept of the audit society is complex and multifaceted. Power casts doubt on the theoretical validity of professional auditing models, suggesting that auditing is more a social construct than a scientific practice: "**Auditabil- ity** cannot be defined; it is negotiated" (Power 1997, 81). He has referred to auditing's "essentially elusive epistemological character" and has highlighted a circularity in definitions of auditor expertise and expressions of collective audi- tor knowledge: "There is no robust conception of 'good' auditing independent either of auditor **judgments** or of the system of knowledge in which those judgments are embedded and against which particular audits could be judged" (Power 1997, 11, 29). He has also treated with suspicion many of the claims made by professional auditors of the utility of auditing, including the notion of auditing's promotion of the **Three Es** of economy, efficiency, and effectiveness. In addition, he has alerted us to the dangers of auditing slipping into a hollow activity—"at worst auditing tends to become an organizational ritual, a drama-turgical performance"—and he has described the "audit society" as "a symptom of the times, coincidentally a *fin de siècle*, in which a gulf has opened up between poorly rewarded 'doing' and highly rewarded 'observing'" (Power 1997, 141, 147).

Power has identified a simultaneous, interrelated process of "explosion" and "implosion" in relation to auditing. The "audit explosion" refers to a proliferation of auditing both within and beyond its traditional heartlands of **financial auditing** and **internal auditing**: "In addition to financial audits, there are now environmental audits, **value for money** audits, **management audits**, **forensic audits**, **data audits**, **intellectual property** audits, medical audits, teaching audits, technology audits, stress audits, democracy audits, and many others besides" (Power 1994b, 1). At the same time, Power has described as an "audit implosion" the increasing internalization of compliance activities in organizations, accompanied by a "riskification" of internal controls through an ever-stronger focus on **enterprise risk management** and on the establishment of in-house infrastructures to attempt assessments of performance and **account-ability**. (The trend of embedding audit processes within organizations is seen in the ways corporations have implemented Section 404 of the *Sarbanes-Oxley Act*.)

While Power acknowledges that the assurances given by auditors can be valuable in the orderly conduct of human affairs, he warns that the costs and **opportunity costs** of maintaining layers of burdensome and overlapping sys-tems of assurance and surveillance might be symptoms of declining public trust in our institutions. Conversely, he has pointed out that the internalization of auditing within organizations suggests an increase in stakeholder trust in self-auditing. He does not perceive the spread of auditing as evidence of an autocratic surveillance society, but indicative rather of a widespread social anx-iety that seeks signals of reassurance through comfort certificates. The audit society "can be understood as a label for a loss of confidence in the central steer-ing institutions of society, particularly politics. So it may be that a loss of faith in

intellectual, political and economic leadership has led to the creation of industries of checking which satisfy a demand for signals of order" (Power 2000, 188).

Power's critique of auditing was developed at the end of the second millennium. In retrospect, a quarter century after the publication in 1997 of *The Audit
Society: Rituals of Verification*, he raised doubts about the continuing usefulness
of the "audit society" concept "in the face of advances in information technology or 'digitization,' . . . a complex question because these advances have been
taking shape over many years in many different ways . . . for both economic gain
and enhanced social control" (Power 2022). The warnings of an "audit society"
have been a compelling counternarrative to official discourses of auditing. And
the inexorable spread of auditing throughout the sinews of our institutions
shows no signs of abating.

audit step

1 An alternative term for **audit test**. **2** An individual action within an audit
test. Example: the **circularization** of customers is a common step within an
audit test to establish the existence and accuracy of an organization's **accounts
receivable** balances.

audit test

An action to gather and evaluate audit **evidence**. Audit tests may be classified
into (i) the **substantive testing** of transactions, assets, and liabilities; and
(ii) the **compliance testing** of **internal controls**. **Analytical review** procedures
are generally considered to be part of substantive testing, and **walk-through**
tests are a technique within compliance testing. All other things being equal,
a high reliance on compliance testing tends to lead to a decrease in the need for
substantive testing. In other words, an auditor's level of confidence in an organization's internal controls determines the extent of **transactional** testing. The
auditing of the characteristics of large **populations** of transactions and other
items is normally performed through **sampling** techniques. See also **test of controls**, **test of detail**, **test of design**, **inspection**, **observation**, and **verification**.

audit trail

The tracing of the flow of a **transaction** for audit purposes. The chrono-
logical development of a transaction originates in its underlying activity

(e.g., an inventory movement or a sale to a customer), and a satisfactory audit trail is deemed to be in place if the audit **evidence** permits a transaction to be viewed in its entirety. The verification of audit trails is important for both **substantive** and **compliance testing**. **Walk-through tests** (a form of compliance testing) specifically focus on the adequacy of audit trails.

audit universe

The total potential scope of audit activity in an organization. **Audit planning** involves the allocation of resources to individual **auditable** units within an audit universe, normally through a combination of the following considerations: (i) **risk assessment**, (ii) **materiality**, (iii) a cyclical or rotational factor to ensure the periodic coverage of auditable units, and (iv) requests from **auditees**. Example: the audit universe of a **multinational** corporation may include the operational activities of overseas **branches**, and an internal audit function may determine the frequency of audit assignments at individual branches from a balanced assessment of the four factors listed above.

authority

A **right**, defined in law or inherent in an individual's organizational status, to act or make decisions and to use commands to compel compliance from other individuals. The rights and responsibilities underpinning authority are usually delegated through a **chain of command** within a **hierarchical** organizational structure. One may differentiate rights from power in the context of authority: authority is a right to act or make decisions, without necessarily the power to do so. In situations, therefore, where authority exists without power, the authority holder's acts or decisions may be ignored or disregarded (Scruton 2007, 47–48).

The rights and powers implied in authority, whether *de facto* or *de jure*, ought to be restrained by **accountability**, and this can give rise to moral questions in terms of the responsibilities of **subordinates** in chains of command. The ultimate responsibility for a decision tends to reside at the top of a chain of command. Example: a senior official in an organization may initiate a questionable or illegal policy (e.g., **bribery** or a decision to pollute a river in search of economic gains), but the implementation of the policy is likely to occur lower down the chain of command. In such circumstances, the allocation of moral and legal responsibilities among the various levels of the organizational hierarchy may be ambiguous (and is often decided in the courts).

The most unyielding examples of rigid chains of command are found in military hierarchies and authoritarian political and religious organizations, in which the cascade of orders and instructions is strictly enforced. Yet in organizational structures of all kinds ethical dilemmas can arise from the delegation of authority. Recipients of a delegated corporate instruction or a military or political order may face an ethical dilemma when suspecting that the instruction or order conflicts with morality. See **whistle-blower**.

A different type of authority derives less from institutional hierarchy than from presumed expertise and access to a reliable body of **knowledge**. In auditing, the authority of an auditor's work and **opinions** derives from the auditor's **professional** status. This status carries powerful social signals that include a presumed mastery of a formal body of knowledge. It has been noted that an "auditor's opinion must carry authority if it is to have a special utility: if it did not carry sufficient unquestioned authority, it would add little to the unaudited information already available . . . there must be confidence in the technical competence, reliability and integrity of the auditors" (Flint 1988, 45–46).

authorization

The act of granting approval or permission. Authorization is central to many of the **internal controls** in modern organizations, from the processing of **disbursements** to the hiring of employees. The act of exercising organizational **authority** tends to be proceduralized through the providing of signatures or through password-controlled access to **transactions** in computerized information systems. Authorization rights derive from an individual's status in an organizational **hierarchy**.

availability bias

A cognitive shortcut or heuristic **bias** that overrelies on explanatory possibilities that come readily to mind rather than on possibilities not so readily recalled. In auditing, an evaluative bias of this nature is a risk to the integrity of **evidence**-based reasoning (see Kahneman 2011, 131–35). See also **anchoring and adjustment bias**, **recency bias**, and **intuition**.

average
A single number calculated to measure central tendency in a set of numbers. The term is popularly used as a synonym for the **mean**, but it also covers the **median** and the **mode**. See also **weighted average**.

avoidable costs
Items of expenditures incurred at the discretion of an individual or organization. In contrast to **sunk costs**, avoidable costs can be incurred, reduced, or avoided on the basis of a decision. Examples: (i) potential rental fees for additional warehousing space can be avoided by a decision not to occupy the supplementary warehouse area; and (ii) the **raw material** costs of a manufacturing process can be avoided by a decision not to produce the final product in question or reduced by the substitution of alternative raw materials. Avoidable costs may be variable or fixed. See also **controllable costs** and **unavoidable costs**.

backflush costing
A costing method that allocates costs to products when a manufacturing process is finished, or when a sale is made. Backflush costing is normally associated with **just-in-time (JIT)** manufacturing and delivery practices, and with the typically low **inventory** levels of JIT environments. It offers the advantage of avoiding cumbersome and expensive cost-tracking mechanisms.

back office
The administrative functions of a **brokerage** operation that trades in **securities**, **commodities**, or **currencies**. Compare **front office**.

back-up
1 The periodic copying of accounting and other data as a safeguard against the loss of information. Adequate backup procedures are often required for **business continuity** and **insurance** purposes. **2** Moral, financial, or administrative support given to an individual or organization.

bad debt

An accounts receivable balance of questionable collectability. Under most systems of **Generally Accepted Accounting Principles (GAAP)**, an **allowance for bad debts** is raised to acknowledge the reduced likelihood of recoverability of a customer balance. When an item is known with certainty to be irrecoverable, it is usually subjected to a **write-off** to expenses. The term "bad debt" is sometimes distinguished from "doubtful debt" so that the former designates a customer balance likely to be irrecoverable, while the latter indicates a customer balance of potential recoverability. However, the two terms are frequently used synonymously.

bait and switch

1 [*In commercial transactions*] An ethically dubious or **fraudulent** deception of customers, involving the promotion of attractive items at good value followed by the encouraging of customers to substitute the promoted goods with inferior or more expensive items. Example: a car dealership may promote a car of exceptional quality and outstanding value; but when customers show up to make the purchase, they are informed that the attractive car has already been sold, and they are instead offered inferior or poor value cars. **2** [*In employment interviews*] The practice of candidates hiring imposters to take their place in job interviews.

balance

1 The net total of **debit** and **credit entries** in a **general ledger** account. **2** The overall equalizing effect of the total debit and credit entries in a general ledger. An assessment of the integrity of the mechanics of **double entry bookkeeping** is undertaken through preparation and analysis of a **trial balance**. **3** The net total of debit and credit entries in a bank or loan account, or in an **accounts payable** or **accounts receivable** account. Example: "I need to check my bank balance today."

balance sheet

An **accounting** summary of the financial position of an organization or individual at a specific date. A balance sheet offers a snapshot of **assets**, **liabilities**, and **equity (sense 1)**, and it sets out the results of the **accounting equation** that underpins **double entry bookkeeping**. Under most systems of **Generally Accepted Accounting Principles (GAAP)**, balance sheets are based largely on **historical costs** and, therefore, are unlikely to reflect the **market value** of an organization's assets. Along with an **income statement**, the balance sheet is prepared from a **trial balance**. See also **financial statements**.

balance sheet equation, the
An alternative term for the **accounting equation**.

balancing figure
A number inserted into a **general ledger** account, a **trial balance**, or a **balance sheet** to tally the totals of **debit** and **credit entries**. Balancing figures are used to correct mistakes or rounding errors in computations of the **accounting equation**.

bank reconciliation
A periodic **internal control** that identifies differences between deposits or loans held by a bank and the corresponding balances stated in **general ledger** accounts. Errors and timing differences may arise between the accounting of **transactions** by a bank and by its customers. Typical differences include **checks** not yet processed through the bank. To ensure the accuracy of both a bank's balances and a general ledger, an organization or individual periodically **reconciles** bank statements with related general ledger accounts.

In auditing, the regular performance of bank reconciliations is sometimes viewed as a barometer of an organization's internal control environment. The line of reasoning is that problems in this fundamental internal control suggest that more sophisticated internal controls may not be functioning adequately. However, the amplification or **extrapolation** of one observation to unknown potential similarities is not grounded in rigorous logic: see **analogical reasoning**.

bankruptcy [of organizations]
The legal status of an organization unable to settle its **liabilities**. Bankruptcy tends to mean the end of a business as a **going concern**, though bankruptcy laws in most jurisdictions allow for attempts to rescue all or part of the business.

In the United States, for example, Chapter 11 of the 1978 US *Bankruptcy Reform Act* and its amendments provides for the financial reorganization of a business while it continues to operate under defined restrictions. Bankruptcy law relating to individuals tends to be markedly different from corporate bankruptcy law in most jurisdictions.

bank statement
A summary of **transactions** in a bank account prepared by the bank for a customer's attention. Bank statements were traditionally prepared at regular intervals in **hard copy** format, but they increasingly have **real-time** availability. **Bank reconciliations**—the agreeing of bank statement amounts with corresponding **general ledger** accounts—is a fundamental **internal control** procedure.

barriers to entry
Restrictions on the entry of new competitors into a **market**. Barriers to entry may result from technical and economic factors. Examples: the large-scale investment in machinery needed for some production processes may be beyond the economic means of many potential entrants into a market, or a corporation may hold an exclusive **patent** right that confers technical advantages in manufacturing a product. Barriers can also derive from **monopolistic** and restrictive trade practices, from **tariffs** and other **protectionist** measures, and from the requirements of **professional** bodies. Contrast **barriers to exit**.

barriers to exit
Restrictions on the ability of participants in a **market** to withdraw from the market. A common barrier to exit is the existence of a law or regulation that forces an organization to produce goods or provide services deemed to be for the public good. Another common barrier to exit derives from the impact of **sunk costs**: an organization that has made significant investments in costly machinery may find it impractical to abandon the activity for which the machinery was intended.

barter
The exchange of goods or services for other goods or services, without the intermediary of **money**. Although barter systems tend to be cumbersome and inefficient, and have largely been replaced by money systems, individual barter

transactions are not uncommon. Example: some developing countries frequently exchange **commodities** or **raw materials** for manufactured goods. The accounting treatment of the elements of barter transactions normally records their **market values**. Compare **payment in kind**.

base document
1 A document that serves as audit **evidence**. Examples: **bank statements**, **vendor** invoices, and **general ledger** extracts. **2** A document that includes the entire **population** of data from which a **sample** can be extracted for audit purposes.

base period
1 A period of time that serves as a framework or starting point for financial or operational analysis. **2** A specific time period from which an **index** is calculated.

base rate
1 An **interest rate** used for reference or comparative purposes. **2** A term used in the United Kingdom (and other countries with historical British influence) for the interest lending rate set by a **central bank**, equivalent to the Federal Reserve interest rate in the United States. Base rates are used as a monetary control mechanism, and commercial banks calibrate their lending rates with reference to national base rates.

base stock
A minimum level of **inventory** required for day-to-day operational purposes. The level of base stock is a critical threshold, and the falling below it of inventory quantities may adversely affect an organization's operations. Example: an organization with inventories below base stock levels may be unable to fulfil sales orders in a reasonable time frame, thereby losing potential sales and suffering reputational damage.

Basic Standard for Enterprise Internal Control (CHINA-SOX) (2008)
Regulatory requirements issued in China for listed corporations. The Basic Standard is sometimes referred to as "CHINA SOX," as it covers topics similar to those

in the United States' earlier **Sarbanes-Oxley Act** (**SOX**) of 2002. It includes requirements for Chinese corporations to assess (and for financial auditors to audit) the effectiveness of **internal controls.**

bear
1 [*Noun*] An individual who believes that **prices** in a **securities** or **commodities** market will fall. **2** [*Adj.*] A securities or commodities market in which there are general expectations of falling market prices. Contrast **bull** for both senses.

bell (or bell-shaped) curve
See **normal distribution.**

benchmarking
The comparison of data or operations against those of similar (or sector-leading) organizations. Benchmarking, whether **quantitative** or **qualitative**, is usually undertaken to seek improvements to an organization's operations. Auditors frequently use benchmarking in their **analytical review** procedures. Example: an industry average of payroll cost per employee is a common benchmark to assess the reasonableness of payroll expenditures in a specific organization.

best practices
Policies, procedures, or **internal controls** held by consensus to represent optimal conditions. Example: the official guidance of the Institute of Internal Auditors (IIA) is widely viewed as a summary of the leading best practices for internal auditing, and many **internal auditors** who are not IIA members adhere to it voluntarily. Notions of best practices vary over time, in line with evolutions of the auditing *Zeitgeist*.

beta
1 A measure of the degree to which the returns on a **security** track the rest of the market. A beta coefficient is a measurement of the volatility of a security's **systematic risk**, which in **portfolio theory** cannot be reduced through **diversification**. A beta of 1 suggests that a security's returns mirror the movements of the rest of the market, and that it therefore has an average risk. A beta of more than 1 indicates that a security moves in the same direction as the market,

but to a greater degree. A beta of less than 1 denotes that a security moves in the same direction as the market, but to a degree that is less responsive than the market as a whole. A negative beta indicates that a security's returns follow the market inversely. **2** The second letter of the Greek alphabet, used extensively in statistics and financial economics.

betterment
The enhancement of the condition and operational functionality of a **fixed asset**. Betterment costs are normally **capitalized** in a **balance sheet**. Compare **maintenance**.

bias
An impediment to rational or **logical** reasoning, or to the integrity of **statistical sampling**. Bias undercuts auditor judgment and the results of statistical **audit tests**. See **anchoring and adjustment bias**, **availability bias**, **recency bias**, and **judgment**.

big bath reserves
Excessively large **provisions (senses 1 and 2)**. Most systems of **Generally Accepted Accounting Principles (GAAP)** restrict the use of big bath reserves, owing to their tainted reputation as a potential means of **creative accounting** through a subversion of the **accruals basis** of accounting. The creation of bloated reserves can be exploited to release the reserves (and thereby inflate **net income**) during periods of weak financial performance. See also **cookie jar reserves**.

Big Five, The
A collective designation of the five largest global public accounting and **financial auditing** firms before the demise of **Arthur Andersen** in 2002. Since 2002, it has been known as the **Big Four**.

Big Four, The
A collective designation of the largest global accounting and **financial auditing** firms. In 2022 the Big Four were Deloitte Touche Tohmatsu, Ernst & Young, KPMG, and PricewaterhouseCoopers. These firms are more than merely global financial auditors; they provide a range of professional services, from tax advice

to **consulting**. The **co-sourcing** and **outsourcing** of internal auditing services have been an important area of Big Four activity in the early twenty-first century.

billion

1 One thousand million. **2** [*Archaic*] An old British term for one million million. Modern British usage normally conforms to one thousand million, but the visitor to the United Kingdom should be wary of the term's potential ambiguity.

bill of materials (BOM)

A summary of the **raw materials** and other components of a manufactured product. A BOM serves as (i) a record of the materials used in a product and (ii) a control document for the manufacturing process. The term is sometimes also used in reference to the construction of a **fixed asset**.

black, in the [*Adj.*]

The state of experiencing **net income** or a positive cash flow. Contrast **red, in the**. The term derives from the practice of using red ink or font to depict negative income and cash flows, in contrast to black for positive flows.

"black box" audit approach

An audit methodology that sidesteps the technical complexities of a computerized processing system. The "black box" is the computer system ignored by the auditor, who focuses instead on a comparison of inputs with outputs. Example: an auditor may review balances from a computerized accounting system without reviewing the manner in which the system processed the underlying transactions. A "black box" approach is often adopted in the context of an auditor's inadequate technical knowledge of computerized systems, or in cases of restricted time or resources. Auditing around a computerized system may produce valid audit **evidence**, but it is essentially **substantive** and historical in nature, and it does not offer any ongoing **assurance** for **internal controls**.

Black Swan event

A **one-off**, unpredictable occurrence with potentially catastrophic outcomes. The term was coined by Nassim Nicholas Taleb (born 1960) in his book *Black Swan* (Taleb 2007). Black Swan events are troubling for auditors because of their unpredictability: they elude statistical **sampling**, **probability**, and **risk assess-ment** models, and they expose what Talib describes as "epistemic arrogance," the condition of exaggerating the extent of one's own knowledge. A Black Swan event may compromise an organization's **going concern** status.

blind entry
A **transaction** in a **general ledger** or an entry in a **journal** that lacks narrative explanation.

bloodhound, financial auditor not as
The notion that **financial auditing** is not **investigative** in nature. In the 1896 British *Kingston Cotton Mill Company* **case**, judicial reasoning held that finan-cial auditing was not investigative in character; the auditor was compared with a **watchdog** rather than with a bloodhound. The metaphor of the bloodhound refers to the bloodhound's reputation as a scent dog, associated with the tena-cious tracking of both animals and humans. By analogy, the financial auditor is not expected to "sniff out" audit **evidence** beyond the expectations of taking **due professional care**.

blue chip [*Adj.*]
A corporation (or its **common stock**) with a history of impressive and stable returns to investors. Blue chip corporations are perceived as reliable or low-**risk** investments. The term derives from the color of gambling chips used to place high-value bets in casinos.

blue-collar [*Adj.*]
Relating to manual work in an industrial setting. The term derives from the overalls traditionally worn in factories and warehouses. Contrast **white-collar**.

blue sky thinking
A synonym for **thinking outside the box**.

board of directors
A group of individuals with ultimate responsibility for the **stewardship** of an organization. Boards of **directors** have been described as "inescapably, the

centre of the [corporate] governance system" (Cadbury 2002, 33). Boards exercise their governance duties by, among other things, (i) elaborating organizational strategies and plans, (ii) defining **risks** and **risk appetites**, (iii) overseeing and reporting on **internal control** strategies, (iv) providing leadership to an organization, and (v) addressing the concerns of **stakeholders**. A main board of directors (or "top table") may delegate some of its authority to subordinate boards (e.g., in operational divisions and overseas **subsidiaries**), but it retains overall responsibility for an organization's stewardship. The responsibilities of boards of directors can be distinguished from those of an organization's managers—a board has a strategic oversight role, while managers take charge of day-to-day operations.

In English-speaking countries, boards of directors tend to have a unitary (or single-tier or monistic) structure. In contrast, two-tier (or dualistic) boards are the norm in continental Europe and some other parts of the world. Example: in Germany, a corporation's supervisory board (comprising representatives of investors and employees) appoints a management board to run the corporation's day-to-day business. This arrangement is intended to promote social partnership between various parties interested in the organization's stewardship, and thereby to avoid an overconcentration of power within the board structure. Although there is little evidence of moves toward a two-tier structure in the English-speaking world, the increasing importance of **outside directors** may be interpreted as an enhancement of independent oversight within the unitary board structure. See also **audit committee**, **remuneration committee**, and **tone at the top**.

boilerplate [*Adj.*]

Standardized, unimaginative, and uninformative. The term is often used pejoratively to indicate the clichéd content of **audit reports** and institutional statements on **internal control** and **risk management**.

bond

A **financial instrument** issued by a public- or private-sector institution. There are many varieties of bonds: (i) unsecured bonds, and those secured with **collateral**; (ii) **short-** and **long-term** bonds; and (iii) bonds with fixed or variable **interest** rates. The bond issuer commits to paying the bond's owner its **face**

value at a specific **maturity** date, and often also periodic interest payments. Unlike **common stock**, a corporation's bonds do not normally carry voting rights.

book
1 [*Plural noun*] A **general ledger** and related accounting records. See **book value** and **cooking the books**. **2** [*Verb*] To record an **entry** in a **general ledger** account.

bookkeeping
See **double entry bookkeeping**.

bookkeeping audit
An audit of **general ledger** transactions that focuses on the accuracy of **double entry bookkeeping** records.

books of account
See **book (sense 1)**.

books of prime entry [*Archaic*]
Accounting records used to summarize information before transfer to a **general ledger** account. Example: a **petty cash** register. Compare **subsidiary ledger**.

book value
1 The historical cost of an **asset** recorded in a **general ledger**. Compare **face value** and **market value**. **2** An alternative term for **carrying value**. **3** The value of a corporation, defined as total assets (or total **tangible** assets) less total liabilities).

bottleneck
A stage or point in a process or activity hindered by congestion or obstruction. Based on analogies with the slow flowing of liquid through a bottle's narrow opening, the term may indicate many types of restrictions to the flow of activities. In production processes, for example, a bottleneck indicates the exceeding of manufacturing capacities.

bottom line

1 **Net income** as recorded in an **income statement**. **2** The crux of an argument. Example: "The bottom line is that this new recruitment campaign must bring results."

box-ticking approach

An approach to auditing or **compliance testing** characterized by a superficial, unimaginative use of **checklists** and **questionnaires**. The term has powerful pejorative overtones, implying a focus on mechanistic information-gathering to the detriment of genuine insights into the underlying matters. Box-ticking in auditing may be interpreted as the subordination of **judgment** to process formalities.

boycott

The withdrawal of economic relations with an individual, organization, or country. A boycott arises from an economic or political dispute, and frequently involves the actions of pressure groups to discourage the purchasing of the goods and services of corporations or countries of whose actions they disapprove. The term derives from the name of a nineteenth-century British land agent in colonial Ireland, who was the subject of economic protests over high rents. Compare **embargo** and **sanction**.

brainstorming

The spontaneous generation and analysis of ideas by a group of individuals. Brainstorming is often advocated by modern management theory as a means of teasing out a large number of problem-solving ideas, or to enhance the so-called **Three Es** in an organization's operations. Generally, in a brainstorming session, a large number of initial suggestions is gradually pruned down, to produce focused recommendations for action.

branch

An operational or administrative unit of an organization. Many **multinational** corporations have branches around the world, and control over remote operating units of this nature present particular challenges. Organizational **risks** are magnified for branches separated from their head offices by (i) large geographical distances; (ii) cultural dissonance; (iii) linguistic differences; (iv) variations in local laws, regulations, and taxation; and (v) differences in **Generally Accepted Accounting Principles (GAAP)**. The degree of decentralization in an organization and the extent of the autonomy **delegated** to the managers of individual branches are central to the nature of an organization's **internal control environment**. The centralized control over branches may sometimes be channeled through the supervisory role of intermediary **divisions**.

brand
The name or logo of a product or service. Brands are **intangible assets** and their value is notoriously difficult to quantify. The value of brands is often made explicit in corporate **acquisitions**, in which it is reflected in **goodwill (sense 1)** in a **balance sheet**.

brass
1 [*Slang*] A British term for **money**. **2** [*Military slang*] A senior officer. An abbreviated form of "top brass," the term frequently insinuates incompetence and a failure to grasp operational complexity at senior institutional levels. The term is sometimes used in nonmilitary contexts.

break-even point
A level of activity at which total **costs** equal total **revenues**. Break-even analysis can be applied to individual products or services, or to an entire organization. At a break-even point, no profit or loss is made.

bribe
An improper or illegal inducement intended to gain influence over an individual or organization. Bribes may take the form of cash, assets, or services. Most legal and ethical systems forbid bribes, owing to their **corrupting** effects, though in practice the dividing lines between bribes and acceptable **gifts** and entertaining can often be fuzzy. In some cultures, the offering of expensive gifts is a commonplace means of social and business interaction. Significant antibribery legislation includes the United Kingdom's *Bribery Act*, Canada's *Corruption of Foreign Public Officials Act (CFPOA)*, and the United States' *Foreign Corrupt Practices Act (FCPA)*. Compare **facilitating payment**.

Bribery Act (2010)

United Kingdom legislation covering domestic and international **bribery**. The *Bribery Act* is broadly equivalent to the United States' ***Foreign Corrupt Practices Act* (FCPA)** and, like the FCPA, it is considered to be uncompromisingly rigorous. For example, the *Bribery Act* holds "commercial organizations" vicariously liable for bribery undertaken by individual employees or **agents**, unless the organization can demonstrate clearly that it has taken all reasonable precautions ("adequate procedures") over the conduct of individuals to prevent bribery.

broker

An intermediary in financial **transactions**. Brokers typically act as **agents** to purchase and sell assets on behalf of others, and they operate in **markets** for items such as **securities**, **commodities**, **currencies**, and **insurance** policies. Brokers are normally rewarded with **commission**.

buck

1 [*Slang*] One US **dollar**. **2** [*Among investment traders*] A euphemism for one million dollars.

budget

A quantitative plan for future activities. The use of budgets is common in most private- and public-sector organizations. Budgets normally fulfill one or more of the following purposes: they act as (i) a record of planned activities; (ii) a means of communicating an organization's plans to its employees; (iii) a standard against which to compare **variances** with actual performance; (iv) an **accountability** mechanism and a means of motivating and rewarding individuals for performance against budget; (v) a brake on profligate expenditures; and (vi) an **internal control** over operations. The sophistication and methodology of budgets varies widely. Budgets may be limited to high-level data on assets, revenues, and expenditures, or they may consist of detailed financial statements, cash forecasts, and operational statistics for individual areas of an organization.

While budgets may have a positive motivational effect on individuals, they may also have dysfunctional consequences. Example: employees may be tempted to incur inappropriate expenditures to fully exhaust a budget, to ensure that they are allocated a similar budgetary level in future years. More generally, organizational turf wars may erupt over the allocation of budgeted resources, and it has been perceptively noted that "it is a rare organization in which budgets do not create a framework for conflict" (Sawyer and Vinten 1996, 245). See also **appropriation** and **forecast.**

budget committee
A group of individuals responsible for overseeing the development and **authorization** of budgets in an organization.

bug
1 An error or flaw in a computer software program. **2** A slang term for **virus (both senses).**

bull
1 [*Noun*] An individual who expects prices in a **securities** or **commodities** market to rise. **2** [*Adj.*] A securities or commodities market in which there are general expectations of rising prices. Contrast **bear** for both senses.

bureaucracy
An organization or a style of administration characterized by a clearly defined, **top-down hierarchical** structure, with an emphasis on strict adherence to rules and procedures. The term is often used pejoratively to imply an inefficient or authoritarian organization. See **authority** and **chain of command.**

business combination
The amalgamation of two or more organizations to form a new economic unit. Most business combinations take the form of **acquisitions** or **mergers**, and their reporting requirements give rise to **consolidated** financial statements.

business continuity planning (BCP)
Policies and procedures designed to secure an organization's ongoing operations. BCP addresses an organization's resilience in the face of daily challenges, in addition to potentially catastrophic disasters like (i) the loss of accounting data and **institutional memory** through cyberattacks; (ii) the destruction of

buildings, fixed assets, and inventory; and (iii) the disruption of distribution networks by adverse weather conditions. Typical BCP components include (i) the adequate **backup** of accounting information, (ii) procedures for the rapid replacement of key employees, and (iii) guidelines for conducting press relations to explain significant disruptions to operations. BCP covers **preventive**, **detective**, and **corrective** internal controls.

business process outsourcing (BPO)

The transfer by an organization of administrative activities to outside providers. The outsourcing organization retains responsibility for an outsourced administrative activity, the handling of which it typically controls through the periodic monitoring of performance. Compare **co-sourcing**.

business process reengineering (BPR)

Radical changes to an organization's processes and procedures aimed at reducing costs or enhancing the **Three Es** of operations.

by-product

An incidental product emerging from a production process. By-products typically have significantly less value than the main production items from which they derive, and they are sometimes unavoidable. Example: paraffin and lubricants are by-products of oil refining processes. Depending on its **materiality**, a by-product can be accounted for as a separate unit of **inventory**, or revenues from its sale can be offset against the production costs of the principal manufactured items. The **financial auditing** profession tends to consider the detection of **fraud** as a by-product, not the principal aim, of financial auditing. Compare **joint product**.

calendarization

The monthly apportionment of a quantifiable item. Example: yearly expenditures on rent totaling $120,000 may be calendarized over twelve months by simply dividing by 12, unless the pattern in which the rent is incurred falls unevenly between individual months. Calendarization is common in **budgeting** calculations. Compare **annualization**.

call option
The right to purchase an asset or **security** at a specific price within a defined time period. Contrast **put option.**

capacity
1 The maximum amount that can be contained in a defined space. Example: "The corporation rented additional warehouse space after storage capacity in its old warehouse was exceeded." **2** The maximum amount of production that can be handled by a manufacturing process. Typical limiting factors on production capacity include restrictions arising from (i) space, (ii) the availability of **labor**, (iii) the condition of **plant and machinery**, (iv) the supply of **raw materials**, and (v) the adequacy of funding.

capex
An abbreviation for **capital expenditures.**

capital
1 Ownership interest in a corporation's **equity (sense 1).** Under the conventions of **double entry bookkeeping** and the **accounting equation**, stockholders' capital consists of the **par value** of **common stock** plus **retained earnings.** **2** Individuals' wealth as measured by total **assets** less total **liabilities.** **3** **Fixed assets** with wealth-generating potential. **4** [*Archaic*] In classical economic theory, capital was one of the three (or four) **factors of production** alongside land and natural resources, labor, and (under some definitions) **entrepreneurship.** Capital was usually understood in this context as consisting of the industrial tools that served as instruments of production, rather than **money.**

capital asset pricing model (CAPM)
A framework for the analysis of the relationships between the **risks** and returns of securities. CAPM makes a number of assumptions, including these: (i) all the investors in a market hold a **diversified** portfolio of securities, so the activity of any single security will not materially affect the market; (ii) the risk of a particular security can be assessed only in terms of its performance to the rest of the portfolio; and (iii) the price of a security whose returns follow market trends will

tend to be low. CAPM states that a security's risk can be analyzed into **systematic** and **unsystematic** risk. The former is nondiversifiable risk, measured by the use of **beta (sense 1)**, while the latter is diversifiable risk.

capital expenditures

The purchase or **betterment** of **long-term** assets like **property, plant, and equipment**. The term is often abbreviated to "capex." Contrast **revenue expenditures**.

capital gain or loss

A **surplus** or **deficit** arising from the disposal of an asset, calculated as the difference between cash proceeds received and the asset's historical cost. The **historical costs** of assets in taxable capital gains are often adjusted for the effects of **inflation** through **indexation**.

capitalization

1 The classification or reclassification of a cost to an **asset** account. Most systems of **Generally Accepted Accounting Principles (GAAP)** permit the capitalization of assets of a **long-term** nature in the **balance sheet**. Example: the costs of renovating a production machine to extend its life by more than one year may be treated as **capital expenditures** through the addition of the expenditures to the cost of the asset. See also **betterment**. **2** The market value of a corporation's total issued **common stock**.

capital lease

A **lease** with contractual terms and economic effects that transfer the **risks** and **rewards** of an asset. Under most systems of **Generally Accepted Accounting Principles (GAAP)**, a **lessee** capitalizes in its **balance sheet** an asset obtained through a capital lease. This is an example of the principle of **substance over form**: the capital lease results in a lessee's *de facto* ownership of the leased asset. Contrast operating lease.

carrying value

An amount shown in a **balance sheet** for an **asset** or **liability**, net of any **offsetting** items. Example: the carrying value of a fixed asset is normally calculated after deduction of **amortization** charges, and the carrying value of **accounts receivable** is typically shown net of an **allowance for bad debts**. It is sometimes referred to as **book value (sense 2)**.

cartel

An arrangement or conspiracy among two or more **suppliers** of a good or service to restrict **competition** so as to influence **prices**. Cartels are illegal in most countries, through **antitrust laws** and regulations to enhance competition. Some cartels operate internationally. A commonly discussed example: the Organization of the Petroleum Exporting Countries (OPEC) attempts to influence world oil prices by coordinating the production levels of its member states, but OPEC defends itself on the grounds that it seeks merely to establish "fair and reasonable" prices for both suppliers and consumers. Compare **monopoly** and **oligopoly**.

cash

1 Tangible units of **money**. In this sense, cash is restricted to bank notes and coins. Small quantities of cash held for day-to-day expenditures are referred to as **petty cash**. **2** Money deposited in a bank. Sometimes, restrictions on the **liquidity** of some bank deposits may not justify a classification as cash. Example: **postdated** checks and bank deposits with withdrawal restrictions may not have sufficient liquidity to be deemed as cash. **3** Highly liquid assets like **checks** and **matured financial instruments**.

cash basis (of accounting)

The **recognition (sense 1)** of **income (sense 1)** and expenditures in line with the timing of related cash movements. Cash basis accounting is not permissible under most systems of **Generally Accepted Accounting Principles (GAAP)**, which require the **accruals basis**, which recognizes income and expenditures as they are earned and incurred.

cash cow

An activity, product, or organization that regularly and reliably generates a healthy cash flow. Cash cows are typically characterized by (i) low growth and (ii) activity in mature markets.

cash equivalent value
The amount of cash that can be received for the sale of an asset in an **arm's-length transaction**. See also **market value**.

cash float
See **float (sense 1)**.

cash flow forecast
A quantifiable estimate of future cash movements arising from the activities of an organization or individual. Many **budgets** include cash flow forecasts to accompany **accruals-based** estimates of **income (sense 1)** and expenditures.

cash flow statement
A summary of cash movements arising from the activities of an organization or individual. Most systems of **Generally Accepted Accounting Principles (GAAP)** require the inclusion of a cash flow statement in a corporation's **financial statements**. Cash flow statements show cash inflows (e.g., from sales) and outflows (e.g., in the form of operating expenses and investments).

casting
A British term for **footing**.

caveat [Latin]
Warning, limitation, caution, **risk**. (Literally: "Beware.") Example: "There's one caveat. The agreement stipulates that you cannot sell your common stock for at least two years."

caveat emptor [Latin]
Literally: "Let the buyer beware." The phrase is used widely in the common law systems of English-speaking countries. It emphasizes the risks inherent in commercial transactions, indicating that a purchaser has a responsibility to examine carefully an article before acquiring it. In the absence of fraud or misrepresentation by a seller, a purchaser must bear the consequences of a decision to buy. In modern times, the implications of caveat emptor have been significantly diminished by the development of consumer protection legislation.

CEAVOP
See **assertions**.

cell
1 An individual element of a **spreadsheet** grid that contains numbers, mathematical formulas, or text. Cells occur at intersection points between a spreadsheet's rows and columns, from which they derive precise grid references. **2** In manufacturing, an operational unit of machines, personnel, or other resources dedicated to discrete tasks. Production cells are particularly associated with the control of operational flows in **just-in-time** environments.

central bank
A national bank that regulates a country's economic system and acts as a lender of last resort to commercial banks. Central banks normally establish a country's short-term **base interest rate**. The level of political influence over central bank policies varies from country to country.

centralization
A concentration of activities, power, and decision-making **authority** within an organization. Centralization may occur (i) in geographical terms (e.g., at a **multinational** corporation's headquarters); (ii) in **hierarchical** terms, with power concentrated in the hands of a small number of individuals at the summit of a **chain of command**; and (iii) in a combination of geographical and hierarchical terms. The antonym of centralization is **decentralization**.

certainty
With 100 percent **probability** of occurrence. Contrast **uncertainty**.

certification
1 An official **recognition (sense 2)** of achievement in a course of **professional** education. Example: the main certification of the Institute of Internal Auditors is the **Certified Internal Auditor** diploma. **2** See **attestation (sense 1)**.

Certified Internal Auditor (CIA)
The **professional** certification of the Institute of Internal Auditors. The CIA designation confers professional **recognition (sense 2)** as an **internal auditor** but

it does not confer a license to practice, as such a license is not required by law to undertake internal auditing.

Certified Public Accountant (CPA)

The designation of accountants and **financial auditors** in the United States who meet **professional** criteria in terms of certification and length of experience. The uniform CPA examination is set nationally by the American Institute of Certified Public Accountants, while the experience criteria for licensure are established by individual states' boards of accountancy. Since 1908, the national umbrella organization for the latter has been the National Association of State Boards of Accountancy. The historical trend of the characterization of public accounting has been succinctly summarized as follows: public accounting "was born through **bankruptcies**, fed on . . . **fraud**, grew on **liquidations** and graduated through audits" (quoted by Matthews, Anderson, and Edwards 1998, 93).

A number of countries have adopted the term "CPA" to designate their public accounting professions (at least in the English translations of the names of their professional organizations). Examples include Israel (the Institute of Certified Public Accountants in Israel), Japan (the Japanese Institute of Certified Public Accountants), and Kenya (the Institute of Certified Public Accountants of Kenya). Many English-speaking countries use the term **Chartered Accountant** rather than CPA.

chain of command

A term derived from military planning to denote the flows of **authority** and **accountability** within an activity or organization. In a chain of command, individuals **delegate** authority to the next lowest **hierarchical** level. Thus, A has authority over B, who is answerable to A; B in turn has authority over C, who is answerable to B; C in turn has authority over D, who is answerable to C; and so on. In a chain of command, departures from established policies and procedures are usually met with disciplinary measures. Most organizations exhibit chain-of-command features, which offer the advantages of discipline and clarity of purpose. However, chain-of-command arrangements may be inflexible, and management theory in recent years has increasingly advocated the **empowerment** of individuals at different levels of an organization.

challan [Hindi]

A term used widely in India for a **voucher**, form, or document.

channel stuffing

A **creative accounting** technique that temporarily inflates sales revenues. The stuffing of distribution channels preceding sensitive **cutoff** dates is achieved through a commercial organization sending excessive quantities of goods to retailers and distributors close to the end of a **financial reporting period**. Although intermediaries (and final consumers) usually possess the right to return the goods, the effect of the intense activity is to inflate sales. Channel stuffing is unsustainable—eventually, the returns eliminate some or all of the excess sales. However, as a short-term measure to boost **earnings (senses 1 and 2)**, it can be effective, though it may contravene **Generally Accepted Accounting Principles (GAAP)**, if **material**. See **window dressing**.

chaos theory

The proposition that systems are governed by unpredictability, owing to the random behavior of independent variables. Beneath the randomness of day-to-day details, however, deeper patterns may be discerned. "Chaos" in this sense does not therefore refer to an everyday meaning of "utter confusion." Weather patterns are often given as an example of chaos theory in practice, in that they combine predictability with unpredictability. A popular metaphor associated with the theory (and first articulated by Edward Lorenz, 1917–2008) is the "butterfly effect": the notion that the flapping of a butterfly's wings can disturb the atmosphere, contributing to a chain of events that causes an environmental catastrophe elsewhere. The "butterfly effect" suggests that small events contain a potential for major, unpredictable repercussions. Chaos theory is a sophisticated and highly technical branch of physics and mathematics. See **Black Swan** event.

charter

See **audit charter**.

Chartered Accountant (CA)

The principal designation of **public accountants** and **financial auditors** in the United Kingdom and additional English-speaking countries. Equivalent to the term **Certified Public Accountant** in the United States, the status of CA is generally awarded following **certification** and a period of relevant professional experience. In the United Kingdom, the principal professional organizations for CAs are the Institute of Chartered Accountants in England and Wales and the Institute of Chartered Accountants of Scotland.

chart of accounts

A sequentially numbered list of **general ledger** accounts. In some countries, typically those with a Napoleonic Code legal tradition, charts of accounts are defined by legislation and facilitate the gathering of information for the purposes of taxation and national economic statistics. Example: the French *plan comptable général*. In common law countries, organizations tend to have discretion in the design of their general ledger systems.

check

1 The **verification** of the existence or accuracy of something. The performance of checks is central to the obtaining and assessment of audit **evidence**. When unannounced, such verifications are sometimes called "spot checks." **2** A document that instructs a bank to pay a sum of money to a named individual or organization from a specific date. Though still an important **disbursement** mechanism, the use of checks is increasingly giving way to **wire transfers**.

check digit

A digit added to a number to permit verification of its accuracy by a computerized accounting system.

checklist

A documented summary of questions, reminders, or other actions. The creation of checklists is intended to ensure that all steps of a process have been identified. Checklists are often used in the context of **Control Risk Self-Assessment**. Their use is frequently criticized on the grounds of their alleged inability to stimulate creative thought. See also **box-ticking approach**.

cheque

The British spelling of **check (sense 2)**.

cherry picking
A biased selection of a sample that may give a misleading impression of an entire data population. In **judgmental sampling**, the cherry picking of items for an **audit test** is likely to lead to unreliable evidence. This term carries notions of intentional bias.

Chief Audit Executive (CAE)
The most senior **internal auditing** post in an organization. Other titles associated with this post include Auditor General, Chief Internal Auditor, General Auditor, and Head of Audit. In all cases, CAE or its equivalent term designates the individual responsible for managing and administering an organization's **internal audit function**.

Chief Executive Officer (CEO)
The most senior individual responsible for the management of an organization. The CEO sits at the top of a **hierarchical**, **chain-of-command** system.

Chief Financial Officer (CFO)
The individual responsible for an organization's financial and accounting functions.

Chief Internal Auditor (CIA)
An alternative term for **Chief Audit Executive**.

Chinese walls
Voluntary information barriers between organizational departments to limit the dissemination of sensitive information. Chinese walls are intended to preserve confidentiality, and to prevent **conflicts of interest** or the abuse of **price-sensitive information**. In multidisciplinary organizations that include **financial auditors**, Chinese walls can act as a mechanism to ensure the auditors' independence from the delivery of other services to an **auditee**. The term derives from the well-known defensive walls erected around ancient China.

circularization
An auditor's written request for **third-party** confirmation of the existence and value of an item under audit. Examples: the circularization by financial auditors of

an organization's customers to confirm **accounts receivable** balances, and requests to banks for evidence of bank deposits and loans. A positive circularization involves a third party confirming the correctness of a communicated balance. A negative circularization requests a reply only in the case of disagreement with a stated amount. A blank circularization asks the recipient to provide the balance. Third-party **evidence** is generally considered by auditors to be of high value, and the responses to circularizations are therefore viewed as strong audit evidence. Responses to circularizations tend to be sent directly to auditors rather than via an **auditee**, to reduce the likelihood of auditee interference during the transmission of the information.

circulating assets
An alternative term for **working capital**.

classification
An arrangement or grouping of items into categories based on shared characteristics. Example: an organization's expenditures are classified into descriptive **general ledger** accounts.

clean audit / clean opinion [*Informal*]
A colloquial term for an audit with an **unmodified** or **unqualified opinion**.

clinical auditing
The auditing of medical activities. Clinical auditing includes both **qualitative** and **quantitative** reviews of patient care, but often focuses on the latter to measure actual to desired outcomes. The review and improvement procedures undertaken by Florence Nightingale (1820–1910) in military hospitals in the mid-nineteenth-century Crimean War are considered to be among the first examples of modern clinical auditing.

cloud computing
Computer services delivered remotely to users through the Internet.

code of (professional) ethics
Formal guidance for moral conduct in the practice of a **profession**.
An altruistic ethos is perceived as essential to public service concepts of

professionalism, and codes of ethics are therefore common in professional organizations. The codes may be either **principles-based** or **rules-based**, and their content typically includes matters of honesty, competence, **due professional care**, and the avoidance of harming others. The *Hippocratic Oath*, for newly qualified physicians, dates from the fifth to the third century before the common era and is an early example of a code of professional ethics that bears a continuing relevance today. An example of a code of professional auditing ethics is the Code of Professional Conduct of the American Institute of Certified Public Accountants (AICPA), which has six principles: responsibilities, public interest, due care, integrity, objectivity and independence, and scope and nature of services.

collateral
Assets pledged to secure or guarantee a **debt**. Default on a debt normally leads to the lender's possession of the assets provided as collateral. Assets commonly used for collateral include real estate property and **inventories**.

collective bargaining
A labor union's group negotiation of the pay and working conditions of its members. An organization of employees is likely to have greater power than single individuals in negotiating with employers.

collusion
A conspiracy between two or more individuals or organizations for **fraudulent** or improper purposes. Example: an employee in a manufacturing organization may collude with a **vendor** to overcharge the costs of raw materials.

comfort
The **assurance** provided by audit **evidence** in addressing **audit objectives** (senses 1 and 2). Auditors aim to obtain high levels of evidential comfort to support their **opinions**.

comfort letter
An alternative term for **representation letter**.

command and control
See **chain of command**.

command economy
An economy in which the state determines the allocation of economic resources, industrial output, and the **prices** of products and services. In a command economy, **market** forces are subdued or eliminated in favor of centralized economic planning. However, the existence of **underground economies** has tended throughout history to undermine the objectives of command economies. Few command economies exist in the early twenty-first century, after the collapse of the Soviet Union (and the subsequent withdrawal of its support for allies and satellite states) in the late 1980s and early 1990s. Communist countries like China and Vietnam have embraced free market principles to varying degrees. See also **nationalization**.

commission
A **fee** for services provided by an **agent** or other intermediary. Commission is often calculated as a percentage of the value of underlying transactions. Illegal commissions are termed **kickbacks**.

Committee of Sponsoring Organizations of the Treadway Commission (COSO)
An organization based in the United States that aims at improving **corporate governance**, **financial reporting**, and **internal controls**, COSO aims to ameliorate corporate governance and deter fraud. Founded in 1985 to sponsor the **National Commission on Fraudulent Financial Reporting** (1987), which produced the *Treadway Commission Report*, COSO is sponsored by five US accounting and auditing organizations: The American Accounting Association, the American Institute of Certified Public Accountants, Financial Executives International, the Institute of Internal Auditors, and the Institute of Management Accountants (formerly the National Association of Accountants).

In addition to the *Treadway Commission Report*, other landmark COSO publications include the 1992 report *Internal Control–Integrated Framework*, updated in 2013, and the 2004 report *Enterprise Risk Management–Integrated Framework*, replaced in 2017 by *Enterprise Risk Management–Integrating with Strategy and Performance*.

commodity

1 A raw, natural resource. Commodities include agricultural items like grains and other foodstuffs, and items extracted by mining, like iron ore. Commodities are often traded in large quantities through sophisticated, global **markets**.

2 A **fungible** item of economic value. The analysis of commodity exchange has often been viewed through two lenses of value—an exchange value and a value in use. The difference between these two values can be analyzed, respectively, in terms of **price** and **utility**. Examples: A $20 bill has a defined exchange value but very little use value; a cup of water usually has a low exchange value but it may possess (to a thirsty person) immense use value.

common law

The section of the law in English-speaking countries that is derived from judicial precedent and custom. Unlike **legislation**, which is created by the parliamentary enactment of statutes, common law derives from case law and the binding nature of accumulated, prior decisions of judges. Flexibility in the system of precedents is achieved through (i) a differentiation between the judicial reasoning necessary for the decision (the *ratio decidendi*) and the other statements relating to the case (the *obiter dicta*) and (ii) judicial discretion in the application of precedents to current cases. The common law developed in England and is used in most parts of the English-speaking world. It is frequently contrasted with civil law systems originating in continental Europe. The development of **financial auditing** in the United Kingdom and the United States has been heavily influenced by case law (appendix B),

common market

An international trading area created by the reduction or elimination of **customs** duties and other cross-border formalities between nations. Examples: the Andean Community (formerly the Andean Pact), founded in 1969; and the European Union, an earlier form of which was created by the 1957 Treaty of Rome.

common stock

A share of ownership in a corporation. The owners of common stock normally enjoy voting rights and are rewarded for their investment by both **dividends** and **appreciations** in the common stock's **market value**. Common stock is classified as **equity** in a **balance sheet**, in which it is normally shown at **par value**.

Companies Act 1948 [United Kingdom]

One of a series of English legislative acts on corporate law. The significance of the 1948 *Act* for **financial auditing** was that it set out, for the first time, a recognizably modern profile of financial auditing for British corporations: it required independent auditors to provide an opinion as to the **true and fair** view of all corporations' **financial statements**. It restricted financial auditors to the members of specified **professional** associations, and it set out the rights and responsibilities of auditors. Starting in the mid–nineteenth century, previous legislation had slowly accumulated most of these legal aspects of auditing: in 1900, for example, an annual independent audit had been required of virtually all corporations. In the aftermath of the catastrophe of World War II, the 1948 *Act* consolidated the historical developments with additional clarifications and requirements. (At the time of this writing, in 2024, the most recent British *Companies Act* dates from 2006.)

Companies Act 2013 [India]

Indian legislation with wide-ranging provisions for corporate law. The 2013 *Act* was influenced by the United States' *Sarbanes-Oxley Act* **(SOX, 2002)**, insofar as it requires **financial auditors** to provide an opinion on a corporation's "internal financial controls" (in addition to the financial auditor's **opinion** on the **financial statements**). The term "internal financial controls" is considered to refer only to **internal controls** directly affecting financial reporting.

compensating balance

1 An amount **offset** by a bank between a loan and a deposit. **2** Two or more accounting balances that offset one another.

compensating control

A secondary or alternative **internal control** that mitigates the risks arising from the absence or limited effectiveness of a primary internal control. Example: an individual who records bank **transactions** and processes **disbursements** appears *prima facie* to violate a basic principle of **segregations of**

responsibilities. In such a situation, a typical compensating control is the performance of periodic **bank reconciliations** by a different individual.

compensating error
A **compensating balance (sense 2)** that consists of two errors. The compensating error neutralizes the effects of an earlier error. Items of this nature are frequently undetected in **trial balances**, as the compensating error does not give rise to an overall arithmetic difference.

compensation
1 Employee **remuneration**, in the form of **salaries, wages**, and other **fringe benefits**. **2** Recompense for damage, injury, or wrongdoing.

competition
Rivalry in a **market**. Competition is often viewed as a positive means of encouraging **efficient** markets, and **antitrust laws** are among the ways in which countries attempt to promote competitive economic practices. **Prices** in free markets are established by the interplay of competitive forces among buyers and sellers. Contrast **cartel**, and **oligopoly**.

compliance
Conformity with laws, **regulations**, procedures, or the terms of a **contract**.

compliance audit
An audit of adherence to laws, regulations, procedures, contractual obligations, or internal controls. A compliance audit is not to be confused with **compliance testing**: the former has as its **audit objective** the verification of compliance with external or internal requirements, while the latter is an auditing procedure used to gather audit **evidence** on the reliability of **internal controls**.

compliance costs
Expenditures to maintain compliance systems and procedures. Example: an organization facing heavy regulation may be obliged to keep costly monitoring records, and to employ a team of auditors to perform **compliance audits**.

compliance testing
Auditing procedures that evaluate the reliability of an entity's **internal controls**. In contrast to the focus of **substantive testing** on verifying the accuracy of quantifiable amounts, compliance testing aims to gain reasonable **assurance** on the effective and efficient operation of internal controls. Auditors tend to reduce the level of substantive testing if compliance testing indicates the satisfactory operation of internal controls and related procedures: "Where a system of accounting and internal control has been well designed and adhered to in operation, and its integrity secured by effective internal check and internal audit, a high degree of reliability may be placed on the data derived from the system" (Flint 1988, 114). Most audits consist of a mixture of compliance and substantive testing, with the balance between the two determined by the volume of transactions to be tested, in addition to the sophistication and reliability of internal controls. Contrast **compliance audit.**

compound interest
The calculation of **interest** on a sum of money by the application of an **interest rate** to both (i) the original sum of money and (ii) accumulated interest. Contrast **simple interest.**

comprehensive auditing [*Archaic*]
An alternative term for **operational auditing** and **value-for-money auditing.** The term was used widely in the United Kingdom before the 1970s.

***comptroller* [*French*]**
A rather archaic, even quaint, term for **controller.** Taken from Anglo-Norman French, the term is still in use in the **public sector** in some English-speaking countries.

computer assisted audit techniques (CAATs)
Methods of gathering, sorting, and analyzing audit **evidence** through computer software programs. CAATs may cover both **compliance** and **substantive testing.**

confirmation
The **verification** of the existence or accuracy of something.

confirmation letter
See **circularization**.

conflict of interest
An incompatibility between rights and responsibilities. **Rewards** gained by
an individual from a conflict of interest are generally regarded as unethical, and they may also breach legislation or regulatory requirements.
Example: an employee of an organization who negotiates raw material prices
with a family-related **vendor** faces a potential conflict of interest between
(i) minimizing costs to the employer and (ii) maximizing returns to the family
member. Financial auditors are particularly sensitive to accusations of conflicts
of interest that may impair their ability to give an **independent** and objective
audit **opinion**. Examples: the providing of lucrative **management advisory services** to an **auditee** and personal investments in an auditee's business are typical
indicators of potential conflicts of interest in financial auditing.

conglomerate
A large, **diversified** corporation.

conservatism [*in accounting and auditing*]
A cautious, **prudent**, **skeptical**, or even pessimistic attitude. Conservatism
tends to result in the prompt **recognition (sense 1)** of expenses and the slow
recognition of revenues, in its aim to avoid understating the former and over-
stating the latter. The **accruals** basis of accounting, rigorously applied, is an
example of the application of accounting conservatism in practice.

consideration
A legal term for the transfer of **money**, **assets**, or other items of **value** in relation
to a **contract**. Consideration may take the form of (i) cash payments, (ii) waivers of
cash payments, (iii) transfers of **tangible assets**, or (iv) the providing of services.

consignment
1 A delivery of goods relating to (and sometimes in advance of) a sale.
2 An arrangement in which an **agent** or intermediary takes physical custody

of a vendor's **inventory**, pending anticipated sales to **third parties**. The agent earns **commission** for the storage and sale of the inventory. The **risks** and **rewards** of the transactions and the inventory normally remain principally with the vendor.

consistency
The regular treatment over time of an **accounting** item or procedural matter. Consistency is a concept fundamental to both accounting and auditing, and its promotion is one of the main purposes of **Generally Accepted Accounting Principles (GAAP)** and **Generally Accepted Auditing Standards (GAAS)**. See the fifth and sixth of the **postulates of auditing** elaborated in the 1960s by Robert Kuhn Mautz and Hussein A. Sharaf.

consolidation accounting
The presentation of the **financial statements** of two or more organizations as one economic unit. Consolidation accounting techniques require the combination of the financial statements of the individual organizations of a **business combination** (i.e., of a **parent organization** and its **subsidiaries**), subject to adjustments like the elimination of profits on **intercompany transactions** between the consolidated entities.

consulting
The providing of specialist advice or expertise beyond audit services. See **management advisory services**.

consumer
An individual who purchases goods and services for personal use. See also **consumption**.

consumer goods
Tangible merchandise or products for sale to the general public. Consumer disposables for instant, **one-off** use, like food, are differentiated from consumer durables, like dishwashers, for use over a period of time. See also **consumption** and **finished goods**.

consumer society

A society or country in which individuals place excessive importance on the accumulation and **consumption** of material goods. In a consumer society, the conspicuous display of material wealth is deemed to be indicative of social achievement. The term has implications of alienation and anomie arising from an inordinate fascination with materialism.

consumption

The use of economic resources. Consumer consumption refers to the final enjoyment of an item's **worth**; in this sense, consumption is the final point in the economic process of production, distribution, and exchange. Consumption may be characterized as the main purpose of economic activity.

consumption tax

An **indirect tax** charged on a good or a service. The burden of a consumption tax falls on the individual or organization that enjoys the full **worth** of the good or service: it is levied at the final stage of the economic process of production, distribution, and exchange. Example: consumption taxes on cigarettes. See also **sales tax** and **value added tax**.

contingent liability

A potential **liability** of doubtful existence or quantification. Most systems of **Generally Accepted Accounting Principles (GAAP)** require the **disclosure** of **material** contingent liabilities in **financial statements**. Contingent liabilities normally depend on the occurrence or outcome of a specific event, such as a court case. Financial auditors use **attorney letters** to gather or corroborate **evidence** of contingent liabilities.

continuing operation

An activity in an organization that is expected to stay in operation. Contrast **discontinued operation**.

continuous auditing

Auditing activity sustained over an extended time period. Example: daily stocktaking checks to monitor the reliability of a **perpetual inventory** system.

A continuous audit is not necessarily an uninterrupted process—it may involve
short breaks in audit activity—and it usually requires specialized software.

continuous improvement (CI)

A Japanese management philosophy that constantly aims to ameliorate all
aspects of an organization's activities. CI tends to be based on customer needs
and is intended to act as a stimulus to improve (among other things) the **Three
Es** of **economy**, **efficiency**, and **effectiveness**. CI is often known by the Japanese term *kaizen*.

contra account

A **general ledger** account that **offsets** another account. Example: **allowances
for bad debts** are recorded in contra accounts in relation to **accounts receivable**.
The Latin word *contra* means "against" or "opposite." See also **contra entry**.

contract

An agreement between two or more parties that is enforceable in law. Contracts
may be written, verbal, or even implied by circumstances. To be legally binding,
a contract must normally be accompanied by some form of **consideration**.

contract auditing

The auditing of **contracts**. A specialization of internal auditing, contract auditing aims to provide **assurance** that contractual terms are correctly followed.

contra entry

An item booked to a general ledger **account** to **offset**, cancel, or partially reduce
a balance. A contra entry is not restricted to the same general ledger account as
the item to which it relates.

control

The exercising of **authority**, regulation, or restriction over an activity, process, or individual. In an auditing context, a control refers to a procedural or
physical mechanism to address a **risk** or to enhance the **economy**, **efficiency**,
or **effectiveness** of operations. A control may or may not be embedded in an
organization's day-to-day operations. Organizational control is often analyzed

into **external control (sense 1)** effected by **stakeholders**, and **internal control** effected by **boards of directors**, managers, and employees.

control account / controlling account
A **general ledger** account used to record and monitor the accuracy of amounts transferred from **subsidiary ledgers**.

control framework
A conceptual basis for understanding and analyzing **internal controls** and **external controls (sense 1)**. A well-known example is the *Internal Control-Integrated Framework* of the Committee of Sponsoring Organizations of the Treadway Commission (COSO).

controllable costs
Expenses incurred at the discretion of an organization's managers. The performance of individuals is often appraised, at least in part, in relation to the efficient and effective stewardship of controllable costs. Most controllable costs are **variable**, but some **fixed costs** may also be discretionary. See also **avoidable costs** and **unavoidable costs**.

controllable risk
A **risk** that can be mitigated, transferred, or eliminated. See **risk minimization**. Contrast **control risk (sense 1)** and **uncontrollable risk**.

controller
See **financial controller**.

control risk
1 In financial auditing, the risk that items in financial statements are misstated as a result of problems in an organization's internal control systems. Control risk is considered alongside inherent risk (sense 1) and detection risk as one of three components of audit risk (sense 1), and it is usually assessed through compliance testing. A system of weak internal controls implies a high control risk. **2** In internal auditing, the risk of a breakdown in internal controls.

control (risk) self-assessment (CRSA/CSA)

A **risk assessment** methodology in which an organization's employees identify and assess areas of **risk** and **internal control** for which they are responsible. CRSA processes include the use of **questionnaires** and the gathering of information through interviews, workshops, and **brainstorming** exercises. Although CRSA processes involve risk assessments made by an organization's employees, the concept is often facilitated by an organization's **internal audit function**.

conversion costs

Production costs incurred in converting **raw materials** into **finished products**. The costs of the raw materials are usually excluded from conversion cost calculations, which focus on direct labor costs and production **overhead.**

convertible security

A **financial instrument** that can be converted into **common stock** during a defined time period. The exercising of rights over convertible securities may **dilute** a corporation's common stock, affecting **earnings per share** calculations.

cookie jar reserves [*Informal*]

A semihumorous term for **accrued expenses** created with the intention of manipulating **financial statements.** The term derives from the image of dipping at one's convenience into a jar of cookies; by analogy, reserves of this type are released at the convenience of the managers of an organization to inflate **earnings** at times of weak financial performance. The selective misuse of reserves in this manner is a subversion of the **accruals basis** of accounting and is forbidden by most systems of **Generally Accepted Accounting Principles (GAAP).** The term "cookie jar reserves" was used in a speech in 1998 by Arthur Levitt, then chair of the US Securities and Exchange Commission. See also **big bath reserves** and **creative accounting.**

cooking the books

A semihumorous term for **false accounting** or the **fraudulent** manipulation of accounting data.

cooperation

A process of working with a partner or partners for a common purpose. Cooperation between auditor and **auditee** is central to the search for **assurance** that lies at the heart of auditing, Auditing, especially **financial auditing**, is nearly impossible under **adversarial** conditions. Auditors act as intermediaries between third parties to report on **accountability** arrangements, but a direct confrontation between an auditor and one of the parties to an agreement or contract is likely to be resolved through approaches other than auditing, including **arbitration** and **investigation.**

copyright

An exclusive legal right to benefit from the authorship of a text or artistic creation. A copyright is **intellectual property** and an **intangible asset.** Payments to copyright holders are often termed **royalties.**

corporate audit

Depending on the context, an alternative term for either **financial audit** or **internal audit.**

corporate governance

The ways in which an organization is controlled, regulated, and held **accountable** for the conduct of its activities. It has been suggested that the "basic [corporate] governance issues are those of power and accountability. They involve where power lies in the corporate system, and what degree of accountability there is for its exercise" (Cadbury 2002, 3). Corporate governance frameworks are molded by many influences, including legislation, custom, ethics, **stakeholder** pressure, public opinion, and the professional and academic literature. In classical economic theory, profit-seeking firms seek to maximize revenues above all other considerations. Corporate governance theory does not necessarily seek to contradict or undermine this objective, but it also attempts to establish socially acceptable rules for the pursuit of profit. In addition, corporate governance is applicable to **public-sector** and **not-for-profit** organizations, for which the alternative terms "institutional governance" and "organizational governance" are frequently used.

Corporate governance tends to be differentiated from the management of an organization. Governance is concerned with strategy and overall oversight, while management addresses the day-to-day implementation of governance strategies. Some commentators identify two main aspects of corporate governance: (i) an external side with the accountability of managerial **stewardship** to stakeholders; and (ii) an internal side of procedures, risk management, internal controls, and internal auditing. See also **corporate social responsibility**.

corporate social reporting (CSR)
See **corporate social responsibility** and **social and environmental reporting**.

corporate social responsibility (CSR)
The encouragement of organizational **accountability** for social and environmental practices. The term "CSR" is used widely, in contexts as varied as these: (i) environmental considerations and sustainability; (ii) ethical and transparent conduct in relation to an organization's investors, employees, customers, vendors, and other **stakeholders**; (iii) ethical investing; and (iv) contributions to social well-being. CSR is a disputed topic, both in its principles and its advocacy of social and environmental reporting. The economist Milton Friedman argued that "few trends could so thoroughly undermine the very foundations of our free society as the acceptance by corporate officials of a social responsibility other than to make as much **money** for their **stockholders** as possible" (Friedman 1982, 133). See also **Environmental, Social, and Governance (ESG)** and **sustainability**.

corporation
An organization recognized as a legal entity separate from its owners. Corporations are characterized by the limited liability of their **investors**. Large, modern corporations are typically run by professional managers who act as **agents** on behalf of stockholding **principals**. The separation of ownership from management gives rise to questions of **accountability, agency costs**, and a large range of **corporate governance** considerations. Compare **partnership**.

corrective action
Steps taken to resolve a problem, or to minimize a problem's likelihood of occurrence or impact. Audit **recommendations** often include suggested corrective actions to address weaknesses in procedures and **internal controls**.

corrective control
An **internal control** designed to remedy or minimize the damage caused by a breakdown in other internal controls. Compare **detective control** and **preventive control**.

correlation
In statistics, the degree of correspondence between two or more variables. Example: ice cream sales tend to be highly correlated with hot weather conditions. See also **scatter graph**.

corruption
Dishonest, illegal, or unethical behavior. Corruption is normally associated with personal gain, and its pernicious influence on organizations is of perennial concern to auditors. Corruption covers matters ranging from **bribes** to the **fraudulent** manipulation of financial statements.

***Corruption of Foreign Public Officials Act* (CFPOA) (1999)**
Canadian anticorruption legislation. The CFPOA is broadly equivalent to the United States' ***Foreign Corrupt Practices Act* (FCPA) (1977)**.

COSO framework
See **Committee of Sponsoring Organizations of the Treadway Commission** and *Internal Control–Integrated Framework*.

co-sourcing
Collaboration with third parties in the performance of an activity. Compare **outsourcing**, in which the day-to-day handling of activities is transferred rather than shared.

costs
1 **Quantifiable** items of **expenditures**. **2** Nonquantifiable, harmful effects of an activity or action. Costs in this sense may imply a benefit forgone; see also **opportunity costs**. **3** The sales price from a customer's perspective.

cost accounting

The recording and analysis of expenditures for management information purposes. Cost accounting often focuses on the costing of units of **inventory**, for
which there are various methodologies, including **backflush** costing. Cost
accounting is sometimes used to establish a product's selling price through
cost-plus pricing.

cost-benefit analysis

An appraisal of the costs and **rewards** of an undertaking (or potential undertaking). Cost-benefit analysis is often used to determine the economic viability of
capital expenditures and other investments.

cost center

An activity, unit, or individual within an organization with which **direct costs**
can be identified and to which **indirect costs** can be allocated. In contrast to
a **profit center**, a cost center usually incurs only costs and does not generate
income. Cost centers are used for the purposes of expenditure control, budgetary analysis, and decision-making. They are also used to allocate types of **overhead** to manufactured products in **absorption costing** methodologies.

cost driver

An activity with a measurable relation to the costs incurred in the achievement
of an organization's objectives. Example: the number of hours for which a production machine operates may be related to costs in a manufacturing process.

cost of capital

The rate of **return (sense 1)** a corporation requires to satisfy the **capital
(sense 1)** used to finance its activities. As capital is drawn from a combination
of forms of **debt** and **equity** (meaning **common stock**, **preferred stock**, and
retained earnings), the cost of capital is usually a **weighted average** of the
costs of the individual sources of capital. A corporation's cost of capital is normally expressed as a percentage, and it is used as a **hurdle rate** in **discounted
cash flow analysis** and other investment appraisal techniques: a proposed

investment's anticipated return must exceed a corporation's cost of capital to be acceptable. See also **internal rate of return.**

cost of goods sold (COGS)
A British term for **costs of sales.**

costs of sales (COS)
The **direct costs** of a product that is sold or intended to be sold. The costs of sales include **raw material** costs and **expenditures** directly attributable to production, but exclude nonproduction **overhead.**

cost-plus pricing
The establishment of a product's selling price by adding a **markup** to its costs.

coupon
A document or voucher entitling the holder to a benefit or right. Example: an organization may issue gift coupons of a defined monetary worth that customers may exchange for the purchase of items. See also **token (sense 3).**

coupon rate
The interest rate stated on a **bond** or similar debt instrument.

creative accounting
The manipulation of **financial statements** through imaginative or unusual accounting techniques. Creative accounting techniques include (i) the extension of the **amortization** periods of **fixed assets** to reduce amortization expenses in the initial years of an asset's life; (ii) the manipulation of **reserves** through **cookie jar accounting**; (iii) the use of **off-balance-sheet items**; and (iv) **window-dressing** techniques. Creative accounting techniques may or may not contravene **Generally Accepted Accounting Principles (GAAP)**, as creative accountants tend to dance around GAAP's outer boundaries. However, by acting in a fuzzy zone between legitimacy and **fraud**, the activities of creative accountants are generally viewed as misleading **investors** and others (Akpanuko and Umoren 2018).

creative auditing

Auditors' acquiescence to an auditee's **creative accounting** practices. The term is pejorative, and expresses a sense of insufficiently objective auditing, and perhaps of **collusion** with managerial misconduct.

credit

1 The facility to purchase a good or service or to take a loan on the promise of payment at a future date. **2** In **bookkeeping**, an abbreviated term for **credit entry. 3** An abbreviated term for **credit limit. 4** Public praise or recognition.

credit control

A function in an organization that oversees the granting of **credit (sense 1)** to customers and the collection of **accounts receivable**.

credit entry

An accounting transaction in **double entry bookkeeping** that increases **income (sense 1)** or **liabilities**, or reduces **expenditures** or **assets**. A credit entry has a corresponding **debit entry** (or debit entries) of equal value.

credit limit

The maximum amount of **credit (sense 1)** offered to a customer. The use of credit limits is a common internal control over **accounts receivable**.

credit line

A facility offered by a bank to a customer for potential borrowing up to a defined limit. Once it is in place, the credit line may be used at the customer's discretion.

credit note

A document showing an amount owed to a customer. Credit notes are issued to refund or reimburse customers for matters such as (i) **discounts (sense 1)**, (ii) price adjustments, (iii) goods returned, and (iv) the correction of invoicing errors.

creditor

1 An individual or organization with a legally enforceable obligation to receive **money**. Contrast **debtor**. **2** [*Plural*] A slightly archaic British term for **accounts payable**.

credit risk

The **risk** that a borrower may default on amounts owed on a **loan** or other **credit (sense 1)** mechanism.

creeping materiality

The increasing importance and relevance of several items in aggregate. In a financial audit, the **materiality** of individual items may fall below a defined threshold for **misstatements** in financial statements, but the accumulated total of individually small items may exceed the threshold. Creeping materiality may be difficult to detect and to interpret, but it may affect the outcome of an audit.

critical accounting movement

A reformist movement that seeks to unfreeze and challenge conventional discourses relating to the socioeconomic power structures of accounting and auditing, including the official narratives of the accounting and auditing professions. The critical accounting movement is a broad school of intersectional thought, based on various strands of leftist theory, from Karl Marx (1818–79) to Michel Foucault (1926–84), via the Frankfurt School and movements like environmentalism and feminism.

    The movement exposes interdependent structures underpinning inequities in power relations. The practices and institutional structures of auditing, and of **financial auditing** in particular, are frequent targets for its critiques. Auditing is accused of perpetuating inequitable power dynamics, and financial auditors are accused of accruing **monopolistic** power through their **rent (sense 2)**–seeking **professional** associations. Critical theorists tend to treat with skepticism, if not outright disdain, the official professional narratives of auditing's contributions to the public good. The critical accounting movement is one of the most tenacious and compelling challengers of auditing orthodoxies. In the eyes of some of the movement's critics, however, its pretensions to the high moral and

intellectual ground have been weakened by hyperbolic denunciations of the
allegedly unenlightened prejudices of mainstream "bourgeois" values.

critical path analysis (CPA)
An approach to decision-making that seeks to minimize the time required to
complete an activity by reference to the longest (or "critical") path of activity.
The aim of CPA is to improve efficiencies along the critical path so as to reduce
the time taken for the entire process. CPA is normally developed as a diagram
that shows various routes and events occurring in a pattern of sequential
activities.

crore [Hindi]
The term used in India for 10 million. Under Indian writing conventions, note
the position of the commas: 1,00,00,000. See also *lakh.*

crystallization
The process of becoming definite, clear, or unambiguous. The term is often used
to refer to the creation or confirmation of an **asset** or **liability.**

currency
A system of **money** widely accepted as a medium of exchange in a specific country. Gold is often considered to be an international currency, owing to its accept-
ability throughout the world. See also **hard currency**, **soft currency**, **functional
currency.** and **managed currency.**

current asset
A **short-term** asset with an anticipated **useful economic life** or expected period
of use of less than one year. Examples: **accounts receivable**, cash, and **inventory.** See **working capital.**

current costs
The costs of replacing an **asset** with an identical one in the same condition. Current costs can refer to either the purchase **price** or the manufacturing cost of an
asset. Contrast **historical costs.**

current liability
A **short-term** liability with an anticipated **settlement** date of less than one year. Examples: **accounts payable** and bank **loans** repayable within one year.

current ratio
A **liquidity** measure calculated by dividing **current assets** by **current liabilities**. Compare the **acid test ratio**, which is generally considered to be a sharper test of liquidity.

curriculum vitae (CV) [*Latin*]
A summary of an individual's work experience, abilities, educational achievements, and professional qualifications, used typically for job applications. The Latin phrase translates as "the course of one's life." See also *résumé*.

customer
A buyer of goods or services. Organizations manage their **credit (sense 1)** transactions with customers through **accounts receivable** records.

customer return
Postsale items returned from a **customer** to a **supplier** in line with **contractual** terms or industry practice. Common reasons for customer returns include defective or damaged products.

customs duty
A form of **taxation** levied on the **importation** or **exportation** of goods or services.

cutoff date
A point of time at which an accounting or **financial reporting period** ends. Cutoff dates are important in determining the allocation of **transactions** to time periods in accordance with the **accruals basis** of accounting. Example: an auditor may verify the reporting of sales in correct periods by reference to the timing of the underlying sales transactions around a cutoff date. The manipulation of transactions across cutoff dates is known as **window dressing**.

cycle (cyclical) counts
The regular undertaking of **physical inventory** checks so that all categories of inventory are counted within a defined time period. Cycle counts are often performed in the context of **perpetual inventory** systems.

data
Information, facts, and statistics. In its general use, the term refers to collections of both numeric and alphabetic information. The singular form is "datum."

data analytics
The examination of **data** for decision-making purposes.

data audit
1 An audit of the quality and reliability of an organization's methods of capturing, storing, and using information. Data audits may identify faulty, missing, or duplicated data and thereby improve the decision-making and other purposes served by the data. They can also identify the degree of adequacy of the **safeguarding** of information. **2** An audit of the accuracy of data in published academic research in relation to the underlying source data. The data audit is a quality control measure over the accuracy and credibility of published research.

database
A structured repository of **data** in a computerized information system.

database management system (DBMS)
A software program used to maintain and make available, for analysis or processing, the information contained in a **database**.

data privacy
Restricted access to information in a **database**. Data privacy is controlled by legislation in many parts of the world: in particular, the member states of the European Union have stringent privacy requirements, and the penalties for infractions may be severe.

data processing
The operations undertaken in a computerized information system to record, sort, process, analyze, and report data.

Davos man / woman
An individual who participates in (or adheres to the **globalist** philosophy characteristic of) the World Economic Forum in Davos, Switzerland. The term is attributed to the political scientist Samuel P. Huntington (1927–2008), who identified a powerful, transnational elite of well-connected, "gold-collar" individuals. The Davos man or woman operates at the intersections of the worlds of business, academia, and **international organizations**, promoting a globalist agenda that combines hard-headed economics with billionaire philanthropy and a disdain for traditional loyalties to the nation-state.

daybook [*Archaic*]
A **ledger** used to record transactions (typically for sales and purchases) before a daily transfer of the total balances to a **general ledger** account. Compare **subsidiary ledger**.

debenture
A corporate **bond**. The issuer of a debenture agrees to pay the holder the debenture's **face value** at a defined **maturity date**, along with periodic **interest** payments. There are many types of debentures, and (unlike **common stock**) they typically do not carry voting rights.

debit entry
An accounting transaction in **double entry bookkeeping** that increases **assets** or **expenditures** or reduces **liabilities** or **income (sense 1)**. A debit entry has a corresponding **credit entry** (or credit entries) of equal value.

debt
A legally enforceable obligation to settle **money** to an individual or organization.

debt-equity ratio

The ratio of a corporation's **long-term** debt to its **equity (sense 3)**. The elements of equity used in the ratio include **common stock**, **preferred stock**, and **retained earnings**. The debt-equity ratio measures a corporation's **leverage**.

debtor

1 An individual or organization with a legally enforceable obligation to **settle** money due on **credit (sense 1)** transactions. Compare **creditor**. **2** [*Plural, Archaic*] A British term for **accounts receivable**.

decentralization

Organizational autonomy in activities, **authority**, and decision-making. **Delegations (sense 1)** of responsibility may occur both geographically and institutionally. Contrast **centralization**.

decision theory

The systematic analysis of strategies for the optimal selection of alternative courses of action. Decision-making in conditions of uncertainty is fundamental to the management of organizations, and decision theory has developed a sophisticated range of methodologies; see **critical path analysis**, **decision trees**, and **discounted cash flow analysis**. Compare **game theory**.

decision tree

A pictorial decision-making tool that portrays possible actions and alternative choices for the completion of an activity. Decision trees normally include estimated outcomes for individual decisions, and the **probabilities** of success of each decision; this permits the calculation of quantifiable **expected values** for various decisions.

deconsolidation

The exclusion of an organization's **financial statements** from the **consolidated** accounts of a group of organizations. Deconsolidation occurs when a **parent organization** reduces its investment in (or its degree of control of) a **subsidiary** to levels that no longer require inclusion in **group financial statements**.

deductive reasoning
See **logic in auditing**.

deeply discounted bonds
A **bond** issued at a cost significantly below its **face value**. Deeply discounted bonds typically offer very low **interest** payments. The attraction to bondholders is the anticipation of income from **appreciation** in the bonds' **market values**.

deep pockets
In financial auditing, the possession by a financial auditor of significant monetary and other resources. A perception that an auditor has deep pockets may increase the likelihood of litigation against the auditor. This may imply that the auditor's ability to settle a case of **negligence** may outweigh the true balance of culpability in a case. See also **due professional care** and **malpractice insurance**.

de facto [Latin]
Existent in practice, but (as yet) unauthorized by law. Contrast *de jure*.

defalcation
An alternative term for **embezzlement**.

default
1 A failure to honor the terms of a **contract**. **2** A failure to **settle** amounts of **money** by specified **due dates**. **3** In a computerized accounting system, to revert to a predetermined position when no alternative action has been specified.

deferred charge
An alternative term for **prepaid expense**.

deferred income
An alternative term for **unearned revenue**.

deferred (income) tax
An asset or liability that arises from timing differences between **income
(sense 1)** calculated under **Generally Accepted Accounting Principles (GAAP)**
and the same income calculated according to **taxation** rules. See also **temporary differences** and **permanent differences**.

deferred revenue
An alternative term for **unearned revenue**.

deficit
1 An alternative term for a **loss** in **not-for-profit** organizations. **2** A debit
balance in accumulated **retained earnings** in a **balance sheet**. **3** A shortfall in
anticipated cash balances. See **overdraft**.

defined benefit pension plan
A **pension plan** that arranges its funding on the basis of predetermined
amounts payable to retired members. The amounts payable to members on
retirement from employment are usually a function of a combination of some or
all of these items: (i) age, (ii) length of service, and (iii) salary on retirement.
Contrast **defined contribution pension plan**.

defined contribution pension plan
A **pension plan** that determines its payments to retired members on the
basis of (i) the amounts contributed by active members and (ii) the performance of the fund's **investments**. In contrast to a **defined benefit pension
plan**, members are not guaranteed specific levels of payments or other benefits
on retirement.

deflation
A sustained reduction in the sales **prices** of consumer goods. Contrast **inflation**
and **disinflation**.

de jure [*Latin*]
Authorized by law. Contrast *de facto*.

delegation
1 The granting of **authority**, responsibility, and power to subordinates in an organizational **hierarchy**. **2** A group of representatives of an organization.

delinquent account
See **bad debt**.

demand
1 The desire or need of participants in a **market** to purchase a good or service. In unregulated markets, **prices** (in theory) are established by large numbers of buyers and sellers, with the market's "invisible hand" guiding the interactions of their demand and **supply** decisions. **2** A request for payment.

denationalization
An alternative term for **privatization**.

department
A separately identifiable part of an organization that undertakes a discrete, specialized activity. See also **cost center** and **profit center**.

deposit
1 Money invested in a bank. **2** A partial payment of a good or service as a pledge for its subsequent purchase.

depreciation
1 A reduction in the value of an asset. Contrast **appreciation**. **2** A cost allocation method used in **accounting** to record the reduction in the value of a **tangible asset** over its **useful economic life**. See **amortization**.

depression
A severe or prolonged economic **recession**. Depressions often result in high **unemployment** levels and low aggregate **productivity**. The Great Depression in the United States, Germany, and other countries of the late 1920s and early 1930s exacerbated the conditions that led to World War II.

deregulation

The reduction or elimination of **regulations**, government controls, and other **market** restrictions. The aims of deregulation include (i) the stimulation of **competition**, (ii) the encouragement of **price** reductions, and (iii) the removal of **barriers to entry** to a market.

derivative

A **security** whose value correlates to uncertain or variable underlying conditions. Examples: **futures contracts** and **options**. The underlying conditions giving rise to uncertainty include fluctuations in the **prices** of **commodities** and **currencies**. The complexity and high **risk** of some forms of derivative require caution from an auditing perspective: specialist **outside expertise** in understanding and assessing the impact of derivatives is often required for an auditor to arrive at a reliable overall audit **opinion**.

detailed audit

An audit characterized by the extensive **substantive testing** of a large number of **transactions**. In a detailed audit, there tends to be a limited reliance on **compliance testing**.

detection risk

In financial auditing, the **risk** that the **misstatement** of items in **financial statements** may not be found through the auditor's **substantive** and **compliance tests**. Detection risk is considered alongside **inherent risk (sense 1)** and **control risk (sense 1)** as one of three components of **audit risk**. Unlike inherent risk and control risk, detection risk can be considered as directly controllable by the auditor, who can perform **audit tests** devised expressly to minimize it.

detective control

An **internal control** designed to identify the occurrence of an unwanted event. Compare **corrective control** and **preventive control**.

devaluation

A reduction in the value of a **currency** in relation to other currencies. Contrast **revaluation (sense 2)**.

developed country

A country of advanced economic standing. A collective term for developed nations is the **(Global) North**. Contrast **developing country**, the **(Global) South**, and the somewhat archaic **Third World**.

developing country

A country with a low *per capita* income, characteristically dominated by the agricultural and **commodity (sense 1)** sectors and therefore vulnerable to **price** fluctuations in these markets. Alternative terms for developing country include less developed country (LDC), **Third World** country, and (collectively) the **(Global) South.** Many international organizations seek to assist the economic progress of developing countries, including the African Development Bank Group, the Asian Development Bank, the International Development Association of the World Bank, and several agencies, programs, and funds of the United Nations. Contrast **developed country.**

dilution

A reduction in the strength of an item in a **balance sheet**. Example: a dilution of investors' equity ownership in a corporation arises from the corporation's issuance of additional **common stock** or from other investors' exercising of rights to **convertible securities** (without a corresponding increase in the corporation's underlying assets).

diminishing returns

1 A decrease of the incremental satisfaction derived from the consumption of a good or the use of a service with each additional unit. Example: a smoker may derive significant satisfaction, or **utility**, from the first cigarette of the day. The amount of satisfaction obtained from each subsequent cigarette decreases progressively. See **indifference curves**. **2** The theory that the use of an incremental unit of one **factor of production**, with all the other factors held constant, will result in reduced levels of incremental output.

direct costs

1 An alternative term for **variable costs**. **2** Costs (fixed and variable) directly attributable to a manufacturing process for a product or to the providing of a service. Contrast **indirect costs.**

director

An individual with formal responsibility for the **stewardship** of an organization. Directors usually exercise their responsibilities through the structure of a **board of directors**. See **inside directors**, **outside directors**, and **gray directors**.

directors' report

A report from a **board of directors** to an organization's **stockholders** and other **stakeholders**. A directors' report normally accompanies annual **financial statements**, which it amplifies and interprets. Under most systems of **Generally Accepted Auditing Standards (GAAS)**, financial auditors are required to report any **material** discrepancies between a directors' report and the related financial statements.

direct taxation

A tax deducted from the **income (senses 2** and **3)** or wealth of an individual or organization. Contrast **indirect taxation**.

disaster recovery planning

An element of **business continuity planning**.

disbursement

A payment of **money**. Disbursements are effected through (i) transfers of **cash**, (ii) the use of **checks**, and (iii) **wire transfers**.

disclaimer

A financial auditor's declaration of an inability to provide an **audit opinion** on an entity's financial statements. Auditors issue disclaimers in the face of **scope limitations** such as (i) insufficient audit **evidence** or (ii) an uncooperative or **adversarial** attitude from an **auditee**. Under most systems of **Generally Accepted Auditing Standards (GAAS)**, financial auditors are obliged to explain the reasons for a disclaimer. Compare **adverse opinion**, **qualified opinion**, and **unqualified opinion**.

disclosure

Information provided in **financial statements** or as supplementary information to financial statements. Disclosure is either (i) required by **Generally Accepted Accounting Principles (GAAP)** or (ii) offered voluntarily to amplify and explain financial statement items. The legal writer L. C. B. Gower stated in 1969 that "as the fundamental principle of investor protection [disclosure] only works if the information disclosed can be safely taken as accurate. Unless checked by some independent authority this cannot be relied on; so as far as the accounts are concerned the auditors are this **independent** (and usually reliable) **authority**" (quoted by Chambers 1995, 73).

discontinued operation
An activity that has been terminated or sold, or that is expected to be terminated or sold within a short time period. Most systems of **Generally Accepted Accounting Principles (GAAP)** differentiate between discontinued and **continuing operations** in financial statements.

discount
1 An amount deducted from the standard **price** or **cost** of an item, service, or **security**. In the context of **sales (sense 1)**, discounts are offered to customers (i) as inducements to purchase, (ii) to encourage the prompt settlement of **accounts receivable**, and (iiii) to generate customer **goodwill (sense 3)**. **2** To recalculate future cash flows in **present value** terms. See **discounted cash flow** analysis.

discounted cash flow (DCF) analysis
An investment appraisal method that assesses the **net present value** of future incremental cash flows arising from a decision. In acknowledgment of the **time value of money**, future cash flows are discounted to present values by an appropriate **cost-of-capital** rate. DCF analysis is frequently used to assess **capital expenditure** proposals. See also the **internal rate of return**.

discretionary costs
An alternative term for **controllable costs**.

diseconomies of scale
Increases in the unit costs of manufactured items in line with increases in production levels. Diseconomies of scale indicate disadvantages to large-scale production, and they usually occur at a point that reverses initial **economies of scale**.

disinflation
A temporary reduction in the **inflation** rate. Contrast **deflation**.

disinvestment
See **divestment**.

distress price
A low sales price offered by a seller owing to financial or operational difficulty. A distress price is often established in relation to a seller's **fixed costs**,
which must be covered if a seller is to continue as a **going concern**.

distribution
1 The mechanisms of **supplying** goods and services to consumers. Distribution
covers the storage, delivery and (under some definitions) the **wholesaling** and
retailing of items. **2** A corporation's payments to stockholders in the form
of **dividends**. **3** The patterns of items in a **population** of data. See **normal
distribution**.

diversification
1 The holding of a **portfolio** with a wide range of **investments** to spread and
thereby reduce **risk**. See **portfolio theory**. **2** A The undertaking by an organization or an individual of a broad range and variety of operations. **Multinational**
corporations tend to reduce their risks by geographical diversification and by
entering different sectors of activity, to reduce overreliance on a small number of
markets. However, although diversification generally leads to a spreading (and
therefore a reduction) of risk, overdiversification may be counterproductive.
A corporation that takes on an excessively wide range of operations may lose
strategic focus, and the variety of its activities may absorb an excessive amount
of management time. The negative effects of overdiversification may be mitigated by the **divestment** of some operations.

divestment
1 The sale or liquidation of an **asset** or **investment**. **2** The sale or liquidation
of a **subsidiary** organization, or of a controlling interest in a subsidiary organization. Contrast **acquisition** and **merger**.

dividend
The distribution of part of a corporation's **net income** to its **stockholders**. Dividend payments to holders of **preferred stock** take priority over those to holders of **common stock.** Dividends are normally paid in cash, as a proportion of the **par value** of a share of stock. For investors in a corporation's common stock, dividends are one of two major forms of investment return—the other major source of investment return derives from **appreciations** of the stock's market value.

division
A segment of an organization. Divisions are often organized by function or geographical distribution, or by a combination of the two. Divisions are used to control activities in large organizations and **multinational** corporations, as the direct control of dispersed or varied operations may exceed the capacity of a centralized management function. Compare **branch, cost center, profit center**, and **subsidiary.**

division of duties / division of responsibilities
Alternative terms for **segregation of responsibilities.**

dollar
A unit of **currency** of several countries, including Australia, Canada, New Zealand, and the United States.

dollar unit sampling (DUS)
See **monetary unit sampling.**

dosh [*Slang*]
A colloquial British term for **money.**

***dottore commercialista* [*Italian*]**
An Italian term that approximates to **Certified Public Accountant** or **Chartered Accountant.**

double entry bookkeeping
A system of recording **accounting** transactions through corresponding **debit** and **credit** entries of equal value. The mathematical integrity of double entry

bookkeeping's dualistic nature is established, through preparation of a **trial balance**, by reference to the accuracy of the **accounting equation**. The efficiency of the mechanics of double entry bookkeeping has long been recognized; it has been described as "simple, symmetrical, logical and beautiful" (Sawyer and Vinten 1996, 204). The origins of double entry bookkeeping are widely attributed to the Italian mathematician and monk Luca Pacioli (c. 1447–1517), though Pacioli's achievements seem to have been based largely on a rigorous synthesis and novel presentation of preestablished practices (Sangster 2018).

doubtful debt
See **bad debt.**

dough [*Slang*]
A colloquial term for **money.**

downloading
The transmission of information between computerized information systems.

downsizing
1 A reduction in the scale of an organization's operations, through the sale or closure of activities, assets, or subsidiary organizations. **2** A reduction in the number of employees in an organization.

downtime
1 A period of involuntary operational or administrative inactivity, owing to an external factor like a power outage. **2** A period of voluntary inactivity. Example: "He was exhausted and took some downtime to recharge his batteries at a beach resort."

draft
An interim version of a document.

drone
A craft, usually airborne or seaborne, piloted by someone at a distance, that is used to gather visual or aural information. Drones are increasingly used in

auditing to obtain evidence of **inventory** items that are difficult to observe, owing to their high volume, frequent movements, or widely distributed nature. In particular, a drone may assist auditors' "inventory counts in large warehouses and open air inventories" (Applebaum and Nehmer 2017, 99). Example: an auditor may use an airborne drone to inspect herds of animals in an agricultural setting.

due date
A defined date at which there is a promise or expectation of a **disbursement**, the delivery of an item, or the performance of a service. Compare **cutoff date**.

due diligence
1 The careful appraisal of a proposed investment. The term is frequently used in the context of corporate **acquisitions**, and it covers financial, legal, and operational considerations. **2** The requisite steps to satisfy a legal requirement.

due professional care
The **prudent** and competent application of expert **knowledge**. In auditing, the concept of due professional care refers to the careful application of expertise in reaching **judgments**. Membership in a professional association with exclusive rights to undertake auditing is deemed to carry commensurate responsibilities in terms of prudent and competent behavior, as reflected in the eighth of the **postulates of auditing** developed in the early 1960s by Robert Kuhn Mautz and Hussein A. Sharaf. These responsibilities may make it difficult for financial auditors, especially those perceived to have **deep pockets**, to escape the consequences of litigation arising from allegations of **negligence**.

dumping
1 The offloading at low prices in an overseas market of **commodities (sense 1)** or goods that are difficult to sell in a domestic market. The effects of dumping can devastate a local market, and many countries have antidumping legislation. **2** A large amount of data transmitted between computerized information systems.

duty
1 Money collected through tax and **tariff** mechanisms. **2** A legal or moral obligation.

earnings
1 An alternative term for **net income**. **2** Revenues from sales. **3** Employee **remuneration**.

earnings per share (EPS)
Net income accruing to a corporation's stockholders, expressed in terms of a ratio to individual shares of ownership. EPS is calculated by dividing net income by **common stock**. In practice, this basic calculation may require adjustments to account for the **dividends** of **preferred stock**, which have preference over common stock in the distribution of **earnings**. The basic calculation may also require adjustments to the common stock figure, to take account of the potential dilution of stockholdings from **convertible securities**, stock **options**, and minority interests. EPS is a highly sensitive figure for corporations, and investment analysts place emphasis on the evolution of EPS over time. Pressures to meet market expectations for EPS were a prominent factor in the earnings manipulation scandals at corporations like Enron and World-Com. Reflecting both the humor and cynicism characteristic of **Enronitis**, one commentator joked that the acronym might well stand for the "eventual prison sentence" of individuals tempted to manipulate EPS (quoted by Jeter 2003, 179).

economic life
See **useful economic life**.

economic order quantity (EOQ)
A volume of purchased **inventory** intended to minimize inventory-related administrative, holding, and transportation costs. An optimal EOQ can be calculated through either formal differential calculus or subjective estimation.

economies of scale
Reductions in the unit costs of manufactured items in line with increases in **production** levels. Contrast **diseconomies of scale**.

economy
1 The obtaining of resources at the lowest possible cost. The concept of economy is sometimes envisioned as a ratio between planned inputs and actual
inputs. It is one of the **Three Es** of **operational auditing. 2** The administration
and management of a nation's resources, and of the production and distribution
of a nation's wealth.

educational auditing
The auditing of the quality of teaching and related operational matters in educational establishments. Audits of this type are undertaken to assess conformance
to preestablished measurement criteria for indications of success in teaching: the criteria are usually established by those commissioning the audits.

effectiveness
The degree of success in undertaking activities to meet objectives. In consid-
ering it to be one of the **Three Es** of **operational auditing**, Flint (1988, 175n6)
defines effectiveness as "success in achieving the objective of a policy or course
of action as a consequence of the input of resources." The concept of effectiveness is sometimes envisioned as a ratio of actual outputs to planned outputs.

efficiency
The performance of an activity with an optimal use of resources and minimal
waste. Efficiency is one of the **Three Es** of **operational auditing**, and Flint
(1988, 175n5) defines it as "obtaining maximum useful output from the resources
devoted to an activity; utilising minimum resources necessary to achieve a
required output or objective; or adopting the policy or course of action to
achieve a required objective which requires least input of resources." The concept of efficiency is sometimes envisioned as a ratio of actual inputs to actual
outputs.

efficient markets hypothesis (EMH)
The theory that abnormal profit cannot be made by investing in **securities** in
a **market** in which information is shared by all participants and reflected in
prices. There are three forms of efficient markets: (i) a strong form, in which
the prices of securities fully reflect all available information (as all information

is known publicly); (ii) a semistrong form, in which the value of a security reflects all publicly held information, but there may be some privately held information from which investors might make abnormal profits; and (iii) a weak form, in which the use of secret information makes movements in the prices of securities difficult to estimate. The existence of profits through **arbitrage** and **speculation** suggests that the strong form of market exists only rarely—if at all—in practice.

elasticity
The responsiveness of **demand** for a good or service to changes in its sales **price**.

election audit
An audit of a voting process, such as a political election or a referendum. Some distinguish between an election results audit (which focuses on the outcomes of a voting process) and an election process audit (which focuses on adherence to voting procedures).

electronic mail
The full term for **email.**

electronic office
An alternative term for the **paperless office.**

embargo
The prohibition of economic activity between one country and another. Embargoes tend to be introduced for political reasons. Example: the United States declared a trade embargo on Cuba in 1961 that is still in force at the time of this writing (in 2024): it is the longest-running embargo in current times. See also **boycott** and **sanction.**

embedded
Incorporated within (or intrinsic to) an activity or procedure. **Internal controls** are often embedded in routine operating procedures. Some forms of **audit test** can be embedded in an organization's computer programs: see **computer-assisted auditing techniques.**

embezzlement

The criminal misappropriation of **money** placed under one's custody and control. Embezzlement is a violation of **trust (sense 3)**.

emphasis-of-matter paragraph

In a financial auditor's report, an emphasis-of-matter paragraph draws attention to a matter (already disclosed in the financial statements or its notes) that, in the auditor's view, is fundamental to a user's understanding of the financial statements. The inclusion of an emphasis-of-matter paragraph does not modify an audit **opinion**. It may cover matters such as uncertainty in the expected outcome of ongoing litigation.

empowerment

The **delegation** of decision-making **authority** to individuals at lower **hierarchical** levels of an organization. Management theory frequently advocates the empowerment of employees as a way of mitigating some of the dysfunctional effects of traditional **bureaucratic** and **chain-of-command** structures.

encryption

The protection of **data** transferred between computers by using codes that only authorized individuals can decipher or understand. Data transferred, stored, or processed in this way require decryption before they can be interpreted.

endorsement

1 An authorizing signature on a **check** or other payment order. **2** A public declaration of approval. Example: celebrities are frequently paid to endorse consumer goods for advertising purposes. **3** A clause in an **insurance** policy that amends the policy's terms.

engagement

See **audit assignment**.

engagement letter

In **financial auditing**, a **contract** that sets out the terms, conditions, and costs of an **audit assignment**. An engagement letter usually summarizes the

objectives of the audit, any limitations on the audit, and the rights and responsibilities of both auditor and **auditee.**

Enronitis

A semihumorous term referring to a loss of investor and public confidence in
corporate financial reporting and **financial auditing.** The term was coined
after the demise of Enron Corporation, which filed for Chapter 11 bankruptcy
reorganization in December 2001. Example: "Wall Street began talking regularly
about Enronitis infecting stocks, as pundits ascribed various declines in the
broad market to worries about corporations' accounting" (Fox 2003, 294). The
uncovering of false accounting and **fraud** forced Enron to make **write-downs**
of stockholder equity of more than $1 billion in its 2001 **financial statements.**
One of the contentious accounting mechanisms used by Enron was a web of
Special Purpose Entities—some of these **off-balance-sheet** investment mechanisms skirted the looser frontiers of **Generally Accepted Accounting Principles
(GAAP)** at the time, and many were essentially elaborate accounting hoaxes to
hide liabilities (Bryce 2002; Schwartz and Watkins 2003). After its collapse, the
activity around Enron has been described in terms of "greed and hubris, deceit-
ful accounting, and Wall Street favors" (Fox 2003, v).

The importance of Enronitis for financial auditing in the twenty-first century
is hard to overstate. First, it was a major exacerbating factor in the demise of
the **Big Five** firm **Arthur Andersen,** Enron's financial auditor. A perception of
improper collusion between the senior management of Enron and Arthur Andersen, or at least of poor **judgment** exercised by Arthur Andersen, led to a hemor-
rhaging of the firm's **auditees,** the secession of some of the firm's international
practices and, eventually, the firm's criminal indictment. Most notoriously,
Arthur Andersen's reported destruction of literally tons of Enron-related audit
evidence left the firm's reputation in shreds, an appropriate analogy for the vast
quantity of documents the firm was alleged to have shredded. The destruction of
evidence also, arguably, left the reputation of the entire financial auditing profession in tatters. Even worse was to follow for Arthur Andersen in 2022, as the
Enron accounting scandal was followed by an even larger one at WorldCom,
another of its clients. Arthur Andersen collapsed in 2002.

The second way in which Enronitis has been important for auditing has been
the effect of the scandal on the law. The Enron affair changed the legal climate

of auditing, with shifts in the parameters of both legislation and regulation. One of the most tangible effects of Enronitis crystallized in the **Sarbanes-Oxley Act** of 2002 in the United States. At the time of this writing (2023), the extent to which the financial auditing profession has fully exorcized the ghosts of the reputational damage arising from Enronitis is questionable.

enterprise

1 A **profit**-seeking undertaking or activity. See also **entrepreneur. 2** A display of initiative and **risk**-seeking attitudes.

enterprise risk management (ERM)

An all-encompassing, holistic, integrated, and strategic administration of the perceived **risks** facing an institution.

Enterprise Risk Management–Integrating with Strategy and Performance

A 2017 report by the **Committee of Sponsoring Organizations of the Treadway Commission (COSO)** that updated and replaced an earlier report, *Enterprise Risk Management-Integrated Framework* (2004). COSO intended the report to be complementary to another of its publications: the ***Internal Control–Integrated Framework.***

entity

A separately identifiable economic unit that can be subjected to auditing. An entity in this sense does not necessarily have a separate legal identity; it can refer to a **corporation**, **partnership**, or **public-sector** institution, or to a **subsidiary** or **department** within an organization.

entrepreneur

An individual who uses the **factors of production** to create **wealth**. In classical economic theory, a **profit**-seeking entrepreneur operating in the **private sector** takes **risks** to achieve income. The term is taken from French, and it literally translates as "an individual who undertakes an **enterprise**," and the term has connotations of energy, flair, and inventiveness.

entry

A record of an accounting **transaction** in a **general ledger** account or in a **subsidiary ledger**. Under the conventions of **double entry bookkeeping**, entries take the form of **debit entries** and **credit entries**.

environmental auditing

The auditing of adherence to laws, regulations, and good practices for environmental matters. This branch of auditing assesses the impact of an organization's activities on interrelated areas like pollution (including air and water quality), climate change, energy efficiency, the handling of waste (including plastic waste), the protection of ecosystems, and the safeguarding of natural resources (from fish stocks to forest maintenance). The Switzerland-based International Organization for Standardization (ISO) issues the 14000 family of standards, which covers environmental matters.

The Environmental, Social, and Governance (ESG) movement

A **corporate social responsibility** initiative of the United Nations. ESG concerns an organization's approach to (i) environmental, (ii) social, and (iii) ethical issues within its **corporate governance**. The coverage of the environmental aspect of ESG is immediately clear from its terminology, while the social aspect typically has a diffuse focus on labor matters and human rights, ranging from employee engagement to the promotion of diversity among the workforce. The **corporate governance** aspect is driven by ethical considerations, including the levels of executive pay and the rights of **stockholders** and other **stakeholders**. It may also cover anti**corruption** measures and security concerns (e.g., **cybersecurity** arrangements).

ESG goals vary between organizations, but perhaps the most frequent common denominator across ESG-conscious organizations and ESG-conscious investors is a commitment to the United Nations' 2015 **Sustainable Development Goals (SDG)**. This reflects the origins of the ESG movement from a review of sustainability organized jointly by the United Nations and the Swiss Federal Department of Foreign Affairs in 2004, and the resulting landmark report *Who Cares Wins* of the next year (Global Compact 2005).

equilibrium
A condition in a **market** in which **supply** and **demand** are in harmony. An equilibrium point establishes a **price** for a product or service, and it can be achieved in both the **short** and **long terms**.

equity
1 The ownership interest of **stockholders** in a corporation. Under the conventions of **double entry bookkeeping** and the **accounting equation**, stockholders' equity is calculated as total **assets** less total **liabilities**, and is represented by the combined value of **common stock**, **preferred stock**, and **retained earnings**. **2** An alternative term for common stock. **3** In a general sense, justice and fairness. **4** A legal right over an asset. **5** A body of English law distinct from (and that generally prevails over) common law. Equitable law derives in part from principles of natural justice, and equitable doctrines are a feature of law throughout the English-speaking world. **6** The fair and unprejudiced treatment of individuals.

equity method
A means of accounting for business combinations in contexts where an investment in an organization is too small to effect control. The equity method operates through (i) the inclusion of an appropriate proportion of the organization's income in the **income statement** of the investor and (ii) the inclusion of the original amount invested (plus a share of **retained earnings**) in the investor's **balance sheet**. Contrast **consolidation accounting**.

error
An inaccuracy, mistake, miscalculation, or misrepresentation. In general, the term tends to be used for unintentional inaccuracies, in contrast to deliberately **fraudulent** irregularities.

escapable costs
An alternative term for **avoidable costs**.

Escott v. BarChris Construction Corp. (1968)
A landmark civil case in the United States that confirmed the liability of **financial auditors** to third parties under the *Securities Act* (1933) for **negligence**

in the auditing of a security issuance **prospectus** and related registration documents. The case was a successful class action by BarChris debenture holders
who claimed to have been misled by auditor negligence in relation to false statements in the registration documents. It was the first judicial interpretation of
this aspect of the 1933 *Act*, occurring more than three decades after the *Act* was
passed (O'Reilly et al. 1998, 5–17).

ethical investment

An investment in activities or organizations that avoid immoral or questionable
activities. The concept of ethical investing is open to dispute, owing to the
subjectivity of some of the ethical judgments that underpin it. Criteria used
to define ethical investing include (i) the nature of an organization's activities
(tobacco and armaments tend to be among frequently disapproved activities),
(ii) a record of good environmental practices, and (iii) equitable treatment
of employees. See also the **Environmental, Social, and Governance (ESG)
movement**.

ethics

Systematic moral judgments, and principles of intrinsic value. High ethical
standards are central to the credibility of **professions**, and to the **corporate
governance** standards of organizations, and they are often formalized in written codes of practice.

evaluation

1 An assessment of evidence that involves a **judgment** rather than merely a
description. Evaluative skills are central to auditing, in both the assessment of
audit **evidence** and the critical reasoning used to arrive at audit **opinions**. See
also **assurance**. **2** A **quantitative** or **qualitative** assessment. Example: evalua-
tions of personnel performance are common in most large organizations.

event

1 A **transaction** or significant happening in an organization that can influence
an audit **opinion**. **2** In **critical path analysis**, a point that represents the start
or end of an activity or a series of sequential activities. **3** In **probability** analysis, an outcome of an activity to which a probability estimate can be applied.

event after the balance sheet date
A **material** occurrence that can potentially affect **financial statements**, despite it taking place after a **balance sheet** date. An event of this type may lead to **disclosure** in the notes that accompany financial statements, or to adjustments to balances in the financial statements. See also **contingent liabilities**.

evidence
Information that supports or refutes an **audit objective** or hypothesis. Evidence is central to an auditor's **judgment** in arriving at an **opinion**: "There is general agreement amongst auditors, academics and regulators that the search for evidence is central to the activity of auditing" (Dennis 2015, 79). In the words of Ratliff and Reding (2002, 377): "Evidence is the foundation upon which all audits must stand."

Auditors gather evidence from a wide variety of sources, and common examples include (i) inquiry (oral and written), (ii) the **observation** of activities, (iii) the **inspection** of assets, (iv) the **circularization** of **third parties**, (v) **examinations** of documents, (vi) the reperformance of activities, and (vii) analytical procedures. Example: an auditor wishing to substantiate the existence and accuracy of an organization's **inventory** balances may apply the above-mentioned methods as follows: (i) discussions with the organization's managers, (ii) observing the **auditee**'s **physical inventories**, (iii) the inspection of warehousing arrangements and items of inventory, (iv) obtaining **confirmations** from **vendors** of the purchases of items that constitute the inventory, (v) a review of vendor and customer **invoices**, (vi) the counting of a sample of inventory items, and (vii) an **analytical review** of trends in inventory balances over time, and of the relationships between inventory levels, purchases, **accounts payable**, sales, and **accounts receivable**. If any of the individual methods proves difficult or expensive to undertake, an emphasis on the other steps might be adequate to fill any evidential gaps. For example, an auditor unable to observe the performance of an auditee's inventory count (item ii above) might obtain adequate evidence through the performance of a sample of counts (item vi above). Auditors record the evidence used to support their judgments and **opinions** in **work papers**.

Some distinguish between "evidence (the overall basis for audit reporting) and evidential material (the various means by which auditors construct their evidence to support their conclusions)" (Lee 1993, 172). Mautz and Sharaf (1961, 82) differentiate between three "classes" of evidence: "(1) natural evidence, (2) created evidence, (3) rational argumentation." Ratliff and Reding (2002, 383–84) identify three "dimensions" of evidence: (1) relevance, (2) sufficiency, and (3) competence/credibility. Irrespective of the conceptual framework one uses, the reasoning process in the interpretation of evidence is a fundamental aspect of auditing (Dennis, 2015, 95–99). Auditors' **judgment** is central to assessments of audit evidence, and the evidence itself should possess adequate diagnosticity.

Auditors seek reasonable **assurance** on an audit objective after gathering and assessing a sufficient amount of evidence. However, **audit risk** is almost always ineliminable, and the evidence gathered by auditors is often persuasive rather than conclusive. This arises because auditors are almost always both cost-constrained and time-constrained, and this requires a tempering of the gathering and assessment of evidence with **efficiency** considerations. As Mautz and Sharaf note: "The auditor must frequently be content with something less than the best possible evidence pertinent to a given problem. . . . Auditors must live with the hard fact of economics" (Mautz and Sharaf 1961, 35).

The handling of audit evidence is also an important consideration for auditors, ranging from confidentiality and legal concerns to reputational issues. The latter was reflected in the demise of the then Big Five financial auditing firm **Arthur Andersen**, after its destruction of significant quantities of audit evidence related to Enron Corporation. See **Enronitis**.

examination

1 The analysis of a matter. The examination of records and procedures is central to the gathering and **evaluation** of audit **evidence**. An 1888 editorial in *The Accountant* magazine described an audit as "an intelligent examination of the **books**" (quoted by Chambers 1995, 73); in the nineteenth century, the term "examination" was often used as a synonym for audit. The *American Institute of **Certified Public Accountants*** issued guidance in 1936 after the enactment of the ***Securities Act* (1933)** and the ***Securities Exchange Act* (1934)** that carefully differentiated between an examination (auditing by the testing of selected items) and a verification (auditing by the review or testing of all or most of the available information) (O'Reilly et al. 1998, 1.9). **2** A formal test of competence or knowledge. Along with supervised work experience, examinations of knowledge are central to the certification of auditors by **professional** associations.

ex ante [Latin]

Before an event, or earlier in time. Contrast **ex post**.

exception

An item that does not follow a general or expected pattern. Example: an organization's **internal control** policies may specify that all **disbursements** over a given threshold should be **authorized** by a senior employee. If this procedure is followed for the most part, any cases of nonadherence to the policy may be considered exceptions. Auditors apply **judgment** to **errors** to decide whether they (i) are merely isolated exceptions or (ii) indicate a systematic breakdown in procedures and internal controls.

exceptional item

A **transaction** separately reported or **disclosed** in an **income statement** on account of its **materiality**, unusual nature, or infrequency. Exceptional items arise from normal operating activities, and examples may include the write-off of a significant **accounts receivable** balance, or unusually large reorganization expenditures. A material, unusual transaction arising from events beyond the scope of normal operating activities is usually referred to as an **extraordinary** item.

exception report

A summary of errors, irregularities, or unexpected outcomes arising from an activity or procedure. Exception reports are convenient mechanisms for focusing on potential breakdowns in **internal controls** and are frequently used as audit **evidence.**

exchange

The buying and selling of items in a **market**. The simplest form of exchange is effected through **barter** transactions, but in modern economies **money** is the main medium of exchange.

exchange rate

1 The rate at which one unit of a **currency** can be exchanged for one unit of a different currency. **2** The **value** of a **commodity (sense 1)**, good, or service measured in terms of its ability to be exchanged for other items, without the intermediary of **money**. See also **barter**.

executive

An individual with high level decision-making **authority** in an organization.

executive director

A British term for **inside director**.

executive remuneration

Compensation paid to an organization's **directors** and senior managers. Levels of executive remuneration are a sensitive topic, and they tend to be subject to **disclosure** requirements in the notes to **financial statements** under most systems of **Generally Accepted Accounting Principles (GAAP)**. Other **corporate governance** measures in this area include (i) the use of **remuneration committees** to determine executive remuneration and (ii) the linking of remuneration levels to individual and organizational performance (including changes in the **market value** of a corporation's **common stock**).

exemption

1 The releasing of an individual from an obligation or responsibility. **2** A deduction or exclusion from computations of taxable income.

***ex gratia* [*Latin*]**

On the basis of a moral decision rather than a legal imperative. It tends to refer to **gift** giving or payments of **money**. The term derives from the Latin expression for "out of grace."

exercise price

See **option**.

existence

Objective, verifiable reality. The **verification** of the existence of both **tangible** and **intangible** items is a fundamental financial auditing objective.

expectations gap

Discrepancies in views of the main purpose of **financial auditing**, between financial auditors on one hand and **auditees**, other **stakeholders**, and public opinion on the other. The expectations gap tends to be most apparent when financial auditors are perceived to have failed to detect **fraud** or other **material** irregularities in a corporation's **financial statements**. While financial auditors have tended to identify the managers of an audited organization as bearing the primary responsibility for the prevention and detection of fraud, public opinion has doggedly pinned these responsibilities on financial auditors (Porter 2018). The expectations gap has been described as "the difference between how financial auditors are perceived (responsible for the detection of fraud) and how they see themselves (primarily responsible for forming a professional **opinion** on the financial statements)" (Power 1994a, 24). Some commentators identify two elements of the expectations gap: (i) a "feasibility gap," covering what auditors may reasonably be expected to do; and (ii) a "performance gap," a shortfall in the quality of audit work.

Disputes arising from the expectations gap are often settled in the courts. In the 1896 *Kingston Cotton Mill Company* **case**, a landmark British common law case for financial auditing, the judicial description of financial auditors as **watchdogs** rather than **bloodhounds** established the principle that financial auditors' duties involve the exercise of **due professional care** rather than an **investigative** remit: "an auditor is not bound to be a detective" (cited by Chambers 1995, 82). The case determined that it was reasonable for the financial auditor of the Kingston Cotton Mill to rely on a management **representation letter** for **inventory** balances, and the auditor was not held liable for failing to detect a **fraud**. The *Kingston Cotton Mill Company* case was an early articulation of the existence of the expectations gap.

The persistence of an expectations gap is, perhaps, inevitable: "It can be argued that the expectation gap can never be resolved—so long as people compare an auditor's ex ante opinion to ex post outcomes" (Hay 2020, 28). The financial auditing profession's approach has tended toward the "education" of public opinion on the role of the financial auditor vis-à-vis fraud, but it has to date been largely unsuccessful in its attempts. Example: Olojede and others (2020) discuss the persistence of the expectations gap in Nigeria despite the financial auditing profession's attempts to promote its perspective. The purposes of auditing are socially constructed, and the stubbornness of public opinion might constitute an educative message for the financial auditing profession; research has indicated that the public's expectation that financial auditors are responsible for fraud identification "cannot be eradicated entirely from society" (Deepal and Jayamaha 2022).

In relation to the expectations gap, there is a degree of asymmetry between auditor failure and auditor success. The public frequently saddles the financial auditor with most of the responsibility for failures in corporate fraud detection, but the success of auditing in ensuring accountability and assurance "will not usually yield public acclaim" (Power 1997, 27). The feverish outbreak of **Enronitis** after the corporate failure in 2001 of Enron Corporation and the demise of the auditing firm **Arthur Andersen** in 2002 has not been matched by any such outbreak of excited praise for the quiet success of financial auditors in more recent years. Perhaps blunders are more likely than successes to be noticed and remembered. The asymmetrical treatment of auditor failure and success may be seen as a microcosm of wider social tensions around auditing; the topic features prominently in the commentaries of the **critical accounting movement**.

expected value (EV)

The quantifiable, anticipated result of a course of action whose outcome is uncertain. Expected values are often used in **decision theory** and are calculated by multiplying the expected outcomes of individual decisions by the **probabilities** of their occurrence. See also **decision tree**.

expediting payment

An alternative term for **facilitating payment**.

expenditures

The act of funding **costs** through the payment of **money** or the incurring of **liabilities**. See **capital expenditures** and **revenue expenditures**.

expense
1 A **cost** incurred during a defined time period. Expenses are deducted from revenues in an **income statement** to calculate **net income**. The costs of **long-term** assets are expensed to individual time periods through the mechanism of **amortization**. The terms "costs" and "expenses" are often used synonymously. **2** [*Plural*] Travel expenses incurred for a business journey.

***expert-comptable* [*French*]**
A term used in Francophone countries that approximates to **Certified Public Accountant** or **Chartered Accountant**.

export
A sale to a customer located in a foreign country. Contrast **import**.

***ex post* [*Latin*]**
After an event, or later in time. Contrast *ex ante*.

exposure draft
A draft **accounting standard** or **auditing standard** disseminated for public comment and discussion before being finalized and published.

extended trial balance
A mechanism for the preparation of **financial statements** from a **trial balance**. The listing of **general ledger** balances in a trial balance is "extended" by the recording of adjustments (e.g., **accrued expenses** and reclassifications), and finally by the allocation of each account to either the **balance sheet** or the **income statement**.

external audit
An alternative term for **financial audit**.

external auditing
An alternative term for **financial auditing**.

external auditor
An alternative term for **financial auditor**.

external control

1 Aspects of **corporate governance** related to oversight exercised by **stakeholders**. Elements of external control include (i) the publication of **financial statements**, (ii) **financial audits** of financial statements, and (iii) **directors' reports**. **2** The monitoring of **internal controls** at a third-party organization. Example: some retail corporations monitor the processes and internal controls of important **vendors**.

extraordinary item

A **transaction** separately reported or disclosed in an **income statement** on account of its **materiality**, unusual nature, or infrequency. Extraordinary items arise from events outside normal operating activities, and examples may include large-scale, **one-off** costs arising from natural disasters, fire damage, or government appropriation of **assets**. An unusual event arising from normal operating activities is referred to as an **exceptional item**.

extrapolation

1 Estimating unknown values that are beyond a range of known values. Compare **interpolation**. **2** The extension of the characteristics of a **sample** of data to the entire **population** from which the sample was extracted. Example: if 10 percent of a **random sample** of **accounts receivable** balances exceeds established **credit limits**, an auditor may infer that 10 percent of the entire accounts receivable balance exceeds the credit limits (provided that the auditor has adequate *a priori* knowledge of the context in which the variables were gathered). Caution must be exercised in extrapolating the results of any sample, however, owing to **sampling risk**.

face value

1 The **nominal value** of a **bond** or other debt instrument. The price of a bond when issued may differ from its face value, owing to a **discount (sense 1)** or **premium (sense 2)** on issuance, and the **market values** of traded bonds also tend to differ from face values. However, a bond's **settlement** value at **maturity** and **interest payments** tend to be calculated in relation to face value. The term "face value" is sometimes used synonymously with **par value**, though careful users restrict the former to debt instruments and the latter to **common stock. 2** The monetary value stated on a coin or bank note.

facilitating payment

A minor payment made to an individual or organization in order to encourage the correct and timely performance of existing duties. The term "facilitating payment" (or "expediting payment") is associated with the United States' **Foreign Corrupt Practices Act**, which distinguishes it from a **bribe**. In essence, a facilitating payment is made to ensure the performance of an individual's routine duties, and no more, while the intention of a bribe is to gain influence and procure preferential treatment. However, the distinction between a facilitating payment and a bribe is often decided in the courts. Compare **questionable payment.**

factoring

The sale of **accounts receivable** to a **third party**, known as a factor. The factor purchases accounts receivable at a **discount (sense 1)** to their total value and assumes the responsibility for collection and **credit risks.** The advantages of factoring for the seller include (i) the saving of administrative costs and (ii) improved cash flow and **working capital.** The main advantage for the factor is the **income (sense 2)** arising from the difference between the purchase price and the **net realizable value** of the acquired accounts receivable.

factors of production

In classical economics, the requirements for the **production** of goods. Famously defined by the economist Alfred Marshall (1842–1924) as the "things required for making a commodity," the factors of production have traditionally been grouped into three categories: (i) land and natural resources, (ii) **labor**, and (iii) **capital (sense 4).** Some economists have added **entrepreneurship** as a fourth factor of production. Although an influential model, modern economists make little use of the classical concept of factors of production, preferring to focus on inputs; labor, for example, is more often viewed today as a form of human capital.

fair presentation

The portrayal by **financial statements** of underlying economic conditions in an accurate, reliable, truthful, and **understandable** manner. Financial auditors are required to give an audit **opinion** on the fair presentation of financial statements, an important element of which is that financial statements should not mislead their readers.

fair value

A British alternative term for **market value**.

fallacy

A fault or error in reasoning. Fallacies may arise from both deliberate deception and unintentional self-deception. In auditing, fallacious reasoning may result in inappropriate **judgments** of audit **evidence**, and therefore wrong or unpersuasive audit **opinions**. In the **logic of auditing**, it is suggested that cogent reasoning requires four core elements: (i) clear terms, (ii) warranted premises (i.e., premises that can support reasonable belief), (iii) no omission of relevant evidence, and (iv) valid reasoning. Based on this structure, fallacies in auditing may be categorized under the headings of (i) ambiguous terms, (ii) unwarranted premises, (iii) omitted evidence, and (iv) invalid reasoning. Some fallacies may overlap these categories. Example: a junior auditor is testing a **random sample** of the documentation that supports a warehouse's receipt of goods, and she cannot locate three sets of documentation from her sample of thirty items. She concludes in her **work papers** that the three items she could not locate may have been lost. This conclusion indicates a fallacy of reasoning (item iv above), because a loss of the documents is only one plausible explanation for their unavailability. Other plausible explanations include a possible misfiling of the documents, a temporary removal of the documents by staff members who are looking into specific queries, and a purposeful destruction of the documents to hide fraud. There is also a suggestion of faulty logic in the auditor's failure to review all relevant evidence (item iii above): the undertaking of **alternative audit procedures** might have provided additional, relevant evidence. For instance, computerized records may have recorded scans of the missing documentation, inquiries to the vendors may have confirmed the transactions, and the tracking of cash settlements in **accounts**

payable records might have provided persuasive evidence of the existence and value of the underlying transactions.

false accounting
The **fraudulent** manipulation of accounting data. See **cooking the books.**

fast-moving consumer goods (FMCG)
Tangible **consumer goods** of portable size characterized by low selling prices and a high volume of activity.

favorable variance
In **budgeting**, the incurring of smaller-than-anticipated costs or the earning of larger-than-anticipated revenues. A favorable variance indicates that actual performance was better than expected. Contrast **unfavorable variance.**

feasibility study
An evaluation of the impact of undertaking a potential activity or making a potential investment. Quantifiable evaluation techniques, such as **discounted cash flow analysis** and **payback period** analysis, are commonly used in feasibility studies.

fee
A payment to an individual or organization for providing a service. The term is often used for the remuneration of financial auditors and other **professionals.** Compare **compensation.**

fictitious asset
An **asset** reported in a **fixed asset register** or **balance sheet** that does not exist. A fictitious asset may arise from error (e.g., a failure to delete an asset after its disposal) or from **fraudulent** activity.

fiduciary
An individual or organization responsible for administering another party's assets. **Agents**, for example, act as fiduciaries to **principals**, and trustees are fiduciaries to the beneficiaries of **trusts (sense 1).**

fiddle [*Verb, Slang, mainly British*]
To falsify. Example: "He was fiddling his travel expenses for years before he was caught."

field auditor
An auditor who undertakes assignments away from an organization's headquarters. Example: The **environmental auditing** function of a **multinational corporation** may use field auditors either to cover a single **decentralized location** or to address two or more locations as **traveling auditors**.

fieldwork
Audit tests undertaken away from an organization's headquarters or main premises.

finance
1 The administration of **monetary** resources. **2** An alternative term for **capital (senses 1 and 4)**. **3** An alternative term for **money (sense 1)** or **funding**.

finance lease
A British term for **capital lease**.

financial accounting
The administration of **accounting** records and the preparation of **financial statements** and related documents. Financial accounting, in contrast to **management accounting**, tends to focus on accounting records for use outside an organization—by **investors**, **creditors**, **debtors**, and **tax** authorities.

financial audit
A branch of auditing that provides **opinions** on the accuracy and **fair presentation** of **financial statements**. Financial auditing is often differentiated from **internal auditing** by its synonym "external auditing." The American Accounting Association provided a landmark definition of financial auditing in 1973: "[Financial] auditing is a systematic process of objectively obtaining and evaluating **evidence** regarding **assertions** about economic actions and events to ascertain the degree of correspondence between those assertions and established criteria and

communicating the results to interested parties" (American Accounting Association 1973, 2). In this definition, "assertions" refer to explicit and implicit representations of financial statement items, on which the auditor provides an opinion; the "established criteria" are **Generally Accepted Accounting Principles (GAAP)** and **Generally Accepted Auditing Standards (GAAS)**; and "communication" refers to the auditor's opinion and comments channeled through the **audit report.**

Additional but connected definitions: "an inferential practice which seeks to draw conclusions from a limited **inspection** of documents, . . . in addition to reliance on oral testimony and direct observation" (Power 2000, 111), and a "complex and technical function in which the auditor verifies and reports on the quality of the financial messages which corporate management discloses publicly to external constituents as part of its financial **accountability** to the latter" (Lee 1993, 4). On the social purpose of financial auditing: "The role of [financial] auditing in an advanced economic society can be and has been stated in very simple terms—to add credibility to financial statements" (Robert Kuhn Mautz, quoted by Flint 1988, 6).

Modern financial auditing is the result of almost two centuries of evolution. It emerged as a **professional** discipline in the United Kingdom in the nineteenth century, spurred on by the expansion of limited liability corporations, starting with the East India Company (Giroux 2017, vol. 1, 45–47), as the dominant form of business, which led to a separation of the providers of capital from the managers who administered it. The massive investments that accompanied the country's Industrial Revolution expanded the role of the limited liability corporation. To provide **assurance** that investments were appropriately managed and controlled, financial auditors offered the providers of capital an independent and objective opinion on published financial statements, traditionally the primary record of corporate accountability. The emergence of financial auditing is therefore often understood in terms of **agency theory**, arising from the **asymmetric information** between the managers of a corporation, as **agents**, and its stockholding owners, as **principals**; the financial auditor took on an intermediary role between the principals and agents. As has been suggested, "capitalism is a complicated enterprise, and the system won't work without referees" (Fox 2003, 313).

British legislation incrementally expanded the requirements for the financial auditing of larger corporations and "public interest" organizations, such as the railways. In 1866, the Exchequer and Audit Department was created to monitor the financial regularity and financial statements of a range of institutions of the British state. (In 1983, the Exchequer and Audit Department became the National Audit Office.) By 1900, legislation required a financial audit for virtually all British limited liability companies. With the founding of the American Institute of Certified Public Accountants (initially named the American Association of Public Accountants) in 1887, the center of gravity of financial auditing moved from the United Kingdom to the United States, where it has since remained. However, it was not until the enactment in the United States of the *Securities Act* **(1933)** and the *Securities Exchange Act* **(1934)** to address the economic turbulence of the immediately preceding years that listed corporations in the United States were required to file audited financial statements (O'Reilly et al. 1998, 1.9).

Among other new professions to emerge during the Industrial Revolution, financial auditing has struggled to attain the prestige of the traditional "learned professions" of divinity, medicine, and law. Financial auditors nonetheless have created, over nearly two centuries, a powerful and lucrative profession with high barriers to entry. Legislation in most industrial countries requires the annual financial audit of all but the smallest corporations, in addition to other institutions, and restricts this activity to the certified members of professional accounting and auditing associations. The British **Chartered Accountants**, the American **Certified Public Accountants**, and their global peers have benefited from almost two centuries of continuous evolution.

Two important influences on the development of financial auditing have been the accounting profession and powerful audit firms. The first institutions of modern public accounting (from whose ranks financial auditors are drawn) first appeared in Scotland in 1854 and England in 1870. Regarding the striking longevity of powerful auditing firms, the firms of nineteenth-century England included the forerunners of today's global auditing and accounting firms (Matthews, Anderson, and Edwards 1998, 45); among the names of London's auditing firms in 1886 were several that have survived, in various combinations, to the modern era's Big Four, including Price, Waterhouse, and Cooper Brothers (now combined into PricewaterhouseCoopers) and Deloitte, Dever, Griffiths (now Deloitte Touche Tohmatsu).

An early emphasis of financial auditing on the detection of **error** and **fraud** gradually developed into an assessment of the accuracy and fair presentation of financial statements. Fraud detection was gradually relegated to a **by-product** of the audit rather than its focus (Power 1997, 21), at least in auditors' eyes. Nonetheless, the expectations from an ever-increasing array of stakeholders that financial auditors' responsibilities should focus on fraud detection have remained stubbornly strong, and this enduring divergence of views is referred to as the **expectations gap.** The expectations gap reached its most acute expression after the collapse of Enron Corporation in 2001, and the subsequent demise of **Arthur Andersen**, the public accounting firm, the next year. The widespread loss of faith in the value of financial auditing and corporate reporting at that time was known colloquially as **Enronitis.**

financial auditing

The process or action of undertaking a **financial audit.** The noun gerund "auditing" places a greater emphasis on action than does the simple noun "audit."

financial auditor

An individual who performs a **financial audit.** In most countries, financial auditors are drawn from the ranks of professional accountant-auditors (**Certified Public Accountants**, **Chartered Accountants**, or licensed individuals of equivalent standing).

financial controller

An individual with the principal "hands-on" responsibility for an organization's finance and accounting functions. In large organizations a financial controller typically reports to a **Chief Financial Officer**; in smaller organizations, the two roles may be combined.

financial instrument

A tradable **investment** that confers a claim or a potential claim on income. There are many types of financial instruments, including **common stock**, **bonds**, and **derivatives**; they are issued by corporations and governments. However, some users of the term reserve it only for traded bonds.

Financial Instruments and Exchange Act (J-SOX, 2006)

Japanese legislation of 2006 that updated the country's **securities** laws to encourage greater transparency and enhance investor protection. Its requirements for financial auditors' **independence** and the **disclosure** of the effectiveness of **internal controls** in listed corporations was influenced in part by the United States' 2002 *Sarbanes-Oxley Act* **(SOX)**. For this reason, it is often referred to as the "Japanese SOX," abbreviated to J-SOX.

financial reporting
The preparation and dissemination of **financial statements**. "Corporate financial reporting is essentially an information system designed to construct and represent abstractions of the state and effects of specific empirical events which comprise the business activity of a corporate organization" (Lee 1993, 138). Financial reporting in most countries is guided by a combination of **legislation**, **Generally Accepted Accounting Principles (GAAP)**, and custom.

financial reporting period
A period of time covered by **financial statements**. An **income statement** usually reports revenues and costs for a financial reporting period of twelve months, and a **balance sheet** reports the totals of **assets, liabilities,** and **equity (sense 1)** on the final date of the reporting period. See also **fiscal year**.

financial reporting standard
Rules and guidance on **accounting** practice and **disclosure** in **financial statements**. Along with **legislation** and custom, financial reporting standards (sometimes referred to as "accounting standards") are the foundation of **Generally Accepted Accounting Principles (GAAP)**. The international harmonization of GAAP is promoted by the International Accounting Standards Board (IASB), for accounting standards, and the International Sustainability Standards Board (ISSB) for sustainability disclosure standards.

financial statements
Summaries of the **accounting** transactions and financial position of an organization at a specific date. The main elements of financial statements are the **balance sheet**, which offers a snapshot of **assets, liabilities,** and **equity (sense 1)** at a given date; and the **income statement**, which sets out operating results and **net income** for a defined time period leading to the balance sheet date. Under most systems of **Generally Accepted Accounting**

Principles (GAAP), other components of financial statements typically include a **cash flow statement**, explanatory notes, and a **directors' report. Financial auditing** is concerned with **opinions** on the "accuracy, clarity and completeness" (Mautz and Sharaf, 1961, 94) of financial statements. See also **fair presentation.**

financial year (FY)
A British term for **fiscal year.**

finished goods
The final products of a manufacturing process held as **inventory**, pending their sale. Compare **raw materials** and **work-in-process.**

firm
1 [*Noun*] An organization established to undertake business or professional activity. A firm is not necessarily a **corporation**, as the term also covers **partnerships** and other legal forms of collective endeavors. **2** [*Adj.*] Not subjected to uncertainty or negotiation. Examples: "a firm order" and "a firm sale."

first-in first-out (FIFO) method
An **inventory** valuation method that assumes inventory is consumed or sold in the order in which it is purchased or manufactured. FIFO methodology, which allocates older inventory costs to **costs of sales**, is acceptable under most forms of **Generally Accepted Accounting Principles (GAAP)**. Compare the **last-in first-out (LIFO)** and **next-in first-out (NIFO)** valuation methods.

fiscal [*Adj.*]
Relating to government finances, including **taxation.**

fiscal year (FY)
A **financial reporting period** of twelve months' duration used for **taxation** assessments. Fiscal years vary between countries—the fiscal year of the United States begins on October 1, while for Bangladesh the date is July 1; for India, April 1; and for the United Kingdom, April 6. In some countries, like Ireland and South Korea, the fiscal year coincides with the calendar year.

Five Es
See the **Six Es**.

fixed asset
1 A **long-term** asset, **tangible** or **intangible**. Contrast **current asset**. **2** [*Plural*] A British term for **property, plant, and equipment**, usually the main category of tangible fixed assets in corporate financial statements.

fixed budget
An alternative term for **static budget**.

fixed charges
1 An alternative term for **fixed costs**. **2** Costs related to the setting up of production batches. All other things being equal, large production batches minimize the impact of fixed charges like the installation and calibration of production machinery, owing to **economies of scale**. **3** The right of a lender to take possession of a specific asset should a borrower **default (sense 2)** on the repayment of a **loan** (or if another specified event—e.g., **bankruptcy**—takes place). A fixed charge establishes a specific asset as **collateral** for a debt. Example: a **mortgage** on a property. Compare **floating charge**.

fixed costs
Items of **expenditures** that are not directly influenced by changes in activity levels. Rental and insurance costs are typical fixed costs for many organizations. Contrast **variable costs** and **semivariable costs**.

fixtures
Fixed assets that take the form of attachments to larger assets. Example: depending on their **materiality**, security devices attached to automobiles could be classified as fixtures.

fixtures and fittings
An alternative term for **fixtures**; but the term distinguishes between attached items (fixtures) and free-standing items (fittings). This distinction may be important for valuation purposes in the sale of buildings.

flag of convenience
In international maritime practice, the registering of a ship in a country other than the ship's country of origin. Flags of convenience tend to be used to simplify administrative requirements, or to avoid or minimize **taxation** and **regulatory** burdens.

flash report
1 A report that summarizes important or sensitive information in advance of a more detailed report. Sales information in commercial organizations is a typical component of flash reports. **2** An alternative term for **exception report**.

flexible budget
A **budget** that provides (or is capable of providing with minimal adjustments) information on various potential levels of activity. In contrast to a **static** budget, a flexible budget is dynamic, catering to changes in operational circumstances.

float
1 An amount of **money** held as **petty cash**. **2** The time difference between the depositing of **checks** in a bank and their processing by the bank. During this processing time, the funds are unavailable to both payer and payee.

flotation
The launching of a new **corporation** through the issuance of **securities** in a **market**.

floating charge
The right of a lender to take possession of unspecified assets if a borrower **defaults (sense 2)** on the repayment of a **loan** or if another specified event (e.g., **bankruptcy**) takes place. Compare **fixed charge (sense 3)**.

flowchart
A diagram that depicts a sequential flow of transactions and activities. Conventional flowchart symbols include (i) rectangles for descriptions of activities, (ii) diamonds for decision points, and (iii) circles for links.

follow-up

In auditing, the periodic monitoring of the status of auditors' findings and **recommendations**. The follow-up process focuses on the sufficiency and timeliness of **auditee** actions to implement auditors' recommendations.

footing

The addition of individual items in a list or **account** to arrive at a total. If a list or account includes both **debit** and **credit entries**, the footing process calculates the **net balance**. Traditionally, in manual **bookkeeping**, footing was an important verification of the arithmetical accuracy of vertical columns of numbers in the **books of account**. Cross-footing referred to the practice of tallying a series of columns of numbers.

forecast

A quantifiable estimate of future activities. The term is sometimes used as a synonym for **budget** but it can also refer to periods of time shorter than or longer than that of a typical budget. It is also sometimes used synonymously with **projection**, but some users of the term differentiate between short-term forecasts and long-term projections. See also **cash flow forecast**.

foreclosure

The forced sale of a property following a mortgage holder's **default (sense 2)** on payments.

Foreign Corrupt Practices Act (FCPA) (1977)

Anti**corruption** legislation passed in the United States in 1977. The FCPA and its amendments (like the *International Anti-Bribery Act* of 1998) forbid the **bribery** of foreign officials and require corporations to maintain adequate **internal control** systems throughout their international operations. In some countries, the exchange of small **gifts** is an essential means of doing business; the FCPA acknowledges this by permitting **facilitating payments**, popularly known as **grease payments**, which are intended merely to encourage foreign officials to perform their routine duties in a correct and timely manner and not to solicit favorable decisions from the recipients. However, the difference between a bribe and a facilitating payment is often thin and the matter is sometimes decided in the courts. Contravention of the FCPA can result in severe fines and custodial sentences, and it has had an enormous impact on how US **multinational** corporations manage their affairs. Owing to the increase in auditing and monitoring that it stimulated, the FCPA has been described as the *Internal Auditor Full Employment Act*—and similar sentiments have been expressed since the passing of the **Sarbanes-Oxley Act** in 2002.

foreign currency
A **currency** used in a different country.

forensic audit
An audit undertaken specifically to support actions in a court of law. Forensic auditing is associated with practices like the **investigation** of **money-laundering** transactions, and it tends to be focused on the uncovering of **fraudulent** and other illegal activity.

forfeiture
The loss or deprival of an **asset** or legal right. Forfeiture may be a punishment for wrongdoing, or it can arise from the nonoccurrence of an event in a commercial **contract**. An example of the latter is the loss of a deposit of **money** required for the submission of bids to win a contract, in circumstances when the deposit is refundable only to the winner of the contract.

forgery
The **fraudulent** copying or imitation of an item. Items typically subjected to forgery include (i) signatures, (ii) **money**, and (iii) works of art.

format
The manner in which an item is structured and presented. The format of an **audit report**, for example, is often central to its success as a communication medium for audit **recommendations**.

forward rate
An **exchange rate** specified in a foreign currency **contract**. The contract in this context involves either a commitment or an **option** to buy or sell a specified amount of a foreign currency at a specified date.

Four Lines Model

An extension of the **Three Lines Model** of organizational risk mitigation activities through the addition of a fourth line of **financial auditing** and regulation.

franchise

1 A **contractual** authorization given by one party (the franchiser) to another (the franchisee) to undertake economic activity using the franchiser's **brand** name. The franchisee usually pays a **royalty** for the use of the brand name. Fast-food outlets are a classic example of a franchise arrangement. **2** The granting by a state of **monopoly** rights to an organization. In this context, franchising is often used for the supply of **public goods**.

fraud

Illegal, dishonest, or improper activity. Fraud takes many forms, including (i) the manipulation or misrepresentation of **accounting** data (or **cooking the books**) and (ii) the theft of **assets** and **intellectual property**. Fraud may be committed by an individual working alone, or in **collusion** with two or more conspirators. Fraud involving deceit by an organization's **directors** or senior managers may be difficult to detect by auditors, yet it can have potentially disastrous consequences. The difference between fraud and **error** originates in the intentions behind the actions—the former encompasses deliberate actions, while the latter arises from innocent mistakes or from negligence.

Fraud has always been of concern to auditors, particularly during the development of financial auditing in the nineteenth and twentieth centuries; in 1843, the accounting writer B. F. Foster remarked that "no system of accounts is secure from the designs of the fraudulent" (quoted by Chambers 1995, 72). The legacy of the importance of fraud in financial auditing is evident in the **expectations gap**—the continuing discrepancy between public and professional opinion on the extent to which financial auditors are responsible for fraud detection.

free market economy

An economy dominated by private enterprise. In a free market economy, industrial output, the **prices** of products and services, and the allocation of economic resources are all determined by the unhindered interplay of the forces of supply and demand. In practice, authentic free market economies are rare, as most nations have significant **public-sector** activity and **regulations** over commerce and trade: a **mixed economy** is therefore currently the norm.

free port
1 A seaport or airport that does not charge **customs** duties on transactions conducted through it. **2** A seaport or airport that is open to traders of all nationalities.

frequency
A measure of the rate of occurrence of an event or item.

frequency distribution
An analysis of the number of times an item appears in a **population** of data. See **normal distribution.**

fringe benefit
An item of **compensation**, other than **money**, transferred to an employee of an organization. Sometimes referred to simply as benefits or **perquisites**, common fringe benefits include (i) the use of an automobile and (ii) health care insurance.

front office
The trading (as opposed to administrative) functions of a **brokerage** operation that buys and sells **securities, commodities (sense 1)**, and **currencies.** Compare **back office.**

functional currency
A **currency** used in the primary location of an individual or organization, which is normally adopted for **financial reporting** purposes. For example, **multinational corporations** based in the United States usually adopt the US dollar as their functional currency.

fund
An amount of **money** set aside for specific operational or **investment** purposes. Examples of funds include **pension funds** and **petty cash** funds.

funding
The providing of **money (sense 1)** to support activities or investments.

fungibles
Items that can be interchanged without any loss in **value**. Examples: bank notes of the same denomination and identical units of a **commodity (both senses)**.

furniture and fittings
A category of **property, plant, and equipment** that consists of **fixed assets** found typically in administrative offices.

futures contract
A **contract** to buy or sell a defined quantity of a **commodity (sense 1)**, **currency**, or **security** at a specified date at a specified **price**. Unlike an **option**, a futures contract involves a commitment to buy or sell in accordance with the terms of the contract.

future value (FV)
The quantifiable amount to which a sum of **money** will grow if invested at a defined **interest rate**.

gain
1 An increase in **value**. Gains arising on the **appreciation** of the value of an **asset** may be **realized** or **unrealized**. **2** An alternative term for **income (sense 2)**.

galloping inflation [*Archaic*]
An alternative term for **hyperinflation**.

game theory
The systematic analysis of strategies for the optimal selection of alternative courses of action in competitive or conflictual conditions. In game theory, unlike **decision theory**, the outcomes of an individual's decisions depend on

the actions of other participants. An important assumption underpinning game theory is that participants act rationally in their self-interest. Very often, as in **zero-sum games**, the participants have conflicting interests. In other cases (so-called cooperation games), collusion and cooperation between participants is possible. The relevance to auditing, which can be described as a **cooperative** search for assurance, is clear. See also **prisoner's dilemma**.

Gantt chart
A graphical portrayal of a project or activity that shows a comparative distribution of operations and responsibilities over time. Gantt charts typically plot bands of activity across a horizontal time scale, offering an overall perspective on the timing (and, possibly, the resource requirements) of a group of related activities. They are named for Henry Gantt (1861–1919), a pioneer of management theory.

gearing
A British term for **leverage**.

General Auditor
An alternative term for **Chief Auditing Executive**.

general ledger (GL)
A group of **accounts** used as a foundation for the preparation of **financial statements**. The general ledger contains accounts for **assets, liabilities, equity (sense 1)**, **revenue**, and **expenditures,** and the accounts are traditionally summarized in a **trial balance** to facilitate the preparation of financial statements. Some accounting **transactions** may be recorded in **subsidiary ledgers** before their transfer to a general ledger account.

Generally Accepted Accounting Principles (GAAP)
Rules, guidance, and concepts for accounting practices and the content of **financial statements**. GAAP covers the **recognition (sense 1)**, **measurement**, **reporting**, and **disclosure** of accounting items, and it is derived from several sources: **financial reporting standards** (often referred to as "accounting standards"), **legislation**, custom, industry-specific arrangements, and the

pronouncements of authoritative professional associations. The importance of each of these elements varies from country to country. Example: in continental Europe, legislation has tended to be the main source of GAAP; but in the United States, GAAP has been derived mainly from the standards of the Financial Accounting Standards Board, the pronouncements and interpretations of professional bodies like the American Institute of Certified Public Accountants, industry customary practices, and academic literature. The international **harmonization** of GAAP gathered significant momentum around the turn of the twenty-first century and continues under the umbrella of the *International Financial Reporting Standards Foundation*.

The fifth of the **postulates of auditing** elaborated by Robert Kuhn Mautz and Hussein A. Sharaf states that the "consistent application of generally accepted principles of accounting results in the **fair presentation** of financial position and the results of operations," emphasizing the importance of assessing the adherence of financial statement **assertions** to GAAP.

Generally Accepted Auditing Standards (GAAS)

Rules and guidance for the conduct of **financial auditing**. Although financial audits are tailored to specific organizational contexts, auditing standards aim to provide a consistent approach to auditing that balances judgment and guidance: "'Cookbook' rules are not and never will be sufficient to cover every possible combination of circumstances and thereby allow [financial] auditors to shed their responsibility to exercise professional **judgment**; on the other hand, a framework exists to provide guidance for exercising judgment in all significant aspects of audit practice" (O'Reilly et al. 1998, 3.5). GAAS is derived from several sources, including **legislation**, custom, industry-specific conventions, academic and professional literature, and, above all, from the announcements of professional auditing organizations. In the United States, the Auditing Standards Board of the American Institute of Certified Public Accountants issues *Statements on Auditing Standards*. On a global scale, the International Auditing and Assurance Standards Board of the International Federation of Accountants aims at the global **harmonization** of GAAS through its standards and pronouncements.

Generally Accepted Government Auditing Standards (GAGAS)

An alternative term for **Government Auditing Standards**.

geometric progression
A sequential pattern of numbers in which the ratio of each number to its predecessor is constant. An example is 2, 4, 8, 16, 32, and so on. Contrast **arithmetic progression.**

ghost ticking
See **phantom ticking.**

gift
An item presented free of charge to an individual or organization. Gifts are generally intended to express gratitude or friendship, and are common in business circles in some cultures. However, a gift may become a **bribe** if it is intended (or is perceived as intended) to gain undue influence over an individual or organization. Typical **internal controls** over the giving of gifts in an organization include (i) the timely recording of gifts, (ii) a statement of a gift's purpose, (iii) prior authorization by a senior official, (iv) value thresholds to discourage the giving of expensive or extravagant gifts, and (v) the forbidding of certain types of gifts.

gilt
A British term for a **Treasury bond (sense 1).** The term originated from the United Kingdom's practice of issuing its **bonds** on paper with gilded edges.

global corporation
An alternative term for a **multinational corporation.**

globalization
1 The internationalization of economic, political, and cultural activity. Globalization is both characterized by and stimulated by improvements in telecommunications and travel infrastructures that facilitate the movement of people, capital, ideas, and consumer goods across geographical and political borders. Deregulation has also stimulated globalization, notably through the economic liberalization in recent decades of China, India, and the former Soviet Bloc. **2** The emergence and impact of international organizations: "Globalization does not mean merely the expansion of communications, contacts, and trade around the globe. It means the transfer of social, economic, political, and juridical power to global

organizations . . . in the form of **multinational** corporations, international courts, or transnational legislatures" (Scruton 2002, 127). See **Davos man / woman.**

going concern

The assumption used in accounting and financial auditing that an organization will continue to operate for the foreseeable future. Worries over an organization's going concern status (e.g., if mounting debts raise the prospect of **bankruptcy** or a significant curtailment of activities) are normally reflected in changes to a range of assumptions concerning the valuation of **assets** and the **matching** of revenues and costs across accounting periods.

golden handcuffs

Contractually agreed-on **remuneration** or other benefits designed to induce an employee to continue to work in an organization. The term is semiformal, and it is normally used to refer to generous **compensation** packages that discourage the poaching of employees by rival organizations.

golden parachute

A **contractually** agreed-on element of **executive remuneration** that guarantees an individual a significant amount of **money** or other benefits in the event of a forced departure from an organization. Golden parachutes tend to be devised with the potential effects of corporate **acquisitions** in mind.

golden share

An investment by a government in a **privatized** organization that confers special rights. Governments retain golden shares in denationalized corporations to keep a degree of strategic control. Examples: a golden share may give a government the right to block a **takeover** bid or to regulate the **prices** of **public goods.**

goods

See **consumer goods.**

goodwill

1 In a corporate acquisition, an **intangible asset** that measures the excess of **consideration** paid by an acquiring corporation over the **fair value** of the acquired **net assets**. Contrast **negative goodwill**. **2** The value of an organization's income-generating **brands** and reputation. This sense of goodwill refers to the total value of an organization over its separable net tangible assets. **3** A favorable or friendly disposition toward an individual or organization.

Government Auditing Standards (GAS)
Public-sector auditing standards in the United States. Often referred to as the *Yellow Book*.

graduated tax
An alternative term for **progressive tax**.

graft
1 Dishonest, **fraudulent**, or improper behavior. See also **bribe** and **corruption**. **2** [*Especially British*] Hard work. Example: "He grafted away for many years with little recognition, only to die just after he achieved success."

grand livre (GL) [French]
The French term for **general ledger**. The expression *grand livre* literally means "big book" or "main book," and by coincidence its abbreviation is identical to that of its equivalent English term.

grant
Assistance given by a government to an individual or organization for a particular purpose. Grants can take several forms; examples include (i) sums of **money**, (ii) donations of **assets**, (iii) training and technical assistance, and (iv) **tax** advantages.

gratis [Latin]
Free of charge. The term derives from a Latin expression meaning "out of kindness."

gray director
See **outside director**.

gray economy
Economic activity that combines legitimate behavior with elements of the
underground economy.

grease payment [*Informal*]
See **facilitating payment.**

Great Salad Oil Swindle (1963)
The popular name of a landmark 1963 US legal case that featured the **Allied
Crude Vegetable Oil Refining Corporation.**

green audit
See **environmental audit.**

greenwashing
The paying of lip service to environmental concerns to give a false impression of
a serious commitment to such matters.

gross
1 [*Adj.*] Without a deduction for **allowances, discounts (sense 1)**, or **taxation.** Contrast **net. 2** [*Noun, Archaic*] Twelve dozen: 12 × 12 = 144.

gross domestic product (GDP)
The total **value** of a country's economic output over a defined time period. GDP
comprises the output of both goods and services, and *per capita* GDP is a frequent comparative measure of a country's economic prosperity.

gross income / gross margin
Total sales revenues less the costs of goods (or services) sold. Nonproduction
overhead (e.g., administration and distribution costs) is excluded from the calculation of gross income. Contrast **net income.**

gross margin
An alternative term for **gross income.**

gross risk
A **risk** before the application of **risk management** procedures. See **net risk** and **residual risk**.

gross sales
Total sales before the deduction of **discounts (sense 1)**, **allowances for bad debts**, and **customer returns**.

group financial statements
The **consolidated** financial statements of a business combination.

guarantee
1 A **contractual** undertaking by a third party, a guarantor, to take on the **liabilities** arising from a transaction if one of the main parties to the transaction fails to fulfill its requirements. **2** An alternative term for **warranty**. **3** A statement of the accuracy of an item. Example: A mint's assay certificates for its gold coins guarantees the coins' gold content.

hacker
An individual motivated by attempts to gain unauthorized access to computer networks or files. Hackers may be motivated by a desire to disrupt or embarrass an organization, to steal information or money, or to enjoy a sense of danger in testing the security of a computerized system.

haircut [*Informal*]
A reduction in the amount repaid on a **liability**. Example: "The bank had to take a 20 percent haircut on its loans to the troubled corporation." Originally, the term was used, starting in the 1960s, to refer to a reduction in an asset's value in the context of the US Securities and Exchange Commission's regulatory requirements.

hard asset
An alternative term for **tangible asset**.

hard audit

An audit that presents difficulties of interpretation arising from complexity and from the availability and nature of audit **evidence**. Hard audits place strong demands on auditors, and different, competent, **professional** auditors may reasonably differ in the **opinions** they reach based on the same evidence. In contrast, for a straightforward or easy audit, one would expect different competent and professional auditors to reach the same conclusions from the same evidence. The term arises by analogy with legal cases in which competent, professional lawyers may reach different opinions. The implications of differing opinions are that there is either (i) no standard answer, based on the available evidence or (ii) the correct answer is difficult to ascertain. In situations in which there is a clear cause for the hardness (difficulty) of an audit, including limitations on evidence or adversarial behavior by an **auditee**, a **financial auditor** may resort to a **modified opinion**. See also **logic in auditing** and **outside expertise**.

hard copy

A tangible document.

hard currency

A **currency** widely accepted throughout the world and freely convertible in currency **markets**. Contrast **soft currency**.

harmonization

The process of increasing consistency between things. In a **financial auditing** context, the term is frequently used to refer to the elimination or narrowing of variations between different international systems of **Generally Accepted Auditing Standards (GAAS)** and **Generally Accepted Accounting Principles (GAAP)**.

Head of Audit

An alternative term for **Chief Audit Executive**.

hedge

An arrangement or transaction intended to protect against fluctuations in the **price** of an asset. Hedges are typically used as **risk management** measures to mitigate the price movements of **currencies**, **securities**, and **commodities** **(sense 1)**.

hierarchy

An organization or system in which concepts or people are arranged, pyramid-like, in **top-down** layers of decreasing **authority** and status. In hierarchical institutions, authority is **delegated** downward through **chains of command**, while **accountability** runs upward through the same chains. In society more broadly, a hierarchy indicates divisions into levels of power and privilege; the **critical accounting movement** has criticized auditing, especially **financial auditing**, for exacerbating the maintenance of the *status quo* of social hierarchies.

hire purchase (HP)

A British term for **installment credit**.

historical costs

The unadjusted, original costs of purchasing an **asset** or an item of **inventory**. Historical costs do not reflect the effects of **inflation** or **revaluations**.

holding company

A corporation created to control one or more **subsidiary** organizations. Control can be achieved through either a majority of **common stock** voting rights or through dominant influence on a subsidiary's management or operating policies. A holding company does not usually have any purpose or operational activity beyond holding investments in subsidiaries.

holding costs

Expenditures on storing items of **inventory**. Holding costs typically include (i) warehousing expenditures, (ii) **insurance** premiums, (iii) inventory **shrinkage**, and, perhaps, (iv) inventory **obsolescence**.

holding gain

An **appreciation** in the **value** of an asset over a period of time, obtained simply through possession of the asset rather than through efforts at enhancing the asset's **value**. Contrast **holding loss**.

holding loss
A **depreciation** in the **value** of an asset over a period of time. Contrast **holding gain**.

holiday [*Mainly British*]
An agreement between a lender and a borrower to pause payments on a **loan** or other liability. Payment holidays typically cover disbursements related to **mortgages**, **interest payments**, and **rent (sense 1)**.

horizontal analysis
The analysis of information in **financial statements** over time. The reasonableness of changes in the amounts of financial statement items between **financial reporting periods** is a common aspect of financial auditors' **analytical review** procedures. Also known as trend analysis, horizontal analysis may be used to forecast future activity through the patterns of past trends. Compare **vertical analysis**.

hostile takeover
An **acquisition (sense 2)**—or attempted acquisition—that is unwelcomed by the acquired or targeted organization.

housekeeping internal controls
Internal controls that relate to routine, day-to-day activities. Example: the written **authorization** of individual **petty cash** vouchers. Although the internal controls addressed by housekeeping controls may not be of **material** significance, the rigor of such internal controls is often considered to be indicative of the quality of an organization's wider internal control environment. See also **analogical reasoning**.

humor in auditing
The ability of auditors to see the funny side of their activities. The established **professions** are targets of long-running jokes. This is most notable for the "learned professions" of physicians, lawyers, and priests, but it also covers other professions. Example: in Monty Python's *Ministry of Silly Walks* sketches, John Cleese (b. 1939) lampooned the formalities of elite British civil servants in a

merciless satire of the futility and absurdity of government routines during the United Kingdom's postimperial decline. Perhaps a profession's capacity to laugh at itself is an indicator of maturity, and an inability to do so is likely a sign of insecurity.

The philosopher of humor, Henri Bergson (1859–1941), considered comedy to have a moral function in society, in overcoming inflexibilities of character and promoting greater elasticity and sociability in our lives. Humor can be literally healthy, as an antidote to stress, and metaphorically healthy, by unfreezing social awkwardness. Jokes about auditing tend to exploit stereotypes of auditors as dull and charmless. The following ten jokes reached this book's author via oral transmission over an occasionally amusing period of more than three decades. The author cannot vouch for their origins, only for their circulation:

(i) Q: How do you identify an extrovert auditor? A: Someone who looks at *your* shoes during a conversation. (ii) Q: Why do auditors avoid gazing out of the window during the morning? A: Because that would give them nothing to do in the afternoon. (iii) Q: How did the auditor propose to his girlfriend? A: He sent her an **engagement letter**. (iv) Q: Why did the auditor break off her engagement to her fiancé? A: They couldn't **reconcile** their differences. (v) Q: How does an auditor's spouse deal with her insomnia? A: "Tell me, darling, what you did at work today." (vi) Those who can, do. Those who can't, teach. Those who can't teach, teach the teachers. And those who can't teach the teachers go into auditing. (vii) He quit auditing after he started to hear invoices. (viii) She quit auditing after she decided it was an accrual world. (ix) They all quit auditing after realizing their days were numbered. (x) Auditor A: "A strange thing just happened. I met the financial controller in the hallway and I asked him about his inventory cost flow assumption—was it LIFO or FIFO? And he responded by repeating to me, over and over again, the acronym FOFO. FOFO, FOFO. . . . What on Earth did he mean?" Auditor B: "I think his message was clear: he was telling you to Fuck Off and Find Out."

hurdle rate
A **rate of return** used as a threshold for accepting or rejecting a proposed **investment**. See **cost of capital** and **internal rate of return**.

hyperinflation
A very high rate of **inflation**. A common yardstick for defining hyperinflation is an annualized rate of 100 percent or more. Example: Venezuela, in early 2019, experienced a rate of *daily* inflation estimated at more than 40 percent. Hyperinflationary conditions may lead to a serious degradation or even a collapse of a country's monetary system, with recourse in extreme cases to systems of **barter** or the use of foreign currencies to undertake transactions. Contrast **deflation** and **disinflation**.

illiquid [*Adj.*]
1 Not in the form of **cash (all senses)** or assets readily convertible into cash. Examples: (i) **fixed assets** and (ii) some types of **current asset**, such as **inventory** (which by convention is excluded from the **acid test ratio**, an important liquidity measure). Contrast **liquidity**. **2** Incapable of satisfying **liabilities** owing to the possession of insufficient cash or assets readily convertible into cash.

immateriality
The unimportance of an item. Contrast **materiality**.

impairment
1 A **long-term**, irreversible **depreciation** in the **value** of an asset (including reputational damage to an **intangible** asset). **2** A real or perceived obstruction to an auditor's unhindered exercise of **judgment**.

impartiality
The absence of bias or **conflicts of interest** that might compromise an auditor's **judgment**. Impartiality is a necessary condition for auditing. It has been suggested for financial auditors (although it is relevant to all categories of auditor) that the role of the auditor "is analogous to that of an umpire in sports. Like the umpire, an auditor must perform his or her responsibilities in a manner which assures all interested parties that the **opinion** given is competent and unbiased" (Metcalf 1977). See **independence**.

import
A purchase from a supplier located in a foreign country. Contrast **export**.

imprest fund
An alternative term for **petty cash fund**.

inauditability
See **auditability**.

income
1 A positive flow of **money**, or a promise of money. Income arises from sources that include the proceeds of sales, gains on **investments**, and earned **interest**. See also **payment in kind**. **2** The excess of **sales** revenues over related costs in a defined time period. See also **gross income**, **net income**, **loss**, and **profit**. **3** An increase in the **net assets** of an individual or organization.

income statement
An accounting summary of the results of operations for a defined time period. An income statement establishes **net income** by deducting **expenses** from **revenues**, in line with the conventions of **double entry bookkeeping** and **Generally Accepted Accounting Principles (GAAP)**. Financial analysts place great emphasis on the net income and **earnings per share** derived from income statements.

independence
In auditing, the absence of a relationship, obligation, **conflict of interest**, or **biased** attitude that could compromise an auditor's **judgment**. While **impartiality** is considered essential for the **professional** credibility of all categories of auditor, independence has been described as "the most critical attribute" of **financial auditors** (O'Reilly et al. 1998, ix). Independence is therefore considered to be necessary for an objective, unbiased financial auditor's **opinion**: "It is primarily on the basis of its independence that the [financial] audit derives its authority and its acceptance" and "the full potential of an audit cannot be realised if it is not wholly and truly independent" (Flint 1988, 29, 55). Expressed

more evocatively: "the [financial] auditor, like Caesar's wife, must be above suspicion" (Toffler and Reingold 2003, 251).

An auditor's independence has been described as a "multi-dimensional concept" (Lee 1993, 100), and a financial auditor's independence can be subverted (or perceived to be subverted) by many factors. Matters that might threaten independence include (i) a financial connection to an **auditee**; (ii) family or personal relationships with an auditee; (iii) lavish entertaining, hospitality, or **gifts** offered to or received from an auditee; (iv) **scope limitations** on audit work; (v) an auditor's economic overdependence on fees from one auditee; and (under some circumstances) (vi) the provision of lucrative **management advisory services** alongside the financial audit. In addition to these threats to independence, most of which are manifestations of potential conflicts of interest, the concept of independence is often discussed in terms of a state of mind, involving personal character, ethics, and honesty. On this basis, therefore, it has been argued that independence "is an attitude of mind which goes deeper than any formal rules or standards" (Newman 1964, 148). Nonetheless, the "confidence of shareholders and others in the honesty of corporate [i.e., financial] auditors and their reports is likely to be focused on . . . visible signals of . . . independence, rather than [a] relatively hidden state of mind" (Lee 1993, 100)—in other words, independence in appearance is as important as independence in fact.

Many observers claim that financial auditors are never truly independent, as they tend to be selected and retained for permissible tenure periods by their clients. The phenomenon of **opinion-shopping** for compliant financial auditors adds to perceptions that true independence cannot be achieved under the current arrangements for the appointment of financial auditors. In 2020, *The CPA Journal* noted the damage to perceptions of financial auditor independence arising from "the institutional arrangement of the audit and the [resulting] conflicts of interest" in "a patronage system that rewards cozy relationships between auditors and clients."

indexation
The process of adjusting a variable in line with changes in another variable. Example: the value of **pension** payments or taxable **capital gains** may be indexed to **inflation** records.

indifference curves
Graphical depictions of economic preferences between two alternative goods providing equal satisfaction (or **utility**) to a consumer.

indirect costs
Expenditures that are difficult or impossible to attribute to specific units of production in a manufacturing context.

indirect taxation
A tax unrelated to, or not contingent on, the income of an individual or organization. Examples: **consumption taxes** and **sales taxes**. Indirect taxes bear a far less obvious relation to an individual's ability to pay than is the case with **direct taxation**. In the case of the corporation tax, the distinction between direct and indirect taxation is to a degree blurred; it is a direct tax on the corporation, but the corporation may deflect the burden by passing on some of the costs to customers (through increased selling prices) and employees (through lower **compensation**). See also **regressive taxation**.

inductive reasoning
See **logic in auditing**.

inflation
A sustained increase in the sales **prices** of goods and services. Inflation causes an erosion in the value (or purchasing power) of units of **money**. See also **deflation**, **disinflation**, and **hyperinflation**.

informal economy
An alternative term for the **underground economy**.

information risk
Risk arising from incorrect, incomplete, or outdated information. Information risk can potentially cause harm by distorting decision-making, subverting the assessment of investments, encouraging inappropriate behavior, or misleading the public on the performance of an organization or an activity. In the context of financial auditing, "by providing an **independent**, external perspective,

an audit enhances the credibility of financial information, and thus reduces the information risk to financial statement users" (O'Reilly et al. 1998, 1.12). See **reliability.**

information technology
The gathering, storage, retrieval, and dissemination of information through computerized and rapid telecommunication systems.

inherent risk
1 In financial auditing, the susceptibility of **financial statement** items to **misstatement**. With **control risk (sense 1)** and **detection risk**, it is one of the three components of **audit risk (sense 1)**. Inherent risk is deemed to be outside the auditor's control, but it can be mitigated by the gathering and assessment of sufficient audit **evidence** to provide **reasonable** expectations of detection. **2** See **uncontrollable risk.**

inside director
A member of an organization's **board of directors** who is also an employee of the organization.

insider dealing / insider trading
The illegal or improper use of **price sensitive information** not in the public domain to benefit from an increase in the value of a corporation's **securities.**

insolvency
The condition of being unable to **settle** liabilities and debts. See also **bankruptcy.** Contrast **solvency.**

inspection
A careful **examination**. Inspection is a technique used in auditing to evaluate audit **evidence**, usually in relation to **tangible assets**; the term is not synonymous with "auditing." See also **physical inspection** and **verification.**

installment
One of a series of payments of sums of **money**, usually of equal amounts.

installment credit
A **lease** agreement in which a **lessee** takes ownership of a leased **asset** after the
completion of an agreed-on number of payments. Installment credit is a common means of financing the sale of **consumer goods.**

institutional investor
An organization that invests on a large scale in **securities, bonds,** and other
assets. Institutional investors are often **pension funds** or **insurance** companies, and (owing to the size of their investments) they tend to enjoy significant
influence in the corporate investment environment. In recent years, institutional investors have altered the nature of **corporate governance** with their
increasing willingness to assert their stockholding rights over corporate **boards
of directors.** This has reversed a trend toward the dispersion of stockholder
power after the end of World War II; as stockholding became more diffuse,
it became increasingly difficult for investors to combine forces to challenge the
directors of corporations. The large institutional investors have reversed this
trend to a significant degree.

institutional governance
An alternative term for **corporate governance** commonly used in the **public** and
not-for-profit sectors.

institutional memory
Collective, aggregated knowledge held by the members of an organization.

insurance policy
A **contractual** arrangement to compensate for potential future illness, or loss
of life, or for the loss or **impairment** of assets. Insurance is a means of **risk
management,** and insurance coverage is normally arranged through the regular
payment of a premium.

intangible asset
A **long-term** asset that does not possess physical substance. Examples: **brands,
goodwill,** and **intellectual capital.** The recognition **(sense 1)** of intangible
assets in financial statements is carefully controlled by most systems of **Generally Accepted Accounting Principles (GAAP).** Contrast **tangible asset.**

integrated audit

An **audit** that combines two or more purposes. Example: an integrated audit may combine a **financial audit** of an organization's **financial statements** with an assessment of the effectiveness and efficiency of the organization's **internal controls.**

intellectual capital

Knowledge, competencies, and good **judgment.** An organization's sum of its employees' intellectual capital can be a source of competitive advantage. See also **institutional memory** and **know-how.**

intellectual property

An **intangible asset** created by human invention and intelligence. Examples: copyrights and patents. See also **goodwill (sense 2).**

intellectual property audit

An audit to establish the existence, value, and ownership of **intangible assets. Intellectual property** audits are common in corporate **mergers** and **acquisitions,** in which they often focus on the risks and opportunities of this potentially valuable class of assets, including the risks of infringements on intellectual property rights.

inter alia **[*Latin*]**

"Among other things." Example: "The framework for corporate governance includes, inter alia, legislation, custom, stakeholder pressure, and public opinion." The use of the term *inter alia* is common in auditing. One should take care with using this phrase; the term refers to inanimate or intangible things, and when referring to people, the phrase *inter alios* ("among other people") should be used.

intercompany transaction

A **transaction** between two members of a **business combination.** Intercompany transactions like **sales** and **loans** are normally eliminated under **consolidation accounting.**

interest

1 The cost of borrowing **money,** or the **reward (sense 1)** for lending money. Interest may be envisioned as a reward for sacrificing the immediate use of

liquid assets. Interest is calculated by applying an **interest rate** to a principal sum of money. See also **compound interest, simple interest, Islamic finance,** and **usury. 2** A legal right or a share in an asset or corporation. See **minority interest. 3** Curiosity, concern, or fascination (with something).

interest cover / interest coverage ratio
The extent to which an organization's **interest** expenditures are covered by income before interest and taxation. An organization with interest expenditures of $10 million and income thus defined of $30 million has its interest covered three times. The ratio measures organizational **leverage (sense 1)**, and it can indicate the vulnerability of an organization in meeting interest payment commitments when faced by risks of fluctuations in the levels of either **interest rates** or income.

interest rate
A percentage rate applied to a sum of **money** to calculate **interest** charges.

interest rate risk
The potentially adverse consequences of unexpected fluctuations in **interest rates.**

interim audit
A preparatory audit performed in advance of a main audit. In financial auditing, interim audits often focus on **audit planning** and **compliance testing**, and are intended to reduce the burden of work undertaken at the subsequent, final audit.

internal auditing
A branch of auditing developed in the twentieth century as a means of monitoring an organization's operational procedures, **risks**, and **internal controls**. The Institute of Internal Auditors defined internal auditing in 2017 as follows: An "**independent**, objective **assurance** and **consulting** activity designed to add value and improve an organization's operations. It helps an organization accomplish its objectives by bringing a systematic, disciplined approach to evaluate and improve the effectiveness of risk management, control, and governance

processes" (cited by Woller 2017, 22). Another definition of internal auditing is provided by the Institute of Chartered Accountants in India: "an independent management function, which involves a continuous and critical appraisal of the functioning of an entity with a view to suggest improvements thereto and add value to and strengthen the overall governance mechanism of the entity, including the entity's strategic risk management and internal control system" (Institute of Chartered Accountants of India 2009, x). An alternative definition is provided by the Philippine Government Internal Audit Manual: "Internal audit is the evaluation of management controls and operations performance, and the determination of the degree of compliance of internal controls with laws, regulations, managerial policies, accountability measures, ethical standards and contractual obligations. It involves the appraisal of the plan of organization and all the coordinated methods and measures, in order to recommend courses of action on matters relating to operations audit and management control" (Systems and Productivity Improvement Bureau 2020, 5). As private- and public-sector organizations became increasingly complex in the twentieth century, and "as direct, personal contacts of managers with the respective operational areas for which they were responsible became more restricted, a greater need developed for the kind of managerial service provided by internal auditors" (Brink 1977, 9). The remit of internal auditing is therefore internal to organizations, in contrast to the focus of financial auditing on **financial statements.** In 1945, one of the founders of the Institute of Internal Auditors (established in 1941) declared that although internal auditing's "roots are in accountancy, its key purpose lies in the area of management control" (quoted by Flescher 1991, ix). Among other things, the matters addressed by internal auditing include (i) the safeguarding of assets, (ii) legal and regulatory compliance, (iii) reviews of operational practices, (iv) assessments of internal controls, and (v) reviews of risks.

The importance of internal auditing has been strengthened by international corporate governance developments and legislation. In terms of corporate governance, as early as 1999 the United Kingdom's *Turnbull Report* explicitly endorsed internal auditing alongside other corporate risk-monitoring mechanisms. The *Turnbull Report* required corporations listed on the London Stock Exchange to assess annually the need for an internal audit function and, to review annually the scope of work, authority, and resources of any existing internal audit function (*Turnbull Report* 1999, section 46). In terms of legislation, in the United States one of the consequences of the Enron and WorldCom corporate scandals in the early twenty-first century was the ***Sarbanes–Oxley Act*** of 2002, formally titled the *Corporate and Auditing Accountability, Responsibility, and Transparency Act* and informally known in auditing circles as the *Internal Auditors' Full Employment Act*. Section 404 of the act requires the documentation and testing of internal controls, a task for which the internal auditor has been well positioned.

The evolution of internal auditing through paradigmatic shifts has been described in these terms: "Internal auditing . . . has passed through two dominant paradigms and is poised on the edge of a third. The first internal auditing paradigm focused on **observing** and counting; . . . [later] a new concept of the system of internal control . . . changed the internal audit paradigm from a focus on *reperformance* to a focus on *controls*. . . . A third paradigm for internal auditing is emerging, based on auditing the business process through a focus on **risk**" (emphasis in original) (McNamee and Selim 1998, 6).

The concept of internal auditor independence differs from that of financial auditors. Internal auditors are normally employees (and sometimes are also stockholders) of the organizations they audit, and they cannot sever all formal links with an audited organization. "Independence" in the context of internal auditing does not refer to the formalities of financial independence, but to a state of mind characterized by objectivity and **impartiality**.

The reference to "assurance and consulting" in the Institute of Internal Auditors' definition of "internal auditing" prior to 2024 indicates an oscillation of emphasis between compliance and consultancy. While it is impossible to hold the jar of internal auditing to the light and expect compliance and consultancy to separate like oil and water, it is nonetheless clear that a suitable balance between these two characteristics is at the heart of all internal auditing activity. The precise weighting of the two strands of internal auditing is often a matter of taste, and of meeting the needs of an organization's particular circumstances.

internal audit charter

A document that sets out the purpose, authority, scope of work, and responsibilities of an **internal audit function**. The charter is often considered to be an audit function's constitution, and its subject matter typically includes some or all of the following: (i) the internal audit function's reporting lines within an organization, (ii) the scope of the internal audit work, (iii) the internal auditors' rights of access to information, (iv) a formal statement of the internal auditors' adherence to **professional** standards (the Institute of Internal Auditors), and (v) the internal auditors' independence from management influence.

internal audit function
The department within an organization responsible for internal auditing. It is headed by a **Chief Audit Executive**.

internal auditing
The process or action of undertaking an **internal audit**. Although the verbal noun "auditing" places greater emphasis on action than does the simple noun "audit," the two terms are largely used interchangeably (when grammatical compatibility between the simple nouns and noun gerunds permits).

internal auditor
An individual who performs an **internal audit**.

internal audit shop [*Semiformal*]
An alternative term for **internal audit function**.

internal control
A physical or procedural mechanism that monitors and mitigates **risks**. The existence of a satisfactory system of internal control is the fourth of the **postulates of auditing** elaborated in the early 1960s by Robert Kuhn Mautz and Hussein A. Sharaf. The postulation of a satisfactory system of internal control does not imply that internal control weaknesses are unlikely to exist in practice.

Although many of the concepts of internal control appear to be relatively recent ones, the underlying philosophies of internal control (e.g., the **safeguarding of assets** and **segregations of responsibilities**) have a long history. Example: the concept of internal control has been analyzed from Talmudic sources on Jewish practices in the centuries leading to the Roman destruction of the Second Temple in 70 CE (Fonfeder, Holtzman, and Maccarrone 2003). See also **control risk (both senses)**, **detective control**, **preventive control**, and *Internal Control–Integrated Framework*.

Internal Control–Integrated Framework

An influential report of the **Committee of Sponsoring Organizations of the Treadway Commission (COSO)**, published in 1992 and updated in 2013, that sets out a comprehensive vision of an **internal control framework**. The report defines reasonable assurance regarding the achievement of objectives relating to operations, reporting, and compliance.

The COSO Report identifies five interrelated and overlapping components of internal control: (i) the control environment, (ii) **risk** assessment, (iii) control activities, (iv) information and communication, and (v) **monitoring**. Classified under these five components are seventeen principles of internal control, ranging from the enforcement of **accountability** to the deployment of control activities through policies and procedures. Despite some criticism of its complexity, the COSO control model has exerted immense influence on global **financial auditing**, **internal auditing**, and **corporate governance** more widely.

internal rate of return (IRR)

The **rate of return** on an investment is derived from comparisons of the **net present value** of future, incremental cash flows with the initial investment. The IRR is used as a hurdle rate and an investment is normally accepted only when the IRR exceeds an organization's **cost of capital**.

international organization

An intergovernmental institution established for a specific purpose. Examples: the United Nations, the International Atomic Energy Agency, the World Health Organization, and the North Atlantic Treaty Organization.

International Standards on Auditing (ISA)

Financial auditing standards issued by the International Auditing and Assurance Standards Board of the International Federation of Accountants.

interperiod income tax allocation

An alternative term for **temporary difference**.

interpolation

The estimation of an unknown, intermediate value by comparing mathematical relationships between known values that surround it. Interpolation is commonly used in **internal rate of return** calculations. Compare **extrapolation.**

intranet

An organization-specific information network. Unlike the Internet, an intranet is devised for use solely by members of a specific organization.

intuition

Understanding through instinct rather than through conscious reasoning or logical persuasion. In auditing, as in other fields of activity, expert intuition is generally considered to be unreliable and vulnerable to inaccuracy, especially in comparison with deductive and inductive reasoning (but not necessarily in comparison with some forms of abductive reasoning; see **logic in auditing**). Intuitive reasoning is not necessarily irrational; it may be considered nonrational. However, intuitive reasoning sometimes appears to be little more than the articulation of a cognitive bias or a knee-jerk, oversimplified metaphor. Psychologists have long recognized the mind's use of heuristics (i.e., often-unreliable educated guesses or intellectual shortcuts) that seek to simplify the search for answers to complicated questions (Chin 2022; Kahneman 2011, 109–95). And in **analogical reasoning**, rash **extrapolations** of already-known characteristics of a topic to new situations are frequently spurious and unreliable, and present dangers to auditors' **judgments**.

Although it is prone to error, intuitive thinking often delivers accurate results. The rapid detection of old patterns in new situations may reflect the skill and expertise gained through years of practical experience and should not be dismissed entirely. Auditors often make intuitive, instinctive, creative, or inspirational judgments on grounds that are difficult to articulate but nonetheless prove valid. Flint (1988, 114) refers to the way in which "the mind of an experienced auditor develops acute sensitivity to recognition of the abnormal or unexpected which is highly relevant to an opinion on the audited propositions." Schandl (1978, 129–130) provides an example of an auditor's "flash of insight" during the conduct of **audit tests** of **accounts payable:** the auditor noticed a clean, unfolded invoice among a set of vendor invoices that had been folded and showed typical signs of having been mailed and handled. Through intuitive insight and a hunch that something was unusual, the auditor dug deeper into the background of the pristine invoice, and thereby uncovered extensive fraudulent activity. In this way, a small clue led to major consequences for the audit, owing to an auditor's intuitive inspiration.

Intuitive insight therefore has a role in the auditor's intellectual tool kit, but it is best viewed as a supplementary rather than a primary tool. See also **auditor's luck, slippery slope** reasoning, and **Occam's Razor.**

inventory

1 Items used in **production** processes or held for sale. Inventory is normally categorized into (i) **raw materials,** (ii) **work-in-process,** and (iii) **finished goods.** Under most systems of **Generally Accepted Accounting Principles (GAAP),** inventory is valued at the lower of cost and either **market value** or **net realizable value. 2** An alternative term for **physical inventory (both senses).**

investigation

Research or a formal enquiry to thoroughly ascertain facts. Auditing is not an investigative activity, except for (i) specialist **forensic audits** that explicitly aim to review potential **fraud** and other illegal **irregularities** and (ii) individual **audit tests** of an investigative or exploratory nature within the overall scope of an audit. Schandl (1978, 122) describes the difference between an audit and an investigation in terms of the relationship to **evidence,** as follows: "In the audit process we are dealing with purported evidence. In the investigation process we have no evidence, and our procedures are geared to the creation or restoration of the evidence." See also **adversariality,** the auditor as **bloodhound,** the **expectations gap,** the *Kingston Cotton Mill Company* **case,** and the comments on inductive reasoning under **logic in auditing.**

investment

The allocation of economic resources to activities, **assets,** or **securities** in the hope of obtaining a satisfactory **rate of return.**

invisible asset

An alternative term for **intangible asset.**

invoice
A document that formally records, quantifies, and requests payment for the sale of goods or services.

Irish Woollen Company Ltd. v. Tyson and Others case (1900)
A colonial Irish legal case of importance for its early definition of **negligence** by **financial auditors**. The auditors were judged to be responsible for not detecting significant **fraud** despite their knowledge of suspicious circumstances. The auditors had obtained evidence that the auditee had manipulated **cutoff dates** for **material** transactions and therefore had subverted the **accruals principle**, yet they did not pursue the logical implications of their suspicions with a sufficient duty of care, and thereby failed to "discover or prevent" (Dicksee 1902, 319) serious, fraudulent transactions.

irregularity
An inaccuracy, mistake, or occurrence outside normal patterns. An irregularity may be intentional (as in a **fraud**) or unintentional (as in an **error**), but the term is perhaps loaded toward matters arising from intent. Two of the **postulates of auditing** elaborated in the early 1960s by Robert Kuhn Mautz and Hussein A. Sharaf Mautz addressed accounting irregularities: "**financial statements** and other information submitted for **verification** are free from **collusive** and other unusual irregularities" (postulate 3), and "the existence of a satisfactory system of **internal control** eliminates the **probability** of irregularities" (postulate 4) (Mautz and Sharaf 1961, 49). These authors described an irregularity as "any departure from the truth," and defined truth as "conformity with reality" (p. 142).

Islamic banking
A slightly archaic term for **Islamic finance**. The term "Islamic banking" suggests that *Shari'a* finance concepts apply exclusively to banking institutions, while Islamic finance more accurately places the concept in a wider economic and social context.

Islamic finance
Financial practices in accordance with Islamic *Shari'a* law. Among other things, *Shari'a* forbids **usury** and the charging of **interest**. *Shari'a* law is considered by

Muslims to be divine, and its principles are therefore considered immutable; its financial practices operate in their purest form in countries like Iran and Saudi Arabia. In some other Muslim-majority nations (like Malaysia), *Shari'a* law coexists with Western financial practices; for example, some Malaysian financial institutions charge interest, while others do not.

itemization
The preparation of a detailed (often numbered) list of the elements of a **data** population or set of information.

job
1 A customer **order** to purchase goods or services. The term is often used for goods or services tailored to a customer's specific requirements. **2** An employment position.

joint costs
Costs incurred in a manufacturing process before a point at which differentiated products can be identified.

joint products
Items of equal importance produced by a common manufacturing process. Example: leather and beef are joint products of the cattle industry. Compare **by-product**.

joint venture
An agreement made between two business enterprises to conduct an activity together. Joint venture arrangements are often adopted in high-**risk** circumstances. Example: **multinational corporations** sometimes use joint venture arrangements to operate in countries with challenging legal, regulatory, or cultural environments, to tap the expertise of local partners.

journal entry
A **transaction** recorded either directly in a **general ledger** account or recorded in a **subsidiary ledger** before transference to the general ledger.

journal voucher

A document used to record and describe (or justify) a **journal entry**. The **authorization** of journal entries is traditionally effected through approval signatures on **hard copy** journal vouchers.

judgment

An **opinion** based on an assessment of **evidence**. In auditing, judgments on the intelligibility and accuracy of a matter are based on a combination of **knowledge** and diagnostic skills, and are central to both the selection and the **evaluation** of audit evidence. The 1877 English case *Leeds Estate Building and Investment Company* was an early articulation of the requirement that **financial auditors** should go beyond checks of the arithmetical accuracy of **bookkeeping** records to judgments of (i) the **substance** of accounting records, (ii) the internal **logical** correspondences of accounting information, and (iii) the analytical connections between accounting records and financial statements.

The establishment of a comprehensive basis for auditor judgment has been elusive. The close relationship between financial auditing and **accounting** implies that the formalities of double entry bookkeeping and the application of **Generally Accepted Accounting Principles (GAAP)** largely underpin the knowledge base of financial auditing. The *Cohen Commission Report on Auditors' Responsibilities* of 1978 explicitly stated that while judgment "pervades accounting and [financial] auditing," it "should be exercised within the existing accounting framework, not independently of it" (*Cohen Commission Report* 1978, 14–16). However, despite financial auditing's close association with accounting, judgment is required for a range of nonaccounting considerations, from the reliability of **internal control** systems to assessments of nonquantifiable operational risks to the reliability of **liquidity** forecasts, all of which are prone to informed differences of opinion. The obvious judgment methodology linking such varied topics is that of logic (see **logic in auditing**).

The **professional** frameworks within which auditors work aim to channel auditor judgment along rational lines according to defined principles, but some critics have doubted the effectiveness of professional frameworks in the exercise of judgment and have suggested that a large element of auditor reasoning is either (i) **intuitive**, and therefore potentially unreliable or (ii) subject to cognitive **bias**. Professional guidance for auditing judgment has been described as "often a case of matching particular judgments, hunches and intuitions formed under economic constraints to more abstract and formal metaphors of best practice; . . . the prevailing humble and craftlike nature of auditing is constantly being attached to models and frameworks which promise a new operational potential" (Power 1997, 77–78).

Irrespective of the extent to which one might support such views of auditing as an activity of skilled technicians rather than accomplished **professionals**, it is indisputable that the auditor's tool kit for critical thinking is crammed with a variety of techniques and approaches, ready for tailoring to the specific circumstances of assessing audit evidence. The auditor's critical thinking processes include causal and probabilistic inference, assessments of evidential validity and reliability, the reconstruction of past events and transactions, the evaluation of testimony and **outside expertise**, the weighing of logical possibilities, and, overall, assessments of the coherence and consistency of all the evidence taken together. The large number of judgment techniques is, perhaps, a means by which auditors protect themselves from unsound judgments and false conclusions arising from any one of the individual techniques: a varied selection of judgment methodologies allows for occasional mistakes, favoring consistency over completeness of evidence and thereby subsuming the risks of individual errors of judgment within a wider range of counterbalancing judgments.

A significant characteristic of auditor judgment is that auditing is usually a time-constrained activity. Auditors tend to make judgments not as a leisurely pursuit; more commonly, they work in contexts of limited time and large volumes of information (Dierynck and Peters 2022). It has been noted that "time is of the essence in the collection of audit evidence and the formation of audit judgments" (Mautz and Sharaf 1961, 95). Cognitively busy auditors resemble jugglers with several balls in the air, and there is an ever-present concern that expediency and arbitrary decision-making may unconsciously replace critical reasoning. This challenge emphasizes the importance of the **supervision** of audit work by more experienced auditors.

The application of judgment to auditing is tested on a massive scale on a continuing basis; auditing sometimes fails, fueling the **expectations gap**, but the vast majority of audits are conducted without dispute or contention. This amounts to pragmatic evidence of the broad success of auditor judgment. (The extent to which such evidence is convincing is, of course, itself a matter of judgment.)

See also **intuition, logic in auditing, psychology in auditing**, and **Occam's Razor.**

judgment [*In law*]
The formal pronouncement of a legal decision.

judgmental sampling
The selection of a **sample** of data from a **population** on the basis of some form of bias. Example: an auditor may skew a test sample of disbursement transactions to those that refer to names suggesting family connections between employees and payees. Compare **statistical sampling, stratified sampling**, and **random sampling.**

junk bond
A high-interest **bond** or debenture of low credit status. The high **interest** rates of junk bonds reflect their high risk of **default (sense 1)**. Junk bonds tend to be issued to finance highly **leveraged** takeovers of large corporations.

junk mail
Unsolicited material transmitted by either physical or electronic mail. See also **spam.**

just-in-time (JIT)
A manufacturing and operating philosophy that aims to supply products to customers in accordance with fluctuations in **demand (sense 1)**. The main advantages of JIT operations include (i) typically low **inventory** levels, (ii) simplified **backflush** costing methodologies, (iii) **efficient** manufacturing operations, and (iv) responsiveness to customer demand. However, JIT operations entail potentially catastrophic **risks** of failing to supply items on time, in the context of interruptions to tight manufacturing or distribution schedules, or to **bottlenecks** in **supply chains.**

kaizen [*Japanese*]
See **continuous improvement**.

kanban [*Japanese*]
"Ticket" or "card." *Kanban* denotes a **real-time** operating methodology used to coordinate activities and to display **inventory** movements in the context of **just-in-time** production and lean manufacturing processes. In *Kanban* systems, items are requested only when necessary.

key performance indicator (KPI)
An important performance measurement or statistic relating to an activity. KPIs are used extensively for management control, **risk assessment**, and **monitoring** purposes.

kickback [*Informal*]
A **bribe** paid for the improper award of a **contract**.

kicking the tires [*Informal*]
A rapid, superficial **inspection** or assessment. The term arose in the early twentieth century, when the solidity and robustness of automobile tires could be readily assessed by a few swift kicks. Example of current use: "They didn't have time for an extensive audit of that small branch, so they visited for only a couple of hours, just to kick the tires."

***Kingston Cotton Mill Company* case (1896)**
A landmark English **common law** case of 1896 that had significant repercussions for financial auditing throughout the English-speaking world. In the rather quaint language of the day, the case's judicial description of the financial auditor as "a **watchdog**, not a **bloodhound**" established the principle that auditors' duties involve the exercising of "reasonable care" (cited by Dicksee 1902, 615) rather than the adoption of an investigative approach. The judge therefore rejected the "the notion that an auditor is bound to be suspicious as distinguished from reasonably careful" and stated that "an auditor is not bound to be

a detective" (cited by Chambers 1995, 82). The specifics of the case determined that it was reasonable (and therefore not **negligent**) for the financial auditor of the Kingston Cotton Mill Company to rely on a management certificate for **inventory** balances, owing to the level of the auditor's trust in the official providing the certificate in this case. The auditor was not held to be liable for failing to detect **fraud**.

The legal and **professional** framework of financial auditing has changed significantly since the *Kingston Cotton Mill Company* case. In particular, the judge's reasoning that "it is no part of an auditor's duty to take stock" would not meet the evidential requirements of due professional care in modern financial auditing. No longer can an auditor rely solely on a management **representation** for a material inventory balance, without undertaking a single **spot check** of inventory quantities. That financial auditors should satisfy themselves as to the existence and valuation of material inventory balances through the physical inspection of inventories was confirmed in the *McKesson and Robbins* **case** of 1939. Nonetheless, the judicial reasoning in the Kingston Mill case is an early articulation of several themes central to modern financial auditing—the **expectations gap**, auditor **negligence**, and the exercise of auditor **judgment**.

kiting
1 A **fraudulent** use of the time taken by **checks** to clear through a banking system to temporarily inflate an organization's cash holdings. **2** In the United Kingdom, the fraudulent use of stolen checks.

know-how
Technical **knowledge** allied to good **judgment**. See also **intellectual capital** and *savoir-faire*.

knowledge, body of
A collection of concepts and terms that provides the theoretical and practical foundations for **professional** activity. A body of knowledge is not merely an accumulation of concepts and theory; it requires an internal structure and logical, orderly patterning to give it coherence. By analogy, a pile of bricks does not make a house—the arrangement of the bricks in systematic and logical patterns is needed to construct a house. The possession of a body of knowledge is

considered a necessary prerequisite for a profession, and professional auditing organizations place significant emphasis on the articulation of their bodies of knowledge to underpin the conduct and standards of their activities (Moeller 2016). The act of defining the norms and criteria of a body of knowledge may be seen as an element in the aspirational "professionalization project" of organizations seeking professional status. The **critical accounting** movement has expressed criticisms of both the coherence and the social utility of the bodies of knowledge of **financial auditing**'s professional associations. See **judgment.**

knowledge management
The gathering, recording, and sharing of information within an organization. A problem central to organizational knowledge is the handling of tacit or implicit information; being undocumented, it is lost with the separation from service of individuals.

labor
Work of either a manual or intellectual nature undertaken to create economic **value.** See also the **factors of production.**

labor union
An organization of employees that seeks to maximize the pay and working conditions of its members. Labor unions operate through the mechanism of **collective bargaining** with employers.

lakh [*Hindī*]
The term used in India for 100,000. Under Indian writing conventions, note the position of the commas: 1,00,000. One hundred lakh = one *crore.*

land
1 An area of the Earth's surface that may be used for economic purposes. Although land not held specifically for **investment** purposes is classified in **property, plant, and equipment**, it is not usually subjected to **amortization** as it is not a **wasting asset** (unless subjected to severe environmental

degradation). Land is one of the **factors of production**, in which it covers all natural resources, including the sea. **2** An area of the Earth's surface protected from economic exploitation, for environmental protection purposes.

lapping
The shifting of accounting entries for cash receipts between **accounts receivable** balances to hide missing cash. Lapping is possible when a **book-keeper** (i) handles cash receipts from customers and (ii) records the cash receipts in the accounts receivable balances. An appropriate **segregation of responsibilities** between these two functions can assist in preventing lapping. Lapping is a smokescreen to hide missing cash and, eventually, it catches up with itself—unless the stolen cash is replaced, accounts receivable will ulti-mately be **overstated** by the amount of missing cash.

last-in first-out (LIFO) method
An **inventory** valuation method that assumes inventory is consumed (or sold) in the reverse order in which it was purchased or manufactured. LIFO method-ology allocates the most recent inventory costs to **costs of sales**. Compare the **first-in first-out (FIFO)** and **next-in first-out (NIFO)** valuation methods.

lead time
The lapse of time between the placing of a customer **order (sense 1)** and the fulfilling of the order. Fulfillment is to be understood here as the delivery of the items or the performance of the services.

lean auditing
A specialism of **operational auditing** that focuses on efficiencies in manufac-turing processes. Lean audits focus on the maximization of productivity.

learning curve
Increases in **efficiency** and output as experience-based knowledge is gained. In a manufacturing context, the learning curve can be measured by a statistical comparison of the increases in cumulative production output and the decreases in cumulative production input. More generally, the learning curve refers to the increasing efficiency and productivity with which an individual or organization

deals with an activity. Example: a junior auditor may initially struggle to efficiently finalize audit tests but is likely to experience increasing efficiency as familiarization with auditing practices increases.

lease
A legal **contract** in which one party (a **lessee**) hires an asset from another party (a **lessor**) for a **rental (sense 1)** charge. In **accounting**, leases are categorized as **capital** or **operating** leases.

ledger
A register of accounting transactions. Traditionally, ledgers were in the form of books, but in modern usage the term normally refers to computerized recording mechanisms. See **general ledger** and **subsidiary ledger**.

Leeds Estate Building and Investment Company case (1887)
An English common law case of 1887 that addressed **due professional care** and **judgment** in **financial auditing**. In the *Leeds Estate* case, it was found that a financial auditor could not rely solely on the verification that a **balance sheet** was a "true copy" of the underlying **bookkeeping** records; the auditor's duty was not merely "the task of ascertaining the arithmetical accuracy of the Balance Sheet, but to see that it was a true and accurate representation of the company's affairs" (quoted by Dicksee 1902, 555). The auditor's responsibility was therefore to assess the **substance** of the transactions underpinning the balance sheet, and to establish logical correspondences and analytical connections between the balance sheet, related accounting records, and the corporation's activities.

legislation
Laws, in the form of decrees or statutes, promulgated by national or local legislative bodies. Example: in the United Kingdom, legislation is passed by the British Parliament. Legislation is sometimes defined as the making of law, but this is an unsatisfactory definition for some legal theorists, who maintain that law can only be discovered, not "made." In English-speaking countries, legislation is often contrasted with **common law**; the latter more clearly demonstrates a "discovery" of law through the accumulated experience of case law precedent.

less developed country (LDC)
An alternative term for **developing country**.

lessee
The acquirer of the temporary use of an asset from another party (a **lessor**) through a **lease** contract.

lessor
The grantor of the temporary use of an asset to another party (a **lessee**) through a **lease** contract.

letter of credit (L/C)
A mechanism used in international trade in which a bank **guarantees (sense 1)** to **settle** the cash payment arising from a transaction, provided that specified conditions have been met. It transfers the **risk** of nonsettlement from the buyer in a transaction to a bank, thereby minimizing (or in some cases effectively eliminating) the seller's risk exposure.

letter of engagement
See **engagement letter**.

letter of representation
A formal, written statement made by an **auditee** and addressed to a **financial auditor**, in which the auditee confirms that representations made to the auditor relating to financial statements are accurate and complete. Letters of representation also usually define the responsibility of an auditee for the **fair presentation** of the financial statements under audit.

leverage
1 The importance of **debt** finance in an organization's capital structure. Most corporations finance their activities through a combination of debt and **equity (sense 1)**, and economists grant significance to determining the optimal mix of the two forms of finance. Excessive leverage may be **risky** to the extent that it obliges a corporation to make high (and often fixed) **interest** payments to service its debts. High leverage may therefore make a corporation dangerously

vulnerable to fluctuations in **interest** rates or the levels of its **net income**. The **debt-equity ratio** and **interest cover** are common measurements of leverage. **2** The risks of high levels of **fixed costs**. This sense of the term is often referred to as "operating leverage."

lex [Latin]
Law.

levy
A **tax**, fine, or seizure of **money**.

liability
A commitment to pay for goods, services, or financing costs. Liabilities possess several characteristics: (i) they give rise to transfers of quantifiable economic benefits, in the form of cash payments or **payments in kind**; (ii) they are applicable to a specific individual or organization; and (iii) their existence is certain (other than for **contingent liabilities**). A liability is recorded as a **credit entry** under the conventions of **double entry bookkeeping**, and **short-term** liabilities are usually referred to as **current liabilities**. Contrast **asset**.

lien
A **creditor**'s contractual right of possession of an **asset** of another party in case of default on a debt or **loan**. A **mortgage** in **default (senses 1 and 2)**, for example, creates a lien over the mortgaged property.

limitation of scope
See **scope limitation**.

limited assurance
See **negative assurance**.

limited audit
An audit with an intentionally restricted scope. Agreed-on limitations on audit work may be determined in reference to (i) time periods, (ii) activities, or (iii) **materiality** thresholds. See **kicking the tires**.

limited liability

A legal liability that does not extend beyond the size of an individual's **investment** in a **corporation** or **partnership**. **Stockholders** do not suffer liabilities for a corporation's debts beyond their investments in the corporation, while a **limited partner**'s liability is similarly restricted in a partnership.

limited partner

A member of a **partnership** who enjoys **limited liability** in line with his or her investment in the partnership.

linear programming (LP)

A method for the optimal allocation of scarce resources to alternative activities. The aim of the decision-making process (termed the "objective function") and related constraints are expressed in mathematical terms and may be plotted graphically in simple scenarios. Typical objective functions include the maximizing of income and the minimizing of costs. As its name suggests, LP is applicable only to contexts in which the relationships between the variables under consideration are linear in nature.

line of credit

See **credit line**.

lines of assurance / defense

See the **Three Lines Model**.

liquid [Adj.]

1 In the form of **cash (senses 1 and 2)** or **assets** readily convertible into cash. **2** Able to satisfy **liabilities** through the possession of sufficient cash or assets readily convertible into cash.

liquid assets

1 Assets held as **cash (senses 1 and 2)**, or readily convertible into cash with a minimal loss of value (as with the case of a marketable **security**). **Inventory** is not generally considered to be liquid, owing to the time delay typically required to convert it into cash: inventory therefore tends to be excluded from the **acid**

test ratio, a popular liquidity measure. Contrast **illiquid**. **2** The condition of assets whereby one possesses sufficient cash resources to meet **current liabilities**.

liquidation
The closing of a business **enterprise**, with the distribution of its assets to creditors and members after the settling of its **liabilities**.

liquid ratio
A British term for the **acid test ratio**.

listed
1 [*Of securities*] Registered and traded on a stock exchange. See also **quoted**. **2** [*Of items and services*] Enumerated and catalogued in a systematic manner. See **itemization**.

litigation in auditing
See **due professional care** and **malpractice insurance**.

loan
An asset—usually but not necessarily **cash (sense 2)**—provided to an individual or organization, for which the return of the asset or repayment of the cash or cash equivalent is anticipated. The cost of a loan is measured by the **interest** costs applied to it.

log
A **register** that records the use of an **asset**, the undertaking of an activity, or other events. A log is an **internal control** mechanism. Example: a log may record the individuals who access a room containing sensitive data or high-value assets.

logic in auditing
Logic refers to structured, systematic reasoning in the context of problem-solving. Many commentators have recognized the centrality of logic to auditing. Mautz and Sharaf (1961, 192–93) judged that financial auditing "has its

primary roots in logic, not in accounting"; Wolnizer (1987, 21) emphasized the importance in auditing of "logical probability"; and Ratliff and Reding (2002, 1) offered the view that "if there is a single secret of successful auditing, it likely lies in the concept of *persuasive* **evidence** . . . [which in turn is] generally governed by the principles of logic" (emphasis in the original).

Despite recognition of the importance of logic in auditing, formal logic is not usually part of an auditor's training (Nelson et al. 2003), and it is extremely rare to see the documentation of logical analysis, in either symbolic or language form, during the conduct of an audit. Nonetheless, logic underpins auditors' reasoning, often in a tacit or informal manner under the threshold of awareness. In the same way that we express ourselves using everyday language without being formally conscious of the grammatical structures we are using, auditors deploy logic without necessarily having an explicit awareness of the logical patterns underpinning their reasoning. (A rare example of explicit references to formal logic in an auditing textbook can be found in Ratliff and Reding 2002.)

There are many forms of logic. Owing to space constraints, and at the risk of some oversimplification, we may identify three types of logic relevant to auditing: (i) deductive, (ii) inductive, and (iii) abductive logic. These three logical approaches offer decreasing levels of persuasiveness in their outcomes: (i) deductive logic provides conclusions of certain validity, (ii) the outcomes of inductive logic offer degrees of probability, and (iii) abductive logic's conclusions provide only degrees of plausibility. These three categories of logic are discussed in the next paragraphs.

Deductive logic (also known as syllogistic logic) has a long history. Initially formulated by Aristotle (384–322 BCE), it has been refined over the millennia. Aristotelian logic envisions three discrete activities of thought, or "acts of the intellect": (i) the apprehension of terms (meaning both concepts and the language used to describe them); (ii) the judgment of propositions; and (iii) the reasoning process to reach conclusions. Under this three-acts-of-the-intellect structure, the instruments of deductive logic are, sequentially, (i) terms, (ii) premises, and (iii) conclusions, and the objectives of the three instruments are, respectively, (i) clarity, (ii) truth, and (iii) validity. Therefore, we seek legitimately to minimize ambiguity in terms, but we should not look to terms for truth and validity—truth relates solely to premises, while validity relates solely to conclusions.

Deductive arguments are logically valid if their conclusions necessarily
follow from their premises. This is the case even if the premises themselves are
false. Therefore, validity is insufficient for cogent reasoning; a valid argument
based on untrue (or unwarranted) premises is sometimes described as having
only "vacuous" validity. For a deductive argument to be fully cogent, (i) its terms
must be unambiguous, (ii) its premises must be warranted (i.e., believable as
true), and (iii) its reasoning must be valid.

Deductive logic might best be understood through the illustration of a
simple syllogism, consisting of two premises (P1 and P2) and a concluding argument (C). In this example, an internal auditor is reviewing **fixed assets** in an
agricultural setting:

Premise (P1)	All fixed assets are items with an economic use of more than one year.
Premise (P2)	The tractors I am auditing are fixed assets.
Conclusion (C)	The tractors I am auditing are therefore all of economic use for more than one year.

Medieval theologians considered the rigorous beauty of syllogistic argument
to be a manifestation of the eternal divine. More prosaically, one may marvel at
the tight structure of syllogistic arguments. The conclusion C follows necessarily
from premises P1 and P2. The validity of C is certain because it does not contain
anything not already included in premises P1 and P2: Premise P1 provides information about a universal population (fixed assets) with a uniform characteristic
(an economic use of more than one year), while premise P2 provides information
about one group of items in that population. Both the premises are simple declar-
ative sentences, in which a subject and a predicate are connected by forms of the
verb "to be" (the *copula*, Latin for "link"). There are three terms spread over P1 and
P2, one of which ("*fixed assets*") is known as the middle term, as it appears in both
P1 and P2. The duplicated middle term cancels itself out, thereby opening the
way for the two remaining terms in P1 and P2 to appear in C. In other words, C has
taken the two nonshared terms from P1 and P2, thereby omitting the middle term.

(*Note:* This example of a syllogism is a simple one. Although going beyond
our discussion, for the sake of completeness, the example given is, in technical
terms, a categorical syllogism of form AAA-1, consisting of three, universal,

affirmative propositions set out in the first figure. In the traditional, mnemonic *Barbara Celarent* system, this form of categorical syllogism is traditionally referred to as being *in modus Barbara*, owing to the three "a" vowels. More complex deductive logic involves hypothetical (if . . . then . . .) or disjunctive (either . . . or . . .) structures, and chains of multiple propositions. The handling of complex deductive logic puts excessive strain on the use of ordinary language, and we eventually reach a point at which it may become more suitable to adopt symbolic logic.)

Auditing's methodology does not rely principally on deductive logic. While deductive reasoning may satisfy the requirements of specific **audit tests**, it is unlikely that an auditor may rely solely on deductive reasoning for an audit in its entirety. Auditing is an inferential practice that provides evidence-based **opinions** rather than cast-iron guarantees. Flint (1988, 113–14) therefore appears to be wrong in claiming that "deductive reasoning is by far the most important . . . source of audit evidence." On the contrary, inductive reasoning is the type of logic most relevant to auditing. Inductive logic often provides persuasive, strong support for **judgments** relevant to the assessment of evidence.

For an inductive argument to be cogent as well as strong, (i) its terms must be unambiguous, (ii) the premises on which it is built must be warranted (i.e., believable as true), and (iii) the reasoning process should clearly link the premises to the conclusions. All this is similar to the cogency of deductive logic. But, as the conclusions of inductive logic do not follow premises with logical necessity, there is an additional consideration—(iv) the premises for inductive arguments should not omit any relevant information. The scope of inductive logic is vast, but we shall focus on two inductive approaches commonly used in auditing: (i) **statistical sampling** and (ii) **analogical reasoning**.

(i) Through statistical sampling, the auditor infers the characteristics of large **populations** of data. The analysis of representative samples of sufficient size usually involves estimates of confidence levels of accuracy, and therefore offers the quantification of expected levels of probability. Here is an example of statistical inference using a premises-and-conclusion structure akin to that used in deductive reasoning; an auditor is assessing the extent to which an organization's consumer goods **inventories** reported in its **financial statements** are in a sellable condition (and do not therefore require a **write-down** or **write-off** on the grounds of a fall in economic worth):

Premise (P1)	Items of inventory of consumer goods may need a write-down or a write-off to reflect any decreases in their **net realizable value.**
Premise (P2)	There are too many items of stock in the warehouse for the auditor to assess them all individually for the purposes of this audit test.
Premise (P3)	The auditor, close to the **balance sheet** date, has assessed randomly selected, representative samples of inventory, and has found the tested sample items to be of unimpaired value.
Conclusion (C)	The inventory balance stated in the financial statements probably requires neither a write-down nor a write-off.

The first thing to note is the looser structure of the logical process compared with that encountered in a deductive syllogism. In inductive logic, we are not dealing with 100 percent certainty; in this example, the auditor cannot be completely sure of the economic worth of all the items of inventory in the extrapolation of the findings of her sample testing to the entire population. In statistical inference, there is always the possibility of error through **sample risk.** Nonetheless, the auditor's conclusion that there is a reliable level of economic worth in the overall holdings of inventory is reasonable and persuasive, because it is based on an inductively strong argument. (In our example, the assessment of the net realizable value of the inventory is likely to be only one of several auditing tests addressing the existence, quantities, legal ownership, and other characteristics of the inventory.)

Inductive inference to broader conclusions based on sample testing is a major part of auditing's logical tool kit. We noted above that in deductive reasoning the certain validity of conclusions arises from the fact that the conclusions do not contain anything not already included in the premises. In contrast, in inductive logic the conclusion may amplify the contents of the premises. This helps to explain why inductive logic does not lead to certainty in its conclusions.

(ii) **Analogous reasoning** is discussed in a separate entry in this book. Unlike statistical sampling, it does not offer quantifiable degrees of probability, but rather general indications of the strength of its conclusions.

Before leaving our glance at inductive reasoning, it is worth mentioning that the inferential practices of the scientific method of hypothesis testing are commonly cited as examples of the application of inductive logic. This is accurate to the extent that scientists observe the effects of their testing on hypotheses, gradually refining the hypotheses and narrowing the probabilities of error. As Ratliff and Reding (2002, xvii) have suggested: "While audits do not generally qualify as scientific research, they do require the same kind of objective . . . process, a similar inquisitive attitude, and thinking skills required by logical research." However, it is problematic to equate inductive scientific methods to auditing. Auditors perform tests to assess **assertions**; but, unlike in the scientist's laboratory, the auditor's tests are generally conducted under time pressure and in nonrepeatable circumstances. Both the scientist and the auditor use inductive reasoning, but in different ways.

Turning to the third category of logic under discussion, abductive logic may be defined as inference to the best explanation. When confronted by matters that seem difficult to interpret, abductive logic seeks the simplest and most likely explanations. Indirect discussions of this form of logic have been traced by some back to Aristotle, but the clarification and naming of inductive logic are attributable to the American philosopher Charles Sanders Peirce (1839–1914). Abductive logic only offers degrees of plausibility; its conclusions are therefore far weaker than those of deductive logic (which provides certainty of validity), and are generally less persuasive than the conclusions of inductive logic (which provides degrees of strength or probability). In Peirce's words, "Deduction proves that something *must* be; induction shows that something *actually is* operative; abduction merely suggests that something *may be*" (emphasis in the original) (cited by Fischer 1970, xvi). Compare the principles of abductive logic with those of **Occam's Razor**.

If abductive logic offers only plausible conclusions, of what value is it to auditing? When can it be an acceptable source of inference for the levels of persuasive evidence required to support most audit opinions? The answer is that abductive reasoning is of value when the auditor is confronted by something unusual or surprising. An example frequently given of the use of abductive logic is the kind of logic-of-discovery associated with Sherlock Holmes, the literary detective created by Sir Arthur Conan Doyle (1859–1930). Holmes needs to think creatively to interpret clues in order to reach a hypothesis. Auditors, of course, are neither detectives nor **investigators**, but they are sometimes required to think innovatively when encountering unexpected things. Example: a financial auditor undertaking an audit of a manufacturer of luxury goods discovers by chance an isolated, basement storage room containing expensive items of inventory—these items are not recorded in the accounting records and the auditee has not mentioned them. The auditor considers possible causal connections underpinning this discovery: (i) the auditee wishes to hide these items so as to mislead the auditor, to cover up a case of **fraud**, like **misappropriation**; (ii) the auditee is unaware of the segregation of these items, and is therefore an unknowing victim of potential fraud that may be taking place; (iii) these items belong to a customer, and have been set aside for dispatch after a confirmed sale; or (iv) these items are damaged and are awaiting donation or destruction. While abductive logic may be considered as "inherently uncertain" (Evans 2017, 4), resulting in conclusions that are at best only plausible, as in this example, these conclusions may in turn be subjected to further analysis to seek stronger levels of persuasiveness. The value of abductive logic for auditors therefore rests in the generation of hypotheses as avenues for further analysis. The process of abductive logic is connected to the concept of **thinking outside the box**, and even to **intuition** in its generation of fresh and creative ideas.

In attempting to articulate aspects of the tacit logic of auditing, we should acknowledge a limitation on our analysis. The borderlines between some types of logic—especially between inductive and abductive logic, and between abductive logic and intuition—are not watertight. Our analysis of three types of logic has nonetheless established broad markers for lines of reasoning in auditing. Whether or not it is explicitly articulated, auditing is founded on logic and, in particular, on inductive logic. Nonetheless, deductive, inductive, and abductive logic all have roles to play in auditing. They may occur in parallel or in sequence in the overall set of tests in the auditor's assessment of evidence.

In summary, auditors' overall opinions should be based on cogent reasoning, achieved through a combination of inductively strong and deductively valid arguments, supported by unambiguous terms and warranted premises (i.e., premises the auditor has reason to believe to be true). Abductively generated hypotheses may generate avenues for both inductive and deductive exploration.

In addition, while auditing is based on logical reasoning, the human mind does not always operate at the consciously rational level. Below the threshold of consciousness, informal logic may operate, in addition to the biases arising from cognitive heuristics. See **psychology in auditing**, **anchoring and adjustment bias**, **availability bias**, and **recency bias**.

London and General Bank case (1895)

An English **common law** case that established the responsibility of **financial auditors** to report to a corporation's **stockholders** (rather than solely to its **directors**). The judicial reasoning also stated that financial auditors cannot be expected to provide guarantees over the accuracy of financial statements, but rather exercise "**reasonable** care and skill" (cited by Dicksee 1902, 588) in reaching an **opinion**. In addition, the judicial reasoning stated that decisions on the exercise of reasonable care are dependent on the circumstances of individual audits.

long term

1 Relating to a period of more than one year. **2** For some categories of **liability**, such as loans and debts, the long term may be defined as more than three or five years.

loss

1 An excess of expenditures over income in a specified time period. **2** A decrease in **net assets**.

lowballing

The offering of a very low sales price to undercut competitors and thereby win a **contract**. In financial auditing, firms are occasionally accused of lowballing to gain audit clients. The low audit fee that results from lowballing might be offset by lucrative **management advisory services**.

lucrative

Generating or capable of generating significant amounts of **money**.

lucre [*Humorous*]

Money or riches.

lump sum

A sum of **money** paid at a specific point in time, rather than in **installments**.

maintenance
The preservation of the condition and operational functionality of an asset. Maintenance costs are normally treated as **revenue expenditures** in an **income statement**. Contrast **betterment**.

make-or-buy decision
An appraisal of the relative costs and benefits of manufacturing an item or buying it from a **supplier**. Both **quantitative** and **qualitative** considerations may be included in the decision-making process. Example of a qualitative factor: the **risk** of excessive reliance on a sole supplier for essential components in a **production** process.

maladministration
The incompetent or fraudulent administration of an activity or organization.

malpractice
Improper, unethical, illegal, or incompetent behavior by a **professional** person. See also **due professional care** and **negligence**.

malpractice insurance
Insurance for **financial auditors** to cover the **risk** of costs that might arise from litigation over allegations of **negligence** or un**due professional care** in the performance of auditing duties.

managed currency
A **currency** with an **exchange rate** overtly manipulated by a government, and therefore not permitted to "float" in response to the flows of demand and supply.

managed risk
A **risk** subjected to **risk management** techniques.

management
1 The process of directing, controlling, and planning in an organization. Much management theory is disputed; it has been suggested that "management is too

unsystematic to make it a science and its knowledge base is too uncertain to call it a **profession**" (Sawyer and Vinten 1996, 18). The "father" of modern management theory is often held to be Henri Fayol (1841–1925), whose *Administration Industrielle and Générale* appeared in 1916. **2** In an organization, a group of individuals that collectively directs, controls, and makes plans.

management accounting

The maintenance, analysis, and reporting of **accounting** information related to an organization's costs, revenues, and activities. Management accounting, in contrast to **financial accounting**, tends to focus on accounting records for an organization's internal purposes, including control, planning, and decision-making.

management advisory services (MAS)

Services other than financial auditing supplied by **financial auditors**. Examples include (i) **taxation** advice, (ii) training, (iii) the **outsourcing** or **co-sourcing** of internal auditing services, and (iv) **consulting** projects. (Some users of the term "MAS" might exclude taxation advice from the definition, so closely is it related to corporate accounting.) Regulators throughout the world have long monitored the extent to which lucrative MAS contracts allegedly compromise the **independence** of financial auditors' **opinions**.

management audit

1 An audit of the extent to which an organization's managers achieve objectives. The term has also been defined as follows: "an examination, analysis and evaluation . . . of the performance of management in regard to the objectives, plans, procedures and strategies of a business enterprise or other organisation, and the expression of an opinion on the effectiveness of management in performance of its responsibilities" (Flint 1988, 175n3). Management audits tend to cover both financial and operational matters. **2** [*Rare or archaic*] An alternative term for **operational audit**. **3** [*Rare or archaic*] An alternative term for **internal audit**.

management by exception

An approach to organizational management characterized by the investigation and analysis of deviations from expected results. Example: managers may concentrate on **variances** from **budgeted** amounts, and on operational anomalies generated by **exception reports.**

management by numbers
An approach to organizational management characterized by an emphasis, or overemphasis, on numerical values and targets. The term carries connotations of an inadequate appreciation of operational realities. It is sometimes referred to as "management by metrics" and "management by spreadsheets."

management consulting
See **consulting.**

management letter
A **financial auditor**'s report that contains recommendations for improvements in procedures and **internal controls.** Alongside an audit **opinion,** financial auditors normally provide a management letter as a service to **auditees.** The management letter has been described as "an important **by-product** of an audit" (O'Reilly et al. 1998, 1.13).

management representation
A statement made to an auditor by the **management (sense 2)** of an organization that confirms an item under audit is correct and complete. See also **letter of representation.**

managerial accounting
An alternative term for **management accounting.**

managerial auditing
An alternative term for both **internal auditing** and **operational auditing.**

manufacturing
The large-scale **production** of **tangible** items.

manufacturing costs
Costs directly attributable to the **production** of **tangible** items.

margin

The difference between the sales price of a good or service and the cost of manufacturing or supplying it. See also **income (sense 2)**.

marginal analysis

The analysis of the effects of small increments or decrements of variable quantities. Marginal analysis is important in economic decision-making, as individuals and organizations often respond to marginal changes in costs and income. In economics, the "marginal principle" holds that it is rational for individuals or organizations to proceed with a course of action until the point at which marginal costs equal marginal benefits.

marginal costs

1 Incremental increases in **variable costs** arising from a course of action. The course of action may include the production of an additional manufactured unit or the supply of an additional measurable unit of a service. **2** A British term for **variable costs**.

marginal tax rate

The **tax** rate paid on the last unit (or extra unit) of taxable income. Under **progressive taxation** systems, the marginal rate is the highest rate of tax that falls on an individual or organization.

margin of error

A **statistical** measurement of an expected level of unpredictability in **random sampling**.

margin of safety

The difference between an individual or organization's current operating activity level and a critical performance measure like a **break-even** or **insolvency** point. A margin of safety can be measured in values, volumes, or percentages, and the concept is an important consideration in **risk management**.

markdown

A reduction in the selling price of a product or service.

market

An arrangement or situation in which goods and services are **exchanged. Money** is the most efficient means of facilitating exchanges in a market. **Prices** in an unregulated or **free market economy** are established by the collective interplay of the decisions of buyers and sellers in achieving an equilibrium point of **supply** and **demand (sense 1)**. Markets may be subverted by **cartels** and **monopolies**, and are often subjected in practice to complex **regulations**. See also **black market, common market, efficient market hypothesis, over-the-counter market, spot market**, and **underground economy**.

market capitalization

An alternative term for **capitalization (sense 2)**.

market price

The selling price of a good, service, **commodity (sense 1)** or **security** negotiated between buyers and sellers in a **free market**. See **arm's-length transaction**. Compare **book value** and **par value**.

market share

The proportion of the activity in a market attributable to a specific organization, activity or product. Market shares are typically expressed in terms of value, volume, or percentage.

market value

The price of an asset in the context of **arm's-length transactions** in a **free market**. Compare **book value**.

markup

An amount added to a product's costs, often to establish its selling price. See also **cost-plus pricing** and **markdown**.

matching

1 The **allocation** of **transactions** to **financial reporting periods** in line with the **accruals basis** of accounting. **2** The allocation of **cash (senses 1** and **2)** receipts to individual balances within **accounts receivable**.

materiality

The importance and relevance of an item. The concept of materiality permeates auditing, and it has been described as "multidimensional" (Lee 1994, 178): it affects **audit planning**, the selection of audit **evidence**, **sample** testing, and the preparation of **audit reports**. Materiality is often judged in terms of potential impact. Example: in **financial auditing**, the potential impact of the omission or **misstatement** of an item on a reader's interpretation of **financial statements** strongly influences materiality considerations. Materiality is also often judged in terms of the **efficiency** of an audit process, to guide the auditor's focus away from trivial and toward significant items.

Materiality is usually assessed **quantitatively**. Example: the materiality of a **balance sheet** item may be calculated in relation to a defined percentage of **net assets**, or the materiality of an **income statement** item may be calculated in relation to a defined percentage of sales or **net income**. However, some items may be material whatever their size; a **bribe**, for example, may be small in relation to balance sheet values, yet its intrinsic nature may ensure its significance. Materiality therefore usually comprises a mixture of qualitative and quantitative considerations. See **creeping materiality**.

maturity date

The date at which a debt, the **principal (sense 2)** of a **loan**, or an **insurance policy**, becomes due for payment.

McKesson and Robbins case (1939)

A legal case relating to a major fraudulent accounting scandal in the United States. The Securities and Exchange Commission (SEC) had been formed in 1934 and, as a consequence of the 1939 *McKesson* case, the SEC established a committee to review the quality of **auditing standards**. Overall, the significance of the *McKesson* case was related less to the specific deficiencies of auditing in the case than to the broader deficiencies in the requirements of standards of **evidence** in support of an audit opinion. Among the subsequent developments were new requirements for stockholder approval of the appointment of financial auditors; new wording for financial auditors' reports; and fresh auditing standards relating to major **balance sheet** items like **accounts receivable** and **inventory**. Regarding the latter, the new auditing standards required financial auditors to have physical interaction with their clients' inventories, instead of reliance solely on managers' **representation letters** as evidence to support inventory balances in the financial statements. See *Allied Crude Vegetable Oil Refining Corporation* **case (1963)** for a later case that prompted financial auditors to tighten further the rigor of the auditing of inventories.

mean

1 [*Noun*] A measure of central tendency of a **population** of data. The arithmetic mean is commonly referred to as the arithmetic **average**, and it is calculated by adding together the values of individual items in a set of numbers and dividing this total by the number of items. Example: the mean of five individual sales transactions of $5, $10, $15, $20, and $30 is calculated as $16—that is, (5 + 10 + 15 + 20 + 30) divided by 5. In this example, the substitution of the $30 sale by one of $150 would distort the mean by skewing it toward the size of the largest transaction, with a potentially misleading mean of $40. Compare **median**, **mode**, and **weighted average**. **2** [*Adj.*] Miserly, ungenerous.

measurability

The condition of being open to an **impartial** quantitative or qualitative assessment. Measurability is central to **auditability**: "If it is not possible to specify the standard of conduct, performance, achievement and quality of information in the relevant report or account in terms which are **understandable** to and acceptable to all parties, there is no basis on which to instruct an audit" (Flint 1988, 33). In other words: without a common understanding of measurement criteria and standards of performance, an audit is impossible. Example: **environmental auditors** may audit the emissions of carbon dioxide, methane, and nitrous oxide (the three main "greenhouse gases") arising from an industrial activity, but they cannot audit the aesthetic qualities of a Richard Wagner music drama. In both cases they can offer opinions, but only for the former exercise are there agreed-on criteria for measurement. Opining on the beauty or otherwise of Wagner's music is the activity of a critic, aesthete, or hobbyist, but not that of an auditor.

median

The midpoint of a **population** of data arranged in ascending or descending order. The median is the item within a set of numbers at which there is an equal number of sequentially arranged items both above and below it. Example: the median of five individual sales transactions of $5, $10, $15, $20, and $30 is $15, as there are two items above it ($20 and $30) and two items below it ($10 and $15). The median differs from the **mean** in that it is less affected by large items; if, in our example, the sale of $30 were replaced by one of $150, the median would be unchanged. See also **mode**.

memorandum account
A record of **transactions** for an asset, liability, or area of revenue or expenditures that is separate from a system of **double entry bookkeeping**. Memorandum accounts serve as reference sources for, among other things, **obsolete** fixed assets and inventory with no monetary value. They are not included in **financial statements**, and they are normally maintained only for information or operational purposes.

merger
The combining of two (or more) organizations that results in the creation of a new legal and economic entity. In contrast to an **acquisition**, a merger implies a voluntary combination by both or all parties. Following a merger, a new organization emerges that tends to reflect the character of the premerger organizations, and the **stockholders** of the amalgamated corporation tend to share on an equal footing the risks and rewards of the newly created entity. However, in practice, one party often dominates a merger arrangement. In many jurisdictions, large corporate mergers that concentrate market power and reduce **competition** are frequently reviewed by regulatory authorities. Mergers have been common among large accounting firms. Example: in 1998, Coopers & Lybrand merged with Price Waterhouse to create a new firm, PricewaterhouseCoopers.

minority interest
Noncontrolling **equity (sense 1)** ownership in a corporation that is controlled by a different, dominant stockholder. Minority interests are rewarded by **dividend** income and **appreciations** in the value of common stock—they are usually unable to determine the strategic policies of a corporation, a consequence of being outnumbered in voting power.

minuted [*Adj.*]
Officially recorded in a summary of a meeting's discussions.

misallocation
The incorrect identification of costs or revenues with specific activities, assets, liabilities, or time periods. Contrast: **allocation.**

misappropriation
The theft of organizational assets or funds for personal use.

mismanagement
See **maladministration.**

mission statement
A formal, written declaration of an organization's high-level objectives and strategies.

misstatement
The inaccurate **valuation** of an item in a **general ledger** account or in **financial statements.**

mixed costs
An alternative term for **semivariable costs.**

mixed economy
An economy in which the **private** and **public** sectors coexist. Most economies are mixed to some degree, though one or two overwhelmingly **command** economies still exist in the twenty-first century.

mode
The item that occurs most frequently in a set of numbers. For example, if ten sales are made at $5, twenty sales at $10, and eight sales at $15, the mode is the most frequently occurring transaction of $10. Compare the **mean** and the **median.**

modus operandi [*Latin*]

"Manner of operating." The term is often used in criminal investigations to describe a suspect's behavioral patterns. It is also used in commercial contexts to describe ways of doing business.

monetary unit sampling (MUS)

Monetary unit sampling (MUS) is an approach to **statistical sampling** that assesses the monetary misstatement that may exist in a data population. Common synonyms for MUS are dollar unit sampling (DUS) and probability-proportional-to-size sampling. In MUS the sampling units are monetary units (e.g., the Japanese yen or the Indian rupee) rather than other types of physical or conceptual unit. Example: a population of 10,000 units of varied inventory items with a total value of one million rupees contains 10,000 physical units and one million rupee units—an MUS technique would use test samples for the one million rupees, and its results would be stated in rupees. MUS is often used by auditors to compare possible monetary **misstatements** with **materiality** thresholds. In MUS, each monetary unit has an equal chance of being selected. The chance of selection of other physical or conceptual units into which the monetary units are grouped (like inventory items or invoices) is proportional to their monetary size.

money

A generally accepted medium of **exchange**. Money has several functions: (i) facilitating **transactions** (contrast **barter**), (ii) storing value and thereby allowing saving, (iii) allowing **credit (sense 1)** transactions, and (iv) offering an easy means of **quantification** and **accounting**. A system of money in a specific country or region is known as a **currency**, and the most **liquid** form of money is **cash (sense 1)**.

money laundering

The transferring of **money** derived from illegal activities through legitimate channels. Money laundering is intended to conceal the illegal origins of funds, and thereby to "cleanse" the funds of their criminal associations. It is commonly associated with drug trafficking and **smuggling**. In the United

States, anti-money-laundering legislation was significantly enhanced by the provisions of the Patriot Act of 2001. Auditing techniques designed to investigate illegal activities like money laundering are often referred to as **forensic auditing**.

modified (audit) opinion

In **financial auditing**, an audit opinion on financial statements that is qualified in some way. There are three forms of modified opinion—the **adverse opinion**, the **disclaimer**, and the **qualified opinion**. Contrast **unmodified opinion** and **unqualified opinion**.

monitoring

The surveillance of an activity, asset, or liability over time. Monitoring is an important means of obtaining audit **evidence**. See also **oversight (sense 1)**.

monitoring controls

Procedures and processes that assess the ongoing performance of **internal controls**. Monitoring controls are usually associated with the second line within the **Three Lines Model**.

monopoly

A **market** with only one **supplier**. The sole supplier in a monopolistic market is likely to be in a position to (i) unduly influence or manipulate the **price**s of the goods and services it supplies, (ii) make profits beyond what would be possible in a more **competitive** market, and (iii) prevent the emergence of competition by erecting **barriers to entry** to the market. Regulations and **antitrust laws** are designed to combat the effects of monopolies.

Concerns over monopolistic power have been central to the human condition for centuries—in England, for example, the *Statute of Monopolies* of 1623 gave **patent** protection to inventors with the intention of promoting temporary monopolies over particular industries, to reward individual talent and to boost the national economy. However, over time, longer-term monopolies became entrenched in England's economy, and further legislation was required to roll back the worst excesses of monopolistic practices. See also **cartel** and **oligopoly**.

moola/moolah [*Slang*]
An informal term for **money.**

moonlighting
The undertaking of work in addition to one's main occupation. The term carries
connotations of (i) secrecy, (ii) irregular hours, (iii) **wages** paid in cash, and
(iv) the **informal economy;** but probably only the second of these characteristics is central to moonlighting.

mortgage
The granting of a property as **collateral** against a **loan.** The loan is often taken
for the express purpose of financing the purchase of the mortgaged property. See
also **lien.**

multinational
1 [*Adj.*] Characterized by activity in two or more countries or by a workforce
comprising several nationalities. **2** [*Noun*] An alternative term for **multinational corporation.**

multinational corporation (MNC)
A corporation with activities in two or more countries. Alternative definitions:
(i) a corporation with a worldwide perspective, in terms of its production, pro-
curement, and revenue markets; and (ii) a corporation producing at least 25
percent of its output outside its country of origin (which may or may not be the
country where the MNC is legally based). To bring coherence to their sprawl-
ing operations and to manage the vast array of **risks** they face, MNCs tend to
develop standardized internal procedures, as far as this is compatible with
local laws, regulations, and cultural practices. The risk of contravention of the
Foreign Corrupt Practices Act is a major concern for MNCs based in the United
States.

mutual fund
A professionally managed **portfolio** of **securities.** For **investors,** mutual
funds offer (i) a **diversification** of **risk** and (ii) the expertise of professional
management.

National Commission on Fraudulent Financial Reporting [Treadway Commission]

A private-sector commission formed in 1985 in the United States to review fraud in **financial reporting**. In 1987, the commission (known popularly as the Treadway Commission, after the name of its first president) issued its findings in a report titled *Report of the National Commission on Fraudulent Financial Information*, known more familiarly as the *Treadway Commission Report*. More than a decade later, a follow-up report, *Fraudulent Financial Reporting, 1987–1997* (Beasley, Carcello, and Hermanson 1999), was published. After the issuance of the 1987 report, the organizations of the Treadway Commission formed the **Committee of Sponsoring Organizations of the Treadway Commission (COSO)**, noted for its influential **internal control framework**; see *Internal Control–Integrated Framework*.

nationalization

1 The transfer to state control of **private sector** economic activity and organizations. The nationalization of the Suez Canal by Egyptian president Gamal Abdel Nasser (1918–70) in 1956 is a well-known example of a nationalization action. Contrast **privatization**. **2** The reinforcement of the national characteristics of an activity, economic sector, or organization. In some countries, organizational quotas define the level of participation of ethnic groups in both public- and private-sector institutions. Example: in Malaysia, Bumiputra ("sons of the soil," from Sanskrit) laws establish affirmative action quotas for ethnic Malays. In several Middle Eastern countries in recent decades, workforce nationalization initiatives (known by terms like Kuwaitization and Saudization) have aimed at reducing dependence on expatriate workers in favor of the more extensive employment of domestic nationals.

negative assurance

1 In **financial auditing**, a weak form of audit **opinion** in circumstances when an auditor does not follow **Generally Accepted Auditing Standards (GAAS)**. Negative assurance is offered by financial auditors in circumstances when standard audit opinions are inappropriate or impractical. The thrust of negative assurance is a statement of auditor unawareness of **material** problems with **financial statements** or a **transaction** under consideration. Negative assurance does not carry the authority and weight of a standard audit opinion issued in line with GAAS. Negative assurance in this context is sometimes referred to as limited assurance. Contrast **positive assurance.** **2** A means of obtaining audit **evidence** by sending written requests to **third parties** to confirm the existence and accuracy of items in financial statements. See **circularization.** With negative assurance, a third party is requested to reply only if a stated balance is incorrect or disputed.

negative goodwill
1 In a corporate **acquisition**, the excess of the **fair value** of acquired **net assets** over the **consideration** paid by an acquiring company. Contrast (positive) **goodwill.** **2** The low esteem in which an organization's **brands** and reputation are held. **3** An unfavorable or unfriendly disposition toward an individual or organization.

negligence
A failure to exercise an adequate duty of care in the performance of an activity that leads to injury or loss to another party. In a **financial auditing** context, accusations of negligence are often based on allegedly inadequate adherence to **Generally Accepted Auditing Standards (GAAS)** in the performance of an audit; but in a broader sense, negligence equates to a failure to exercise **due professional care.** It has been noted that financial auditors "cannot be expected to have an unlimited duty of care because that would be unreasonable and unfair. But they cannot be allowed to practise their skills with no responsibilities" (Lee 1993, 116). In striking a balance between these two extremes, case law has often highlighted the extent of financial auditors' professional responsibilities (see appendix B). See also **deep pockets** and **malpractice insurance.**

net
An amount stated after the deduction of **allowances, discounts (sense 1), taxation**, or other items, or the result of the addition of **debit** and **credit balances.** Contrast **gross.**

net assets
The difference between the total assets and total liabilities of an organization or individual.

net income
Total revenues less total expenses in an **income statement**. Contrast **gross income**.

net off [*Verb*]
To deduct **allowances**, **discounts (sense 1)**, **taxation**, or other items from an amount, or to add together **debit** and **credit balances**. Compare **footing**.

net present value (NPV)
The value of an investment derived from the **present value** of anticipated future, incremental cash flows. The present value of cash flows is calculated by applying an appropriate **cost-of-capital** rate to each period's cash flows. This approach recognizes the **time value of money**. See also the **internal rate of return**.

net profit
An alternative term for **net income**.

net realizable value (NRV)
1 The expected proceeds from the sale of an **asset** (usually an item of **inventory**) after the deduction of relevant selling, distribution, and other incidental expenses. **2** The expected recoverable value of **accounts receivable** balances. The NRV of accounts receivable is stated after the deduction of an appropriate **allowance for bad debts**.

net risk
An alternative term for **residual risk**. Contrast **gross risk**.

net sales
Sales after the deduction of **discounts (sense 1)**, **rebates**, **allowances for bad debts**, and **customer returns**.

next-in first-out (NIFO) method
An **inventory** valuation method that allocates replacement or current costs to
costs of sales. NIFO may be a valuable costing technique in times of high **inflation**
as it focuses on up-to-date (rather than **historical**) costs, but it is unacceptable
under most forms of **Generally Accepted Accounting Principles (GAAP)**. Compare the **first-in first-out (FIFO)** and **last-in first-out (LIFO)** valuation methods.

nominal ledger [*Semi-archaic*]
A British term for **general ledger**.

nominal value
The monetary amount of an individual **security** or other **financial instrument**,
unadjusted for the effects of **inflation** or **market value**. The **par values** of com-
mon stock and the **face values** of **bonds** are examples of nominal values.

nonaudit services (NAS)
An alternative term for **management advisory services**.

nonexecutive director (NED)
The British term for **outside director**.

nongovernmental organization (NGO)
A **not-for-profit** organization, usually outside political control, that is dedicated
to charitable assistance and development. NGOs are often active in **developing
countries**.

nonprofit organization
An alternative term for **not-for-profit organization**.

nonrecurring [*Adj.*]
Infrequent or unusual. See also **exceptional** and **one-off**.

nonsampling risk
In auditing, a **risk** that does not derive from **sample** testing. Examples include
errors in **footing** and the exercise of poor **judgment**.

nonstatistical sampling
An alternative term for **judgmental sampling**.

normal distribution
A graphical portrayal of a **probability** distribution that is symmetrical around the **mean**. A normal distribution shows that values close to the mean occur more frequently than values farther from the mean; it is therefore shaped like a bell curve, with values clustered around the mean and decreasing toward the extremities. The **standard deviation** of the mean measures fixed proportions of items in the population that vary from the mean. Normal distributions have been shown commonly to reflect typical frequency distributions within large, **random** samples. Example: the graphical plotting of the heights of adult males in a population approximates to the classic bell-shaped curve.

normal spoilage
Unavoidable waste, **scrap**, or defective items arising from a manufacturing process. Unlike **abnormal spoilage**, normal spoilage is inherent in a production process. It is uncontrollable in the **short term**, as it is driven by **long-term** technological aspects of production. The costs of normal spoilage are usually treated as regular production costs, rather than as **one-off** items to be expensed as incurred.

North, the [Global]
A collective term for economically **developed countries**. The term (often rendered as "the Global North") derives from the location of most of the world's wealthy countries (in North America, in Western Europe, and on the Pacific Rim) in the Northern Hemisphere. Contrast the **South**.

not-for-profit organization
An institution without a **profit**-seeking motive. Example: charitable institutions. In not-for-profit organizations, **net income** is often referred to as a **surplus** rather than as a **profit**, and an excess of expenditures described as a **deficit** rather than as a **loss**. Organizations of this type are not motivated primarily by profits; they aim to achieve their declared objectives while maximizing the **Three Es** of **economy**, **efficiency**, and **effectiveness**, and they often enjoy exemption from some forms of **taxation**.

objective

1 [*Noun*] The purpose of an audit assignment. Audits are performed to support or refute defined objectives. A financial audit typically has the objective of obtaining **evidence** that an organization's financial statements conform with **Generally Accepted Accounting Principles (GAAP)**, and offer a fair representation of the entity's financial position, the results of its operations, and changes in cash flows. The gathering of sufficient audit evidence to confirm this objectives clears the way for the issuance of an **unqualified opinion**. (Secondary objectives of a financial audit typically include the identification of **material** fraud, or serious weaknesses in **internal controls**.) **2** [*Noun*] The purpose of an **audit test**. An audit test is performed to confirm or refute a defined objective (or objectives), and its results are assessed after gathering and evaluating relevant evidence. An internal audit **work paper** may start as follows: "To obtain evidence that bank balances are accurately stated and correctly classified in the **general ledger**." Or an environmental audit work paper may begin as follows: "To obtain evidence that the levels of pollutants in the river are within agreed[-on] limits." The formal stating of objectives in this manner for individual audit tests encourages the focusing of auditing work to contribute to an audit's overall objective(s). **3** [*Adj.*] Impartial, without bias. Objectivity is fundamental to the credibility of auditing, owing to the importance of unimpaired auditor **judgment**. A common yardstick to assess the **reasonableness** of an auditor's objective judgment is to ascertain that the same judgment would likely be reached independently, in a replicated audit, by a different auditor faced with identical evidence.

objectivity

See **objective (sense 3)** and **impartiality**.

observation

1 A systematic **examination** of an activity or procedure. Observation is an important technique for obtaining and evaluating audit **evidence**, and it includes examinations of the performance of **internal control** procedures. Although the terms "observation" and **inspection** are often used interchangeably in auditing, there is a tendency to restrict the former to the examination of the performance of activities, and the latter to the examination of tangible assets. **2** An auditor's finding, conclusion, or **judgment** in relation to a topic. Compare **opinion**. **3** The act of following or obeying laws, rules, and regulations.

obsolescence

The end (or significant reduction) of an asset's **useful economic life** (or sales value), through technological or other changes. Obsolescence is central to the **amortization** of **long-term** assets and the valuation of **inventory**. The operational effectiveness of an item of plant and equipment can end for many reasons: examples include (i) the inability to obtain spare parts, (ii) the diminishing availability of maintenance engineers, (iii) **wear and tear**, and (iv) inefficiency in comparison with other assets available in the marketplace. If an asset becomes obsolete before the end of its amortization period, it is normally subject to an immediate **write-off** (less any **scrap** value). For items of inventory, shifts in customer demand can signal a drastic reduction in sales value. Some manufacturers rely on the planned obsolescence of their products to maintain ongoing demand.

Occam's Razor, theory of

As popularly understood, the notion of accepting the most straightforward answers to questions or problems. Occam's Razor is often interpreted to mean that simpler explanations are generally better than more complex, competing theories, and it is sometimes called the "law of parsimony" (Latin: *lex parsimoniae*). The simplicity principle of *lex parsimoniae* is that the variables under consideration in problem-solving should not be multiplied beyond what is necessary. The concept more formally is often rendered as "entities are not to be multiplied beyond necessity" (Latin: *"entia non sunt multiplicanda praeter necessitatem"*), although this precise phrasing is not found in Occam's extant writings (Flew 1984, 253). William of Occam (sometimes spelled Ockham; c. 1287–1347), was an English theologian-monk and philosopher; starting in the nineteenth century, his name became associated with the notion of cutting away (or slicing off, as in the use of a razor blade) unnecessarily complex material to favor simplicity.

In auditing, Occam's Razor encourages a focus on readily testable hypotheses. Example: a chronic inventory **shrinkage** of a luxury whiskey from storage containers might at first sight be attributable to theft, in the context of inadequate security safeguards and poor **internal controls.** However, Occam's Razor suffers from the weakness that simplicity does not always provide truth. A strict adherence to Occam's Razor may lead to the neglect of complex but crucial elements in problem-solving, thereby reinforcing a bias toward a glib, superficial type of rationalism. To continue the previous example: the shrinkage of the whiskey inventory may be a result of evaporation caused by excessive heat around the storage vats while the cellars are closed and unattended (and therefore unobserved). Auditors should therefore balance a search for simplicity with a **skeptical** attitude toward the interpretation of audit **evidence.** See also **logic in auditing.**

For a similar concept at a more humorous level, see the **Sutton Rule.**

off-balance-sheet asset / liability (OBS)
An **asset** or **liability** omitted from a **balance sheet. Creative accounting** techniques frequently try to manipulate financial statements through off-balance-sheet transactions, "in which significant corporate resources, income or cash flow are never brought into . . . audited financial statements because of the terms in which the relevant contracted transactions are written (for example, **leases,** quasi-**subsidiary** companies, **joint ventures,** and contingent contracts)" (Lee 1993, 144). **Generally Accepted Accounting Principles (GAAP)** around the world aim to narrow the scope for off-balance-sheet activity. See also **substance over form.**

offsetting
In **accounting,** an amount that reduces or eliminates a balance in a different account. Example: in a **general ledger, amortization** accounts are offset against accounts for **property, plant, and equipment** to arrive at the net **book value** of **fixed assets.**

offshore [Adj.]
1 [*Of corporations and investments*] Located in a **tax haven. 2** [*In the oil and gas industries*] Extracted from the seabed.

oligopoly

A **market** dominated by a small number of participants. In an oligopolistic market, participants may take advantage of their collective power to conspire to influence the prices of products and services. Regulations and **antitrust** laws are designed to combat the anti**competitive** effects of oligopolistic markets. See also **cartel** and **monopoly**.

one-off [*Adj.*]

Unique or unrepeatable.

operating expenses

Costs incurred by a manufacturing organization that are not directly related to production activity. Also known as nonmanufacturing costs.

operating lease

A **lease** whose contractual terms and economic effects do not involve the transfer of the **risks** and **rewards (sense 1)** of the leased asset. Under most systems of **Generally Accepted Accounting Principles (GAAP)**, a lessee does not **capitalize** an asset obtained through an operating lease: ownership remains with a **lessor**. Contrast **capital lease**.

operational audit

1 An audit of an organization's activities, as opposed to its administrative functions or **financial statements**. The first use of the term has been traced to 1954 (as cited by Flesher 1991, 5); before then, the term "nonaccounting audit" was commonly used. Operational auditing often focuses on the **Three Es** of the **economy, efficiency**, and **effectiveness** of activities. Compare **compliance audit, management audit, performance audit**, and **value-for-money audit**. **2** [*Archaic*] An alternative name for **internal auditing**.

opinion

In auditing, a conclusion on the extent to which **evidence** refutes or confirms an **audit objective**. **Impartiality** is central to the credibility of audit opinions; in the context of **financial auditing**, this extends to perceptions of

independence from **conflicts of interest**: "An auditor's opinion is no more than an opinion, but it must be believed to be an informed opinion honestly held" (Flint 1988, 47). Auditors generally do not provide cast-iron guarantees or other attestations of certainty—their activity is the providing of impartial, evidence-based opinions. See **unqualified opinion, unmodified opinion, qualified opinion, adverse opinion**, and **disclaimer**.

opinion shopping

In **financial auditing**, the search by an **auditee** for a financial auditor willing to provide an **unmodified opinion** on financial statements. The practice of opinion shopping challenges the integrity and **independence** of financial auditors, who may be tempted to secure lucrative audit fees in exchange for compromising the **impartiality** of their **judgment**.

opportunity costs

The costs incurred (or income lost) from a decision not to pursue a course of action. Opportunity costs are measured in terms of the reward forgone by choosing the next best course of action. Example: if an organization purchases an **asset** for $100, the opportunity cost is calculated as the most rewarding alternative use to which the $100 could have been put. The alternative action may have included the investment of the amount in a bank to earn **interest**. Calculations of this type consider only the future incremental costs of a decision, thereby excluding costs already committed, such as **sunk costs**. See also **cost-benefit analysis**.

option

The right to buy or sell an **asset** or **security** at a specific **price** within a defined time period. An option confers a right rather than an obligation. The decision to use an option is known as "to exercise an option" (and the option price known as the "exercise price"). See **call option** and **put option**.

order

1 A **contractual** commitment to purchase a good or service. **2** An instruction or command. **3** A logical or sequential arrangement of items. **4** A document instructing a bank to pay a sum of **money** to a specified individual.

organization
1 An institutional arrangement for the association of individuals with a common purpose. Example: "He set up an organization to protect and preserve the urban hedgehog." An organization is usually distinct from its members, and it can therefore outlive changes of membership. **2** The action of making arrangements. Example: "Her organization of the auditing conference was superbly efficient."

organizational governance
An alternative term for **corporate governance**. The term "organizational governance" explicitly extends the theories of corporate governance to unincorporated organizations, like partnerships.

organization chart
A diagrammatic portrayal of an **organization**'s structure. Organization charts tend to depict relations of **accountability**, **delegations of authority**, **hierarchical links**, and reporting relationships.

organization man / woman
1 [*Pejoratively*] An individual molded by the impersonality of large-scale **organizations**, and characterized by conformity, mediocrity, and a mechanistic nature. The term was coined by William H. Whyte (1917–99) in his 1956 book *The Organization Man*, to denote the suppression of individuality and personal morality by the collectivist ideologies of modern **bureaucratic** institutions. **2** [*Admiringly*] An individual who demonstrates selfless loyalty to an organization.

outside director
A member of an organization's **board of directors** who, unlike an **inside director**, is not an employee of the organization. An outside director is considered to act as a kind of quasi-independent watchdog on a board of directors, by bringing an impartial perspective and knowledge of best practices in other organizations. An outside director who has a link or affiliation with an organization, thereby blurring the lines between inside and outside director status, is referred to as a gray director. It has been suggested that the impartiality of individuals may be

affected by **conflicts of interest** rising from gray director status (e.g., by Prasad, Prabhu, and Sankaran 2019).

outside expertise

A provider of specialist knowledge or skills beyond an auditor's normal range of expertise. Examples: **actuaries** provide analysis and opinions to auditors on the valuation of retirement and health insurance funds, and valuation experts advise auditors on the **market prices** of artwork and complex investments like **derivatives**. An auditor using outside expertise is required to reach an opinion on the outside expert's opinion: the auditor's opinion therefore requires confidence in the outside expert's knowledge and objectivity. The consequence is a chain of trust on others' opinions. See also **understandability**.

outsourcing

The obtaining of items or services by an organization from an external **supplier**, rather than from its internal resources. Outsourced **internal auditing** services have grown in importance in the twenty-first century. The advantages of outsourcing internal auditing services include (i) access to expertise and **know-how** and (ii) eliminations of (or reductions in the sizes of) in-house **internal audit functions**. The disadvantages include (i) an organization's dependence on its **suppliers**; (ii) a loss of administrative and cultural control to **third parties**; (iii) security **risks**, as suppliers gain access to confidential or sensitive information; and (iv) a potential loss of collective **institutional memory** of audit-related topics. See also **co-sourcing**.

outstanding [*Adj.*]

1 Of exceptional quality. **2** Unresolved. **3** Unpaid.

overdraft

A deficit in a bank account. An overdraft facility may be provided by a bank in accordance with an agreed-on **credit line**.

overdue [*Adj.*]

Not having occurred by an expected time or date.

overhead
A recurring administrative cost not directly related to a manufactured product or revenue-generating service. See **indirect costs**.

oversight
1 The **monitoring** or **supervision** of an activity or individual over time. Auditing is central to oversight in **institutional governance**. Example: the United Nations has institutionalized its internal auditing activity within its Office of Internal Oversight Services. **2** An unintentional failure to notice an event or to perform an action.

overstatement
The overquantification or exaggerated description of an item. The term is often used in the context of incorrectly measured items in **financial statements**. Example: "The company overstated its sales by millions of dollars." Contrast **understatement.**

overtime
Work undertaken outside of normal hours. Employees are often paid a **premium (sense 2)** for overtime work.

overtrading
The undertaking of business activity that results in **cash flow** problems and potential **insolvency**. Overtrading is characterized by the overstretching of **working capital** arising typically from a simultaneous (i) slowness of cash receipts from **accounts receivable** and (ii) pressing payment demands from **suppliers.**

paperless office
An environment in which computerized, on-screen information eliminates or minimizes paper documentation. Reductions in **hard copy** records have not been met without reservations by those (including regulatory authorities) who prefer to see an adequate level of physical documentation in **audit trails.**

paper profit
Income (senses 1 and 2) that is not mirrored in underlying cash flows. See also **unrealized gain**.

parent organization
See **holding company**.

***pari passu* [*Latin*]**
In proportion, side by side, or at an equal rate of progress. Example: creditors paid pari passu are paid strictly in proportion to their liabilities.

partnership
An unincorporated business entity in which two or more individuals (the partners) agree to share the business's **risks** and **rewards (sense 1)**. Unlike a **corporation**, a partnership does not have a separate legal personality: partners essentially act as **agents** for one another, and individual partners have unlimited personal liability for the debts of the business. (The liability of so-called limited partners is restricted to the value of their investment in the partnership.) The advantages of partnerships include (i) a low level of administrative and regulatory costs vis-à-vis corporations and (ii) flexibility in admitting new partners. The main disadvantage of partnerships is the unlimited liability of individual partners.

par value
The nominal, monetary amount of an individual share of **common stock**. Par value tends to be the legally protected minimum value of common stock, and it is established when the common stock is issued. In practice, stock market values tend to significantly exceed historical par values, and common stock is often issued at a **premium (sense 2)**. See also **face value**.

password
A string of characters that permits access to a computerized information system. Password access is designed to protect the confidentiality and integrity of information, and to channel **authorization** procedures. Password control is strengthened by (i) the maintenance of secrecy, (ii) regular changes to passwords, and (iii) the inclusion of nonalphanumeric characters that make deciphering more difficult.

patent
1 [*Noun*] A license that confers rights over an invention for a defined time period. Typical activities covered by patents are the manufacture and sale of products. A patent is an **intangible asset** and a form of **intellectual property**. See also **trademark**. **2** [*Adj.*] Obvious.

payback period
1 A time period over which the costs of an investment are recouped by the cash flows it generates. Example: a $12,500 investment expected to result in annual, net cash inflows of $5,000 has a payback period of 2.5 years ($12,500 is divided by $5,000). In practice, payback calculations are complicated by uncertainty over cash flow and the effects of the **time value of money**. The latter issue is usually addressed by **discounting** future cash flows to their **present values**. **2** A period of time over which a loan should be reimbursed.

payment holiday
See **holiday**.

payment in kind
The transfer of economic benefits in the form of goods or services, rather than in the form of **money**. Compare **barter**.

payroll
A list of an organization's employees and their **remuneration** details. A payroll records not only **disbursement**s paid to personnel but also employer contributions to items such as pension and health insurance plans.

peer review
The review of an auditor's work by another auditor. Peer review is an important component of self-regulation and **quality control**.

pension plan
An arrangement to fund regular payments to individuals who no longer work. Pensions may be paid by a government on the basis of the recipient's age, or by employers on the basis of employment service. Most pension plans require

contributions from members during their active working lives, through **taxation** (for government pension plans) or **payroll** deductions (for occupational pension plans), but some pension plans are noncontributory. Pensions are often classified into **defined benefit** and **defined contribution** plans, and their often-complex funding requirements are determined by **actuaries**. Pension funds are among the largest **institutional investors**. See also **annuity** and **perpetuity**.

per annum [Latin]
Annually. Compare **per diem**.

per capita [Latin]
By head of population. The phrase is commonly used in the context of economic statistics. Examples: "per capita GDP"; "per capita consumption."

percentage
A number or rate expressed as a proportion of 100.

per diem [Latin]
Daily. The phrase is commonly used to denote expenditures incurred in daily patterns, like travel subsistence allowances and professional fee rates. Compare **per annum**.

performance audit
An audit of the **Three Es** of the **economy**, **efficiency**, and **effectiveness** of operations. Performance auditing is a term associated especially with **public-sector** organizations. In the private sector, the term **operational auditing** is more common. See **value-for-money auditing**.

periodic
Occurring from time to time. The term is used in relation to both regular and irregular time intervals.

perk
See **perquisite**.

permanent difference

A difference between **income (sense 2)** calculated under **Generally Accepted Accounting Principles (GAAP)** and income calculated according to **taxation** rules. Permanent differences are never reversed. Contrast **temporary difference**.

permanent file

A repository of audit documentation of a **long-term** nature. A permanent file typically includes this information on an **auditee**: (i) **organization charts**, (ii) **policies** and **procedures**, (iii) details of significant **internal controls**, and (iv) **minutes** of **board meetings**. The records of **audit tests** for specific assignments are normally maintained separately from the permanent files.

perpetual inventory (PI)

A system of **inventory** control with a continuous or near-continuous updating of inventory quantities. A PI system may be updated in **real time**, or there may be a slight delay between inventory movements and the subsequent updating of inventory balances. Auditors often place reliance on PI systems through the periodic verification of their correct functioning. In such cases, auditors frequently dispense with traditional physical inventory counts at financial period-ends, as they can obtain sufficient audit **evidence** on the accuracy of inventory balances at any date (thereby minimizing disruption to a warehouse's operations). This is an example of the ways in which satisfactory **compliance testing** may reduce the extent of **substantive testing**.

perpetuity

An **annuity** that continues indefinitely, with no specified **maturity date**. The **present value** of a perpetuity is calculated by dividing the perpetuity's periodic, constant payment by an appropriate **discount (sense 2)** rate.

perquisite

An employment-related benefit in addition to a salary or wage. It often carries notions of customary rights. See **compensation** and **fringe benefit**.

petty cash

Small amounts of **cash (sense 1)** kept for minor, day-to-day expenses. Although not usually **material, internal controls** over petty cash tend to be strong in most organizations. Typical controls include (i) a secure storage location; (ii) the **accountability** of specific individuals for cash custody and handling; (iii) **authorization** procedures for individual transactions; (iv) documentary evidence to support disbursements (with the cancellation or other means of identifying the documents as paid, to prevent their duplicated presentation for payment); and (v) periodic counts to verify the petty cash balance. An additional control is the establishment of a defined value for a petty cash fund (sometimes referred to as a float or imprest limit), that is periodically replenished; at any time, the total of cash on hand plus vouchers pending replenishment should equal the defined imprest total.

phantom employee

A fictitious or deceased employee included in a **payroll** register. The inclusion of a phantom employee in a payroll register is usually for **fraudulent** purposes, with **misappropriation** of the **compensation** allocated to the "phantom."

phantom ticking

The falsification of audit **work papers** through the recording of misleading or bogus **audit tests**. The term derives from the **ticking** procedures traditionally used in manual audit work papers.

physical inspection
See **physical verification**.

physical inventory

1 A process to obtain **evidence** of the existence, physical quantities, and condition of **inventory**. The auditor's counting of inventory quantities is normally performed on a **sample** basis, especially when the volume of inventory would make a full count impractical. The results of sample counting can be extrapolated to the entire inventory **population**, provided **compliance testing**

indicates the satisfactory operation of relevant **internal controls**. Physical inventory tests may range from counts performed annually to periodic (or continuous) verifications of the accuracy of **perpetual inventory** information, or a combination of the two. See the ***Allied Crude Vegetable Oil Refining Corporation* case (1963).** **2** A process to obtain evidence of the existence, physical quantities, and condition of **property, plant, and equipment**.

physical verification

The **examination** of a **tangible asset**. Physical verification is an important means of gathering and evaluating audit **evidence** for the existence and condition of **inventory, property, plant, and equipment**, and other assets. It is a form of **substantive testing**. The term is often used synonymously with "physical inspection."

plan comptable général (PCG) [French]

The national **chart of accounts** used in France and some Francophone countries. Translatable as "general accounting plan," the PCG exists in different forms for different industries. Its use of standardized **general ledger** account numbers facilitates tax assessments and the gathering of national economic statistics.

planned economy

An alternative term for a **command economy**.

planning

The establishment of strategies for the achievement of future objectives. Planning is one the main functions of organizational **management (sense 2)**, and it is often analyzed into **short-term** and **long-term** aspects. See also **audit planning** and **budgeting**.

point of sale (POS)

1 The location and time (usually the moment of customer payment) at which a computerized retail system captures sales **transactions**. **2** The principle, in accordance with the **accruals basis** of accounting, that revenue is **recognized** in financial statements only in the accounting period to which it relates. The point of sale for tangible products is usually based on the date of despatch of goods to customers, and for services on the date at which a service is performed.

poison pill

A tactic adopted by a corporation's owners to deter an unwelcomed **takeover** bid through the triggering of an event that makes a corporation a less attractive takeover target. Example: disposals of attractive assets triggered by a takeover attempt may reduce the value of a corporation.

policy

1 A formal rule of conduct. Policies often describe (i) essential administrative **procedures**, (ii) limits of **authority**, and (iii) adherence to **regulations**. **2** An **insurance** contract. **3** A declared course of action in a political or organizational context. Example: "The corporation has declared a policy of reducing its carbon footprint in Africa."

Ponzi scheme

A **fraudulent**, high-**risk**, unsustainable **investment** scheme based on ever-increasing numbers of **money**-paying participants joining the scheme. Investors are promised high **returns (sense 1)**, and the **cash flow** to pay the initial returns comes from new investors' contributions. When the pool of new investors eventually dries up, the system collapses under the weight of its own arithmetic, and participants may lose all or part of their investment. The term is named for the swindler Charles (Carlo) Ponzi (1882–1949), who perfected this type of **fraud**. Example: Bernie Madoff (1938–2021) ran one of the largest Ponzi schemes recorded to date; it was uncovered in 2008.

population

A set of data from which a **sample** may be extracted. Auditors frequently **extrapolate** the findings of representative samples to entire populations of data, to obtain audit **evidence**. See also **judgmental sampling**, **random sampling**, **stratified sampling**, and **statistical sampling**.

portfolio

1 A holding of a group of **securities** or other investments. Investors use portfolios to **diversify** risk, by holding assets with a range of risk profiles. **Portfolio theory** analyzes the composition of efficient portfolios. **2** A bank's list of its **loans** to customers.

portfolio risk
The risk that a **return (sense 1)** on an investment (or on a **portfolio** of investments) differs from expectations. See **portfolio theory.**

portfolio theory
A branch of financial economics associated with Harry M. Markowitz (1927–2023) that analyzes the **diversification** of **risk** in **portfolios** of investments. A major assumption underlying portfolio theory is that investors are rationally **risk averse** by nature, while simultaneously desiring high **returns (sense 1)** on their investments. Investors therefore expect the highest achievable returns from the lowest possible risks; to achieve this, they aim to hold efficient portfolios in line with their risk appetites. An efficient portfolio of investments is one that gives the highest possible return for a specific level of risk, or the smallest possible level of risk for a specific expected return. Although efficient portfolios of investments generally benefit from the spreading of risk through diversification, in any portfolio there is an element of risk—**systematic risk**—that cannot be diversified away.

positive assurance
1 A strong form of **assurance** in **financial auditing.** Contrast **negative assurance**, which conveys an auditor's unawareness or lack of knowledge of a matter. **2** A means of obtaining audit **evidence** by sending written requests to **third parties** to confirm the existence and accuracy of items in **financial statements.** See **circularization.** With positive assurance, a third party is asked to confirm a specific **balance.**

postaudit period
The period of time between the end of detailed **audit testing** and the formal issuance of an audit **opinion.** Financial auditors are obliged to consider the impact on audited **financial statements** of any **material** events during this period. See also **event after the balance sheet date.**

post–balance sheet event
See **event after the balance sheet date.**

post–balance sheet review
A **financial auditor**'s review of **events after the balance sheet date.**

postdated check
A **check** that can be honored only on or after a defined future date.

posting
The recording of an accounting **transaction** or **journal entry.** Some users restrict the term to one of two contexts: (i) the recording of an item directly in a **general ledger** account or (ii) the transfer of **subsidiary ledger** totals to a general ledger account. In practice, however, the term is used freely in both contexts.

postulates of auditing
Theoretical principles and assumptions that purport to define the conceptual basis of auditing. Robert Kuhn Mautz and Hussein A. Sharaf elaborated eight "tentative," interrelated postulates of auditing in 1961: they focused on financial auditing, but many of their postulates are applicable to broader categories of auditing. The postulates are listed as follows (adapted slightly from the original wording by Mautz and Sharaf 1961, chap. 3 *passim*), with additional cross-references to relevant entries in parentheses:

1. **Financial statements** and their supporting information are verifiable. (This postulate goes to the heart of **auditability** and **understandability**.)
2. There is no necessary **conflict of interest** between an auditor and **auditee.** (See **adversariality** and **cooperation**.)
3. The **financial statements** and other information submitted for audit are free from **fraudulent** and other unusual **irregularities**. (See the **expectations gap.**)
4. The existence of a satisfactory system of **internal control** eliminates the **probability** of irregularities. (See **compliance testing.**)
5. A consistent application of **Generally Accepted Accounting Principles (GAAP)** results in the **fair presentation** of financial statements. (See also **Generally Accepted Auditing Standards (GAAS).**)

6. In the absence of clear **evidence** to the contrary, what has held true in the past for the enterprise under examination will hold true in the future. (See **consistency**.)
7. When financial auditors provide **independent** opinions on financial statements, they act exclusively in the capacity of auditors. (See **profession**.)
8. The professional status of the independent auditor imposes commensurate professional obligations. (See **due professional care**.)

Postulates are axioms—that is, fundamental assumptions underpinning a body of knowledge. Postulates are used as starting points for further reasoning and analysis, but they are open to challenges. The main disadvantage of using postulates is that they may turn out to be false or misleading, and may therefore direct reasoning in false directions and down unproductive avenues. Yet the refuting of postulates (or the identification of limitations to postulates) is itself a useful means of clarification in valid reasoning.

Mautz and Sharaf's postulates were developed in the context of **financial auditing**, and have been debated and criticized at length, not least by critics of some of the postulates' apparently "optimistic" nature. Some theorists (Flint 1988; Lee 1993) have attempted to refine Mautz and Sharaf's postulates or develop new postulates. More than half a century after their formulation, however, the postulates remain relevant. Postulates 7 and 8 go to the heart of concerns over the **independence** of financial auditors, a topic of crucial importance in the decades since the demise of Enron Corporation in 2001 and the implosion of the auditing firm **Arthur Andersen** in 2002. The postulates have, in general, stood the test of time.

pound sterling
The **currency** of the United Kingdom.

predatory pricing
A sales **pricing** policy intended to undercut **competitors**' prices. Predatory pricing is undertaken to achieve any or all of these objectives: (i) to maintain or increase market share, (ii) to drive competitors out of a market, and (iii) to erect **barriers to entry** to a market.

preference shares
A British term for **preferred stock.**

preferred stock
An ownership share in a corporation that has preference over **common stock** in the distribution of earnings. Preferred status over common stock also usually relates to payments arising on a corporation's **liquidation.** Preferred **stockholders** take on less risk than common stockholders, as their **dividend** income is usually fixed (in contrast to the variability of common stock dividends). The owners of preferred stock do not normally enjoy voting rights, or may have only restricted voting rights.

preliminary audit
An audit performed in advance of a main audit. In **financial auditing**, preliminary audits tend to occur before the **balance sheet** date and to focus on **audit planning** and **compliance testing.** (In contrast, final audits tend to take place after the balance sheet date and they concentrate more on **substantive testing.**)

premium
1 [*Noun*] A regular payment of **money** for an **insurance policy. 2** [*Noun*] An amount added to a basic or established **price.** Examples include (i) an excess paid over the **par value** of **common stock**, (ii) an excess paid over the **face value** of a **bond**, and (iii) an increase in the sales price of a product. **3** [*Adj.*] Of high or exceptional quality.

prepaid expenses / prepayment
Expenses not yet incurred in a **financial reporting period**, but for which cash payment has already been made. In line with the **accruals basis** of accounting, prepaid expenses are recorded as **current assets** in the **balance sheet** and they are released to expenses in the following financial reporting period. Typical prepaid expenses include **insurance** premiums and **rental (sense 1)** costs.

present fairly [*Verb*]
See **fair presentation.**

present value

The current value of future cash flows. The **time value of money** implies that units of money are worth more at the present time than in the future, owing to the corrosive effects of **inflation**. Present values are thereby calculated by restating future cash flows in current terms through the use of an appropriate discount rate (normally an organization's **cost of capital**). See also **net present value.**

preventive control

An **internal control** designed to anticipate and preempt the occurrence or impact of an unwanted event. Example: **segregations of responsibilities**. Preventive controls have the advantage of avoiding problems, but one cannot rely solely on preventive controls, as errors or exceptions are bound to occur occasionally: "A good system of internal control will reduce the possibilities for irregularities; . . . but it can never guarantee their prevention" (Mautz and Sharaf 1961, 145). **Detective controls** and **corrective controls** are therefore necessary to address problems after their occurrence.

price

The rate at which a good or service can be exchanged for **money.** Price mechanisms are driven by competitive pressures in capitalist or **mixed economies** in the interplay of **supply** and **demand**, and they facilitate distribution and exchange. Price controls are often used by governments in attempts to regulate and control markets.

price discrimination

A sales **pricing** policy in which different prices are established for different buyers. Price discrimination is only possible in a **market** that can be segmented. Example: a transportation corporation may set different prices for different times of the day, and a **multinational corporation** may set different sales prices for a product in different countries.

price/earnings (P/E) ratio

The ratio of the **market price** of a share of a corporation's **common stock** to **earnings per share.** The P/E ratio is a fundamental investment statistic used to appraise the market performance of a corporation's results and its **securities.**

price sensitive information
Information likely to affect the **market value** of a listed **security.** The term carries the implication that the information is restricted in some way, or not widely known. See also **insider dealing.**

prima facie **[*Latin*]**
"At first sight" or "as it first appears." The term is used extensively in legal contexts and not uncommonly in auditing contexts. Example: to describe **evidence** as "*prima facie* convincing" indicates that the evidence is immediately compelling.

prime costs
1 **Direct costs** in a manufacturing process. Prime costs usually comprise directly attributable **raw materials, labor** costs, and production **overhead.** They usually exclude **fixed costs. 2** An alternative term for **conversion costs.**

principal
1 **[*Noun*]** An individual who, in **agency theory**, delegates responsibilities to an **agent.** A principal's remoteness from an agent may be in both physical terms (i.e., geographical distance) and conceptual terms (i.e., an inability to understand the complexity of an activity). **2** **[*Noun*]** The base amount of a financial instrument on which **interest** accrues. **3** **[*Adj.*]** Main, or most important.

principal–agent problem
See **agency theory.**

principles-based approach
[*In corporate governance and ethical standards*] Guidelines that provide for a flexible interpretation and that can be tailored to specific circumstances, rather than a strict compliance with rules. Compare **rules-based approach.**

principles of auditing [*of the International Organization for Standardization*]
Purported essential criteria for auditing identified in the International Organization for Standardization's *Standard 19011:2018, Guidelines for Auditing Management Systems*. The seven auditing principles are (i) integrity, (ii) **fair**

presentation, (iii) **due professional care**, (iv) confidentiality, (v) **indepen-dence**, (vi) an **evidence**-based approach, and (vii) a **risk**-based approach. Com-pare the **postulates of auditing** and see **quality auditing**.

prisoner's dilemma

A branch of **game theory** that systematically analyzes strategies for the optimal selection of alternative courses of action in competitive conditions. The prison-er's dilemma focuses on the complexities of making competitive choices. In a simple version of the game. two criminal accomplices are held in separate prison cells, without a means of mutual communication. They face serious charges, like homicide, and are confronted with the following options: (i) if both prisoners confess to homicide, then both will be sentenced for homicide, but with reduced prison sentences; (ii) if neither prisoner confesses to homicide, then both pris-oners will be sentenced for the lesser charge of manslaughter; (iii) if one pris-oner confesses to homicide, then he or she will be freed and the accomplice alone will be sentenced for homicide. It is clearly against the interests of the prisoners for them both to confess, but this is a likely outcome arising from the prisoner's mutual suspicion of their motivations.

Researchers have applied game theory scenarios like the prisoner's dilemma to decision-making processes in various social settings—for example, in situations of **conflict of interest** and **asymmetries of information** between principals and agents in **agency theory**. Some commentators interpret the out-comes of the prisoners' dilemma as an indication that individual self-interest may run counter to wider social welfare, in the absence of social coordinating mechanisms.

private sector

In **mixed economies**, the elements of economic life not under direct state con-trol. The term encompasses both organizations, such as listed **corporations**, and economic **transactions** between individuals.

privatization

The transfer of economic activity and **organizations** from state control to the **private sector**. Privatization covers a variety of matters: (i) the denationaliza-tion of state-controlled **corporations**, (ii) the **deregulation** or liberalization of

economic activity, and (iii) the subcontracting to the private sector of traditionally **public-sector** activities. Contrast **nationalization.**

probability

The likelihood of the occurrence of an event, measured by a ratio of likely
occurrences to the total number of possible occurrences. Probabilities can be
expressed as (i) **percentages**, (ii) decimals between 0 and 1, (iii) fractions, and
(iv) qualitative estimates (high, medium, and low). Using percentages, a probability of 0 percent indicates than an event is not expected to occur, while a probability of 100 percent suggests that an event is expected to occur with **certainty.**
Auditors use **random sampling**, based on probability theory, as a means of testing large populations of data. See also **expected value**, **risk**, and **uncertainty.**

probability proportional to size sampling
See **monetary unit sampling.**

procedure

A formal rule of conduct. The terms procedure and **policy** are often used interchangeably, but careful users restrict the former to detailed administrative
rules, and the latter to more general statements of organizational conduct.

proceeds
Money received in the **settlement of** a **transaction.**

process

1 [*Noun*] An intentional, sequential series of actions to achieve a defined
purpose. See also **business process reengineering.** **2** [*Noun*] A court
action. **3** [*Verb*] The sorting, analysis, and reporting of **data**, especially by a
computer. See **data processing.**

process costing

A costing method that uses an organization's manufacturing **processes** to allocate costs to **products.** Typically used in the large-scale production of identical
or **fungible** items (e.g., in the chemicals industry), process costing uses **cost
center** activity levels to determine cost **absorption rates.**

product

1 An item created in a **production** process. See also **consumer good**. **2** In auditing, the outcome of an audit process, such as an **audit report** or **attestation statement**.

production

1 The creation of tangible items from **raw materials** and other inputs. See also **by-product**, **joint product**, and **factors of production**. **2** The process of creating and administering an artistic endeavor, such as a stage play, musical product, or film.

productivity

The rate of output from a use of defined quantities of inputs. The concept is typically applied to labor productivity and capital productivity, and is often measured by **ratio analysis**.

profession

An occupation characterized by a high level of expertise and a commitment to serving the public interest. The three traditional "learned professions" of divinity, law, and medicine were supplemented during the Industrial Revolution by new trade and craft associations seeking professional status. Starting in the nineteenth century, the new professions included engineers, teachers, accountants, and **financial auditors** (Giroux 2017, vol. 2). Elements of a profession typically include (i) the existence of a formal body of **knowledge**, (ii) certification as both a signal of expertise and a means of obtaining exclusive or **monopolistic** rights to undertake an activity (Abbott 1988), (iii) an institutional framework, (iv) written standards for work performance and personal conduct, and (v) a commitment to exercise **due professional care** in the performance of duties. That the responsibilities of financial auditors derive from their professional status was the eighth **postulate of auditing** developed by Robert Kuhn Mautz and Hussein A. Sharaf.

In addition to the attributes of a profession listed in the previous paragraph, an ethical dimension attaches to notions of professionalism. Public opinion may, for example, admire the skills (in deceptive eloquence or safe-cracking) of the "professional criminal," but it is unlikely to support his or her moral character. Instead, professionals are expected not only to provide services "essential to the public" (Flint 1988, 88) but also to deliver these services with altruism or, at least, a commitment to the public good. See the ***United States v. Arthur Young & Co. et al.* case (1984)**. That modern financial auditors display an altruistic professional ethos is disputed by the **critical accounting** movement.

Professions tend to erect **barriers to entry** to their professional associations, through rigid requirements for certification and approved periods of practical experience. The restrictions on entry of this type may assist in fostering conditions of high income and high social status for the profession's members. However, with the benefits of professionalism come risks and liabilities; in particular, financial auditors may face legal liabilities arising from allegations of **negligent** performance of their duties. In a narrow sense, negligence may be attributable to the inadequate application of **Generally Accepted Auditing Standards (GAAS)** and **Generally Accepted Accounting Principles (GAAP)** to the performance of an audit, but in a wider sense negligence equates to a failure to exercise due professional care. Popular perception may tend toward the view that litigation related to financial auditing has exploded from the turn of the new millennium, with the spectacular demise in 2002 of **Arthur Andersen**. In fact, there is a long history of case law involving public accounting audit firms and alleged negligence in auditing (see appendix B). And the demise of large audit firms did not begin with Arthur Andersen; in 1990, for example, the seventy-five-year-old firm Laventhol and Horwath, with fifty regional offices, filed for **bankruptcy** as a consequence of litigation problems—it faced more than one hundred lawsuits pending at the time of the bankruptcy (O'Reilly et al. 1998, 5.6).

profit
See **income (sense 2)**.

profitability
The capacity of an activity or organization to generate **income (sense 2)**.

profit-and-loss account
A British term for **income statement**.

profit center

An activity, unit, or individual within an organization with which **income (sense 1)** can be identified. Compare **cost center**.

profit margin

1 The ratio of **net income** to **net sales**. **2** The ratio of **gross income** to **net sales**.

profit-seeking

Motivated primarily by the generation of **income (sense 2)**.

profit-sharing

A **contractual** arrangement to divide the **net income** of an organization between two or more parties. Contexts in which profit-sharing occurs include (i) employee **compensation** plans, (ii) **partnerships**, and (iii) **joint venture** arrangements.

profit-taking

The sale of an investment or asset to **realize** an **appreciation** in value.

pro forma [*Latin*]

"For form's sake" or "as a matter of form." Example: **pro forma** invoices are sent to customers to elicit estimated or preliminary payments in advance of the despatch of related goods.

progress billing

The raising of interim **sales** invoices and the **recognition (sense 1)** of interim revenue in line with the sequential progress of a **long-term** sales **transaction**. It is applicable in particular to large construction and civil engineering projects.

progressive tax

A **taxation** system in which **tax rates** increase with higher levels of taxable income. Under a progressive tax system, the burden of taxation falls more heavily on the wealthy. Contrast **regressive tax**.

project
An undertaking to achieve defined objectives within a defined timeframe.

projection
See **forecast**.

promissory note
A **contractual** document that contains an unconditional promise to pay a speci-fied sum of **money** at a specified date. Some forms of promissory note are traded.

property, plant, and equipment
Long-term, **tangible** assets used for operational or administrative purposes. The term does not normally refer to assets held principally for **investment** or trading purposes. It typically refers to land, buildings, machinery, and office equipment. Other than land, assets in this category are normally subjected to **amortization**. Compare **fixed asset** and contrast **current asset**.

pro rata [Latin]
On a proportionate basis. The term is used to describe the proportionate allo-cation of costs and revenues to activities, assets, liabilities, or time periods. Example: dividends are distributed pro rata to holders of common stock, based on the proportions of stockholders' investments.

prospectus
A document that promotes the sale of an asset or service. In particular, the term is used in the context of corporate documents that promote the issuing of new **securities**.

provision
1 A **liability** arising from the accounting treatment of **accrued expenses**. Provisions are shown as either short-term or long-term liabilities in a **balance sheet**, depending on the nature of the underlying circumstances that give rise to the provision. **2** An amount **recognized** in an accounting period for a reduc-tion of the value of an asset, in line with either the **accruals basis** of accounting

(e.g., **amortization**) or reductions in **net realizable value** (e.g., **allowances for bad debts**). **3** A legally binding condition or **contractual** clause.

provision for doubtful debts
A British term for **allowance for bad debts.**

proxy
The **authority** to represent another individual, or to vote on that individual's behalf. Proxy voting arrangements are common at corporate **stockholders'** meetings.

prudence
1 The exercise of care and restraint. **2** In auditing, prudence refers to the exercise of **due professional care**: a prudent auditor is considered to exhibit "knowledge, skill, caution, and responsiveness" (Mautz and Sharaf 1961, 139). **3** In accounting, prudence underpins the **accruals concept**, whereby revenues and expenses are **recognized** only in the periods when they are earned or incurred. Prudence discourages the anticipation of revenues and the deferment of expenses. See also **conservatism.**

psychology in auditing
The functioning of the human mind in relation to auditing. In the entry **logic in auditing**, various methods of rational reasoning are discussed. While the **judgment** of **evidence** in auditing is founded on logical reasoning, the human mind often operates in a nonrational manner; the production of ideas is often "automatic, operating beneath the level of conscious thought" (Evans 2017, 9). Intuitive expertise is without doubt an important element of auditor judgment, but so are judgment-distorting cognitive biases such as **anchoring and adjustment bias, availability bias,** and **recency bias.** The impact of potentially deceptive heuristics on auditing judgment has been widely acknowledged (e.g., Chin 2022; Maradona 2020).

public good
A resource or service considered essential for the social well-being. Public goods are usually funded collectively through **taxation** because, owing to their

importance, their supply cannot be entrusted solely or largely to **free market** mechanisms. Common examples of public goods and services include (i) children's education, (ii) refuse collection, (iii) postal services, (iv) streetlighting, (v) policing, and (vi) mass transportation. The suppliers of public goods often enjoy state-sanctioned **monopoly** rights. However, in some countries, the supply of some public goods has been **privatized**; examples are (i) the coexistence of private and state-funded schools and (ii) the use of private security arrangements alongside official police services.

public sector

In **mixed economies**, the parts of economic life that are under the control of the state. This sector includes government departments and nationalized **corporations**. See also **Supreme Audit Institution**.

public utility

An organization that provides goods or services deemed essential for the **public good**. Examples include the supply of water and electricity. Public utilities are usually either state-controlled or subjected to close regulation.

put option

The right to sell an **asset** or **security** at a specific **price** within a defined time period. Contrast **call option**.

qualified opinion

A **financial auditor**'s **opinion** that, except for a stated limitation, an entity's financial statements conform with **Generally Accepted Accounting Principles (GAAP)** and fairly present the entity's financial position, the results of its operations, and changes in cash flows. Qualified opinions normally arise from limitations in the scope of audit work or from contraventions of GAAP, like a **material** misstatement of an item in the financial statements. Under most systems of **Generally Accepted Auditing Standards (GAAS)**, financial auditors are obliged to explain the reasons for issuing a qualified opinion. In a qualified opinion, the limitation tends not to be pervasive; if the problems are stronger than those covered by a qualified opinion, the auditor issues an **adverse opinion**. Though not as strong as an adverse opinion, a qualified opinion tends to arouse negative **stakeholder** sentiment. See also **unqualified opinion** and **disclaimer**.

qualitative [*Adj.*]

Relating to measurement by nonquantitative or nonmonetary methods. Examples of topics associated with qualitative assessment: (i) employee morale and (ii) the aesthetic appeal of products. Contrast **quantitative**.

quality

1 The conformity of an item or activity to an objective standard. **2** Excellence.

quality auditing

The auditing of activities and operations with a focus on conformance to standards, especially in relation to the quality management systems of organizations like the International Organization for Standardization (ISO). Based in Switzerland, the ISO publishes standards in a wide range of technological and business areas. One of its most widely used products is the ISO 9000 family of quality management systems, used by corporations around the world. See also **quality control** and ISO's **principles of auditing**. Quality audits are also associated with the search for continual improvement in **total quality management (TQM)** systems.

quality control

Systems or procedures that aim to maintain high standards in an activity. The control of **quality** is often maintained through **sample** testing of the items or activities under consideration. In terms of auditing, quality control may be understood as (i) the *raison d'être* of auditing itself, insofar as auditing is a quality control mechanism over the objects of audits, be they **financial statements**, surgical operations, or assessments of "carbon footprints"; or (ii) a means of securing and evaluating the adequacy and consistency of auditors' performance. The latter activity is achieved through practices like professional certification and continuing education requirements for auditors, the allocation of work to those with appropriate experience, and the careful **supervisory** review of **work papers**. For **financial auditing**, external quality review is delivered through peer review processes. For internal auditing, the Institute of Internal Auditors requires five-yearly external validations—essentially quality control reviews—of an **internal audit function**'s conformance to its professional practices framework.

quality of earnings
The extent to which **net income** reflects and portrays underlying economic circumstances. Financial auditors review the quality of earnings of their **auditees**, obtaining **evidence** that net income in **financial statements** has not been distorted by **creative accounting** or transient factors.

quantitative [*Adj.*]
Relating to measurement by quantity rather than by quality. Example: product sales expressed in dollars or units. Contrast **qualitative.**

quasi [*Latin*]
"Almost" or "similar to." The word is encountered as a prefix in terms like "quasi-**contract**" and "quasi-official."

questionable payment
A potentially illegal or improper payment. Examples: **bribes** and other cash **disbursements** made for **corrupt** purposes. Compare **facilitating payment.**

questionnaire
An interrogative document that lists a series of questions. Questionnaires are a common survey instrument for auditing and **internal control** reviews; in particular, **Control Risk Self-Assessment** techniques are frequently based on questionnaires. Critics have pointed to the limitations of questionnaires by describing them as inflexible, susceptible to bias, and "easy to manipulate" (Toffler and Reingold 2003, 144). However, they offer a cost-effective means of gathering information in large organizations. See also **checklist** and **box-ticking approach.**

quick ratio
An alternative term for the **acid test ratio**.

quid [*Slang*]
A British term for the **pound sterling**.

quid pro quo [*Latin*]
"Something for something." The modern use of the term usually implies an unethical exchange of favors in the context of **bribery** and **corruption**.

quoted
1 [*Of securities*] Registered and traded on a stock exchange. See also **listed**.
2 [*Of a price*] Proposed before the formalization of a **contract**.

random sampling
A **sampling** method in which each item in a data **population** has an even chance of being selected. In random sampling, no **judgment** or bias skews the sample, which facilitates making inferences about the entire population based on the characteristics of the sample. See also **stratified sampling** and **statistical sampling**.

random walk
The theory that the **market prices** of **common stocks** and other tradable items—such as **commodities (sense 1)**—exhibit unpredictable patterns, and do not reflect historical trends. According to random walk theory, future behavior is independent of past history.

rate of exchange
See **exchange rate**.

rate of interest
See **interest rate**.

rate of return
Income (sense 1) from an investment expressed as a percentage of the amount invested. See also **internal rate of return**.

ratio

A **quantitative** relationship between two variables. See **ratio analysis.**

ratio analysis

1 The analysis of **financial statements** through the study and interpretation of ratios. Examples: (i) **acid test ratio**, (ii) **current ratio**, (iii) **debt-equity ratio**, (iv) **interest coverage ratio**, and (v) **price/earnings ratio.** Financial statement ratios are often compared with sector averages. **2** The analysis and interpretation of ratios beyond financial statements. Examples: operating and efficiency ratios, including measurements such as manufacturing output per employee.

raw materials

Inputs to production, typically natural resources or **commodities (sense 1)**, to be subjected to a **manufacturing** process. In manufacturing processes, an **inventory** of raw materials is normally converted into a **work-in-process** before its final conversion into **finished goods.**

realized gain or loss

The difference between cash received for the sale of an **asset** and the asset's **carrying value** before the sale. Contrast **unrealized gain or loss.**

real terms

The value of a variable like **money** or a **price** following an adjustment for the impact of **inflation** and **interest rates.** See also the **time value of money.**

real-time [Adj.]

The immediate (or almost immediate) processing and updating of information in computerized accounting systems.

real-time auditing

Auditing in the context of the **real-time** processing of information in computerized accounting systems.

reasonableness

1 The state of being fair, logical, and justifiable. Auditors are required, through the assessment of audit **evidence**, to judge the reasonableness of matters ranging from the measurement and presentation of **financial statement** items to the reliability of **internal controls**. It is normally impractical for auditors to review every **transaction** in an organization; they therefore review processes, internal controls, and **samples** of transactions to arrive at reasonable **assurance** (rather than absolute assurance or a guarantee) on which to base an **opinion**. **2** Possessing the condition of being good value, or inexpensively priced.

rebate

1 A partial **refund** of a sum of **money**. **2** An alternative term for **discount (sense 1)**.

recalculation

An **audit test** that assesses the arithmetic accuracy of a balance in a general ledger or financial statements. Example: financial auditors may recalculate a fixed asset's **amortization** charges to obtain **evidence** of their accuracy. This type of audit test falls within the category of **substantive testing**. Compare **reperformance**.

receipt

1 A document that records or acknowledges the occurrence of an event. Examples: (i) **invoices** and bills for expenditures, (ii) confirmations of cash payments, and (iii) product delivery documentation. **2** The act of taking delivery of cash or an asset.

receivables

Amounts of **money** owed to an organization or individual. Trade receivables are referred to as **accounts receivable**. Nontrade receivables range from employee salary **advances** to **taxation** rebates. See also **debtor**.

recession

A slowdown in economic activity in a **market** or territory, often defined by economists as a reduction in **gross domestic product** in two consecutive quarters. See also **depression**.

recognition

1 The recording of a **transaction** in a **general ledger** and its inclusion in financial statements. The recognition of expenses and revenues is driven by the **accruals basis** of accounting. See also **realization**. **2** Public or official acceptance of the credibility (or **professional** status) of an individual or organization.

recommendation

A proposed action to remedy a problem or potential problem. Recommendations addressed by **internal auditors** to **auditees** normally form part of the internal auditor's report, while **financial auditors** tend to communicate their recommendations in the form of a **management letter**.

reconciliation

An **internal control** procedure that identifies differences between two accounting **balances**. Common reconciliations include **bank reconciliations** and reconciliations from the **general ledger** to the **subsidiary ledgers**. The results of reconciliation procedures are considered to be a strong form of audit **evidence**, particularly when one of the reconciling balances (e.g., a bank statement) originates from a **third party**.

recency bias

A cognitive shortcut or heuristic **bias** that overrelies on recent events over earlier ones. Recency bias is a memory bias. In auditing, an evaluative bias of this nature is a risk to the integrity of **evidence**-based reasoning. Example: an auditor who relies on oral testimony for a matter may place a greater emphasis on the most recent testimony. Research has suggested that "auditors with higher trait **skepticism** exhibit higher cognitive effort which mitigates the recency bias" (Koch, Köhler, and Yankova 2016, 1). See also **anchoring and adjustment bias**, **availability bias**, and **intuition**.

red flag

The identification and warning of a danger or problem. The term can be used literally (e.g., a physical red flag on a beach to warn of dangerous swimming conditions) and metaphorically (e.g., a computerized indication of a poor **internal control**).

red, in the
To make a **loss** or to have negative **cash flow**. Contrast "in the **black**." Negative cash flows have traditionally been colored red.

redemption
1 The payment of a **liability** on or before a **maturity date**. **2** The exchange of a **coupon** for cash or for an asset. **3** The fulfillment of a pledge or promise. **4** Atonement for poor past behavior or performance.

red herring
An irrelevant item that serves to distract from **relevant** information. In **audit tests**, the existence of a red herring might mislead an auditor into false inferences and inappropriate **opinions**.

reducing balance method
A British term for the **accelerated method**.

reengineering
A redesigning or restructuring of an activity. See **business process reengineering**.

refund
The paying back of a sum of **money**.

register
1 A formal document or repository that lists items. See also **log** and **risk register**. **2** A measure of linguistic formality.

Registeraccountant
The equivalent of **Certified Public Accountant** or **Chartered Accountant** in the Netherlands.

regression analysis
A **statistical** method to analyze relationships between a dependent variable and one or more independent variables. The most common form of regression analysis

is linear regression, in which one finds the line (or a more complex linear combination) that most closely fits the data according to specified mathematical criteria.

regressive tax

1 An individual **tax** in which **tax rates** decrease with higher levels of taxable
income. Under a regressive tax system, the burden of taxation falls dispropor-
tionately on the less wealthy. Contrast **progressive tax. 2** A taxation system
designed to favor the wealthy. Example: a taxation program that derives a large
proportion of its revenues from **sales taxes** may be deemed to be regressive,
in that the burden of taxation is unrelated to individual prosperity.

regulation

A **rule** established and enforced by an institution with legal, **quasi**-legal,
or moral **authority**. See also **policy** and **procedure**.

related party

Two individuals or organizations whose relationship is characterized by **control**,
influence, or emotional attachment. It is assumed that **transactions** between
related parties may not be made at **arm's length**, and the **disclosure** of **material** transactions of this nature in **financial statements** is required under most
systems of **Generally Accepted Accounting Principles (GAAP)**.

relevant costs

Expenditures that have a bearing on, or are affected by, a decision-making process. See **avoidable costs**, **controllable costs**, and **discretionary costs**.

reliability

Trustworthy, credible, and free from error. Reliable audit **evidence** is fundamental to **auditability**; it has the qualities of completeness and representational
faithfulness, and is capable of independent **verification**. The auditor is sometimes viewed as having not only a confirmatory role in relation to the reliability
of audited information, but also a motivational role—the awareness that one's
work will be audited might serve as a mechanism to generate reliable evidence:
"Knowing that an audit will be performed is a strong deterrent to disseminating
erroneous information" (O'Reilly et al. 1998, 1.13).

remote operating unit
An alternative term for **branch.**

remuneration
1 **Salaries** and **wages** paid to an organization's employees. **2** **Fees** paid to an individual for the performance of services.

remuneration committee
A committee of a **board of directors** (or similar governing body) that oversees an organization's **executive remuneration** policy. Remuneration committees are often composed of **outside directors** to encourage **independence** and to minimize potential **conflicts of interest.**

rent
1 The cost of hiring an **asset.** **2** In economic theory, a payment for an item or resource in excess of its **price** in a **competitive** market, or above its **opportunity costs.** In a perfectly competitive market, rents are impossible to achieve. Rents therefore arise from competitive advantages or from market inefficiencies or restrictions, such as a shortage of the supply of an item or service, or a **profession**'s ability to restrict competition through **monopolistic** control of an activity.

reperformance
An **audit test** that repeats or re-creates the operation of an **internal control.** Example: auditors may run a test transaction through an accounts payable system, to obtain **evidence** of the satisfactory operation of the system's internal controls. This type of audit test falls within the category of **compliance testing.** Compare **recalculation.**

replacement costs
See **current costs.**

reporting
1 The providing of information to others. Reporting is central to **management** functions like **planning** and **control.** See also **audit report** and **financial**

reporting. **2** The channeling of **accountability** relationships between individuals in an organization through the **hierarchy** of a **chain of command**.

representation
See **management representation**.

representation letter
A document signed by the management of an organization and addressed to a financial auditor, stating that items in **financial statements** are **fairly presented**, and free from **fraud**, **misstatements**, and other **irregularities**. The representation letter confirms that the primary responsibility for the accuracy of financial statements rests with managers, not auditors. Representation letters can also occur in an internal auditing context; for example, in reviews of compliance with the **Foreign Corrupt Practices Act**, an internal auditor may request written management confirmations of (i) the nonexistence of **conflicts of interest**, (ii) the nonpayment of **bribes**, and (iii) the operation of satisfactory **internal controls**.

reputation(al) risk
The **risk** of damage to an organization's or individual's image or **brand**.

requisition
1 A written demand or request to purchase or take possession of an item, or for the performance of an activity. Example: a documented request for the withdrawal of an item from **inventory**. **2** A decision by a government to make use of, or take ownership of, an **asset**. The requisitioning of assets often takes place in war time, or during a forced **nationalization** process.

research and development (R&D)
Investigations of a **long-term** and scientific nature, intended to develop new knowledge (research) and to apply this knowledge to new products and services (development). Depending on the specific circumstances of R&D activity, R&D costs may be classified as either **revenue expenditures** or items to be **capitalized** and **amortized**.

reserve

1 An alternative term for **provision (senses 1 and 2)**. **2** Additional amounts of inventory, money, or other items maintained for operational or **investment** purposes. **3** [*Plural*] **Retained earnings** set aside for a specific purpose.

residual risk

The **risk** remaining following the application of **risk management** techniques and risk-mitigating **internal controls**. It is often impossible to eliminate risks entirely, but risks can be managed to levels that an organization's managers deem to be acceptably low. Organizational culture and the tolerance of risk (**risk appetite**) tends to determine levels of acceptable residual risk. Contrast **gross risk.**

residual value

1 The value of an asset at the end of its **useful economic life**. Residual values tend to be based on resale or **scrap** values, less any disposal or selling costs. The costs of assets subjected to **amortization** normally exclude residual values. **2** The value of an asset, less amortization charges, at any stage of its useful economic life.

responsibility accounting

A system of **management accounting** in which individual **managers** are held **accountable** for operational and financial performance.

restatement

The correction of an inaccurate balance in a **general ledger** or **financial statements**. Financial statements are normally reissued for restatement purposes only for **material** inaccuracies.

résumé [*French*]

See *curriculum vitae*. Some users of the terms differentiate between a summary or brief *résumé* and a more extensive *curriculum vitae*, but in practice the two terms are often used interchangeably.

retailing

The selling of goods to the final consumer. Compare **wholesaling.**

retained earnings
Accumulated **net income** recorded as stockholders' **equity** in a corporation's **balance sheet**. Retained earnings are normally available for distribution as **dividends**.

return
1 Income **(sense 1)** derived from an **investment**. Returns from investments may be in the form of **cash** or **appreciations** in an investment's value. Example: investors in a corporation's **common stock** hope for returns from both **dividend** income and appreciations in the stock's market value. **2** An abbreviated term for **customer return**. **3** The submission of a formal report or document, like a **taxation** calculation.

revaluation
1 A change in the **value** of an **asset** that is **recognized (sense 1)** in **financial statements**. Revaluations are normally made to bring an asset's **book value** into line with its **market value**. The term carries strong connotations of an increase in asset value; for a downward revaluation of an asset, the more commonly encountered term is **write-down**. **2** An increase in the value of a **currency** in relation to other currencies, usually resulting from an intentional government policy. Contrast **devaluation**.

revenue
See **income (sense 2)**.

revenue expenditures
Expenditures on **short-term** items, charged in full to an **income statement** in the period when they are incurred. Contrast **capital expenditures**.

review
1 An assessment of an item or activity with the intention of suggesting or implementing changes. In the context of **financial auditing**, a review implies an **examination** or limited **assurance** exercise that falls short of an **audit** as defined in **Generally Accepted Auditing Standards (GAAS)**. **2** An abbreviated term for **analytical review**.

reward

1 An increase in wealth through income, the transfer of cash, or the **appreciation** of an asset. The term reward is often used in contrast to **risk**. Example: "The partners all accepted the risks and rewards of entering a new market." **2** A **gift** to recognize an achievement. Example: "The police are offering a reward for information that leads to his arrest."

right of return

A **contractual** agreement that provides an explicit right to customers to return a product under defined circumstances.

risk

The **probability** of the occurrence of an event with negative consequences. Risk leads to **opportunity costs** as well as traditionally understood costs, and it can be quantified in terms of (i) likelihood of occurrence and (ii) consequences or outcomes. While some risks can be quantified only with difficulty, they can at a minimum be categorized as high, medium, or low, in terms of both likelihood of occurrence and the financial or operational outcome.

Risks may be envisioned as general dangers to the well-being of individuals and organizations, but they are also often interpreted as potential barriers to the achievement of the objectives or goals of an activity or organization. Typical areas of risk in modern organizations include (i) strategic and **planning** risks, (ii) **fraud**, (iii) **credit risks**, (iv) operational risks (including health and safety concerns), (v) legal matters, (vi) **regulatory risks**, (vii) accounting risks, (viii) technological risks (including the **obsolescence** of manufactured products), and (ix) **treasury** risks. Many of these risks are not stand-alone items, and their interrelations can be complex. Three underlying primary causes of organizational risk are (i) the random nature of events, (ii) imperfect or incomplete knowledge, and (iii) poor internal control.

Risk also affects the auditor directly, especially the **financial auditor**, in terms of the risk of providing an inappropriate opinion. Financial auditors are **accountable** for legal risks under both criminal and civil law arising from **negligent** or dishonest audit work (but not for reasonable errors of **judgment**).

See also (in addition to the entries that begin with the word "risk") **absolute risk, audit risk (sense 1), Control Risk Self-Assessment, credit risk,** enterprise risk management, portfolio risk, reputation risk, sampling risk, systematic risk, uncertainty, and unsystematic risk.

risk acceptance
A decision to accept the **risks** (and **rewards (sense 1)**) of an activity or **market**. Example: the risks of operating in high-technology markets might be acute, owing to the danger of rapid **obsolescence**, but markets of this type can offer extremely attractive returns to its risk-seeking participants. Risk acceptance decisions may also occur on geographical lines. Example: in the period after the Sri Lankan economic crisis of 2022, some **multinational corporations** may have been tempted to pull out of the country on the basis of unacceptably high economic and political risks. Conversely, other **investors** justified continued activity in Sri Lanka based on an assessment of that country's longer-term economic health. Pulling out of a market only to reenter it later can be a more costly option than remaining throughout a period of crisis.

Risk acceptance also relates to the proportionality of individual risks in **risk management** processes, with the managers of (or the investors in) an organization adopting **risk mitigation** measures to meet their **risk appetites** for individual risks. Example: a reduction of 50 percent of current **shrinkage** of inventory might be an acceptable target to satisfy an organization's risk appetite. Contrast **risk avoidance.**

risk analysis
An alternative term for **risk assessment.**

risk appetite
The willingness to tolerate **risk** in the achievement of defined objectives. Risk appetites range from **risk averse** to **risk seeking.**

risk assessment
The identification, analysis, and measurement of **risks** relating to an activity or organization. Risk assessment comprises the initial stages of **risk management**, and it is one of the five components of effective **internal control** identified in the *Internal Control–Integrated Framework* (the *COSO Report*). Risk assessment practices have spread beyond their historical heartlands of

the **insurance** and financial services sectors to enter the wider organizational mainstream.

Auditors use risk assessment for purposes analogous to the use of **sample** testing—for reasons of pragmatism and efficiency. The testing of entire data populations is often impractical, owing to the high volumes of auditable information in large, modern organizations, and risk assessment offers a pragmatic alternative through the prioritization of areas of perceived high risk. Risk therefore offers the auditor efficiencies by reducing inputs to the auditing process (the burdens of **evidence** assessment) in relation to its outputs (**opinions** on levels of **assurance**). Efficiencies of this nature are important cost control measures in **financial auditing**, especially in the supply of audits to aggressively competitive markets. Example: risk assessment techniques can be used to identify suitable areas for review in a large **audit universe**, and to identify specific **audit tests** for a defined topic. This approach contrasts with the cyclical patterns of **audit planning** common until late in the twentieth century.

risk aversion

An attitude to **risk** characterized by avoidance or minimization. Risk averse investors have low **risk appetites** in their preference for likely but relatively low rates of return over doubtful but higher rates of return. Example: an individual who chooses to receive $100 with certainty over a 50 percent chance of receiving $200 would be classified as risk averse. (Some commentators consider that such cases reflect a preference for outcomes rather than for risks, but in practice it is difficult to disentangle the preferences for risks vis-à-vis preferences for outcomes.) Contrast **risk-seeking**.

risk avoidance

A decision not to accept the **risks** of an activity or **market**. Refraining from involvement in an activity or a market (or disengaging from existing commitments) can sometimes be a costly strategy, as it can involve significant **opportunity costs**. At the end of the Korean War in 1953, for example, South Korea had a *per capita* **gross domestic product** comparable to those of India and many Central African countries. The war had destroyed much of the country's infrastructure and industrial base. But over the next decades, the country's rapid economic growth made it, by the 1990s, one of the most affluent countries in the world.

International **investors** who accepted the risks of operating in war-devastated South Korea in the 1950s were rewarded during the nation's subsequent economic boom, while those who initially avoided South Korea faced expensive entry costs as latecomers to this dynamic Asian "tiger" economy. Contrast **risk acceptance**.

risk-based auditing (RBA)
Auditing in which **objectives** and **audit planning** are driven by a **risk assessment** philosophy.

risk committee
A committee of a **board of directors** (or similar governing body) that oversees an organization's **risk management** activity. Sometimes, there is a combination of functions with an **audit committee**, covering auditing and risk management.

risk elimination
The complete removal of a **risk**. Unlike **risk avoidance**, risk elimination does not necessarily imply nonengagement in (or disengagement from) an activity or **market**; it covers the elimination of a risk while activity is ongoing. Risk elimination techniques can be costly. Example: an organization can eliminate its foreign exchange rate risk by the full **hedging** of foreign currency liabilities, but it can find itself locked into **contractual** exchange rates that turn out to be unfavorable at the transaction **settlement** dates. However, many risks can never be entirely eliminated; the risk of theft in a warehouse, for example, may be mitigated and thereby reduced to acceptable levels, but it can hardly ever be completely eradicated. Compare **risk minimization**.

risk event
An occurrence that gives rise to the creation or **crystallization** of a **risk**.

risk factor
An element of **risk** considered in a **risk assessment** or **risk management** exercise.

risk-free
Involving no **risk**.

risk identification

The process of establishing the existence and definition of a **risk**. Risk identification is the first stage of a **risk assessment** exercise.

riskification [*Semiformal*]

An increasing application of risk concepts to a topic. Internal auditing, for example, became increasingly riskified in the early twenty-first century, through an emphasis on **risk-based auditing**.

risk management

The assessment, evaluation, and monitoring of **risks** in an activity or organization, and the undertaking of appropriate mitigating actions. Risk management aims to be a comprehensive, disciplined process to protect the achievement of an organization's objectives. The monitoring and corrective actions arising from risk management tend to focus on risk-mitigating **procedures** and **internal controls** that reduce risks to within the boundaries of the organization's **risk appetite**. Five strategies of risk mitigation are **risk acceptance**, **risk avoidance**, **risk elimination**, **risk minimization**, and **risk transfer**. It is frequently observed that risk management may increase a corporation's value by reducing risks and, thereby, reducing the **cost of capital**. When undertaken at an organization-wide level, risk management is often called **Enterprise Risk Management**.

risk minimization

A **risk management** technique that reduces the likelihood of occurrence or the potential impact of a **risk**. If a risk has been managed to acceptable levels of **residual risk**, the incremental costs of attempting **risk elimination** may be unacceptably high. Example: an organization may significantly reduce the **shrinkage** levels of its **inventory** by establishing robust security measures around its warehouses. Once an acceptable level of shrinkage has been achieved, it may be counterproductive to incur additional expenditures on security measures, as the additional investment may result in unacceptably small marginal benefits. Only **controllable** risks can be minimized.

risk mitigation

Actions undertaken to reduce, transfer, or eliminate **risks**. See **risk management**.

risk premium
An additional **return (sense 1)** on a high-**risk investment** that **rewards** investors for assuming a high level of risk.

risk ranking
A listing of **risks** in order of severity. Severity may be measured in terms of (i) the likelihood of occurrence of a risk, (ii) its potential financial or operational impact, or (iii) a combination of i and ii. The velocity of risk **crystallization** is often an additional element of a severity assessment.

risk register
A list or repository of **risks** identified in a **risk assessment** exercise.

risk retention
An alternative term for **risk acceptance**.

risk-seeking [*Adj.*]
A readiness to assume significant levels of **risk** to embrace opportunities for high **returns (sense 1)**. Risk-seeking investors are deemed to have high **risk appetites**. Example: a risk-seeker would tend to reject the offer of a certain $100 in favor of a 50 percent chance of receiving $200. Gamblers are classic risk-seekers, driven by the thrill of the wager. Contrast **risk averse**.

risk sharing
A partial or incomplete **risk transfer**.

risk tolerance
See **risk appetite**.

risk transfer
A **risk management** strategy that involves the displacement of a **risk** from one individual, activity, or organization to another. Risk transfer can imply the moving of an entire risk elsewhere, but in practice it often tends to involve the sharing of a risk with another party. **Insurance** cover is a classic risk transfer strategy, and it illustrates that risk transfer strategies can be very costly: In 2001, for example, a guerrilla attack on Sri Lanka's Colombo International

Airport destroyed several commercial airliners and, as a consequence, war-related insurance **premiums** rocketed by over 300 percent for commercial airlines operating to and from that country. Other potential risk transfer parties include **customers, suppliers, agents,** and **joint venture** partners. A transfer of risk does not imply a transfer of **accountability**; an organization's management remains responsible for the results of its risk management strategy.

risk velocity
The speed at which a risk may materialize.

ritualistic audit [*Pejorative*]
An audit of limited value or ambition that is restricted to the performance of predictable, unimaginative **audit tests.** A ritualistic audit might create an impression of reliability and orderliness, but at its worst its overemphasis on formalism does little more than convey hollow signals of **assurance.**

rollover
1 A renewal or prolongation of a **loan** or other **liability. 2** A transfer of **funds** between **investments** after an investment reaches **maturity. 3** A transfer of **taxation** relief between different activities or time periods.

rotation
See **auditor rotation.**

rounding
To restate a fraction or a decimal as the nearest integer (whole number).

roving auditor
An alternative term for **traveling auditor.**

Royal Mail Steam Packet Co. case (1931)
An English criminal case in which a financial auditor was accused of fraudulent collusion with corporate managers in the issuance of a **prospectus** for **debentures.** The case centered on the **disclosure** of the use of **reserves (sense 1).** Although the financial auditor was cleared of the fraud charges, one

consequence of the case was a change in the standard wording to denote **fair presentation** in **financial auditors'** reports—from "true and correct" to "**true and fair.**"

royalty
A payment made for the use of **intellectual property**. Examples: (i) payments by publishers to individuals for the latter's authorship of books, (ii) payments for the use of a **brand** name under a **franchise** agreement, and (iii) payments for the use of an invention for which the inventor holds a **patent.**

royalty audit
An audit of **royalty** transactions for the use of **intellectual property.** Example: an audit of the accuracy of royalty payments by publishers to book authors.

rule
A **regulation** or **procedure** defining **authorized** conduct for a particular activity, the infringement of which carries the risk of disciplinary action.

rules-based approach
[*In corporate governance and ethical standards*] Prescriptive guidelines that require strict compliance and minimize the scope for flexibility of interpretation. Compare **principles-based approach.**

sacred cow [*Cliché*]
An individual, activity, or practice considered immune from change or criticism. The expression derives from the respect and veneration given to the cow in Hinduism. It is often used by auditors, who talk of "slaughtering sacred cows" to convey challenges to received wisdom.

safeguarding
The protection of an asset or activity. The safeguarding of assets is among the main objectives of **internal controls.**

safety margin
See **margin of safety.**

salary
Regular **remuneration** paid to an employee of an organization. In contrast to **wages**, salaries are usually set at fixed amounts and are paid at regular intervals. However, the two terms are often used synonymously.

sale
1 The exchange of an item or service for **money** or for the promise of money. **2** A temporary offer of the sale of a good or service for an unusually low **price.**

sales discount
See **discount (sense 1).**

sales return
An alternative term for **customer return.**

sales tax
An **indirect tax** charged on the selling **prices** of goods and services and collected as **sales** are made. See also **consumption tax** and **value-added tax.**

sample
A collection of items selected from a data **population** for the purposes of inferring characteristics of the whole population. Auditors use sample testing for the interrelated reasons of pragmatism and efficiency, for both **substantive testing** and **compliance testing.** The testing of entire data populations is often impractical, owing to the high volumes of auditable information in large, modern organizations, and sample testing offers a pragmatic alternative through **extrapolation** of the findings of statistically reliable data samples to larger populations. Sampling also offers the auditor efficiencies by reducing inputs to the auditing process (the burdens of **evidence** assessment) in relation to its outputs (**opinions** on levels of **assurance**). Efficiencies of this nature are important cost control measures in **financial auditing**, especially in the supply of audits to aggressively competitive

markets. As Power has suggested, "It is through the problem of sampling that the economic dimensions of auditing become explicit: the auditor must stop checking where the marginal cost exceeds the marginal benefit (incremental confidence) of testing a further item" (Power 1997, 73). However, sample testing is not always an appropriate evidence-gathering technique in auditing, especially in contexts where statistical confidence levels can be assessed only with difficulty, where patterns of **sampling risk** are unpredictable, and where concerns over catastrophic **Black Swan events** are prominent. In such cases, the minimization of inputs to the auditing process is more likely to be based on assessments of **risk** than on the efficiencies of sample testing. See also **judgmental sampling**, **random sampling**, and **statistical sampling**. **2** A representative item or specimen of merchandise given for review to a customer, in the hope of winning future sales.

sampling error / risk

The risk that a sample of data does not accurately represent the population from which it has been extracted. In auditing, sampling risk can lead to incorrect audit opinions.

sanction

A punitive measure taken by one country against another. Often adopted as an alternative to war, sanctions take the form of restrictions of economic activity or cultural exchange. Sanctions are often directed at specific economic sectors, or even at individuals, in contrast to an **embargo**'s more general prohibitions. Example: in September 2022, the US Department of the Treasury's Office of Foreign Assets Control subjected about 300 Russian individuals in leading political, military, and business posts to sanctions in a US protest against Russian involvement in the 2022 Russo-Ukrainian war. See also **boycott**.

Sarbanes-Oxley Act (SOX) (2002)

A legislative act passed in the United States in 2002 that addresses **financial reporting** and related record keeping. Named for two senators, the *Sarbanes-Oxley Act* was designed to shore up investor and public confidence in the regulation of listed corporations (and their **financial auditors**) after the accounting scandals at Enron Corporation (2001) and WorldCom (2002), and the collapse of the **Big Five** accounting firm **Arthur Andersen** (2002). Arthur Andersen had been the financial auditors of both corporations, and it collapsed amid accusations of criminality (Lee 2002).

The *Sarbanes-Oxley Act* has been described as "the most sweeping law on securities regulation and corporate governance since the 1930s" (McElveen 2002, 40). It is complex and wide-ranging, with both criminal and civil law provisions. Among other things, it mandated the creation of the Public Company Accounting Oversight Board to oversee the regulation of the financial auditing process. Another area of particular interest to auditors is the *Act's* stringent requirements for the **independence** of financial auditors (in terms of addressing matters that include **conflicts of interest** and the periodic **rotation** of auditors): Section 303 of the *Act* is titled "Improper Influence on the Conduct of Audits." The *Act* also strengthened the role and responsibilities of **audit committees**, in relation to matters like the handling of **whistle-blowers'** accusations, and it addressed (in Section 401) the disclosure of **off-balance-sheet** activities, a topic that had been central to the accounting fraud at Enron Corporation. **Internal auditors** took a special interest in Section 404 of the *Act*, which requires corporations to file an annual report on **internal controls**. The work undertaken to satisfy the requirements of Section 404 has often been undertaken by internal auditors—not without reason has Section 404 often been referred to informally in auditing circles as the *Internal Auditors' Full Employment Act*. However, some commentators have expressed concern that Section 404 activities belong more to the second of the **Three Lines** model (associated with management monitoring), rather than to the third line associated with internal auditing.

The ramifications of the *Sarbanes-Oxley Act* have had an international dimension, affecting non-US corporations with secondary listings in the United States, as well as US corporations with significant overseas subsidiaries. The *Act* has also influenced related legislation like Japan's 2006 *Financial Instruments and Exchange Act* (often referred to as J-SOX) and regulations like China's 2008 *Basic Standard for Enterprise Internal Control* (**CHINA-SOX**).

savings
1 **Money** accumulated or deferred for future use. Contrast **consumption**. **2** A reduction in costs. Example: "The corporation made immense savings by moving to less expensive rented offices."

savoir-faire [*French*]

"**Know-how.**" This term is often dropped into English sentences as an elegant turn of phrase, yet it coexists with the informal term "savvy" (taken into English, via West Indian creoles, from the French "savoir" or perhaps from its Portuguese or Spanish equivalents).

scam

A **fraudulent** scheme aimed at extracting **money** from **investors** or participants. Example: bogus accident claims are a common **insurance** scam. See also **Ponzi scheme**.

scan

1 The rapid reading of a document to identify its main features. **2** The conversion of a document or image into a digital format for storage.

scatter graph

A depiction of the relationship between two variables set out along x and y axes. From a scatter graph, a pattern of **correlation** between the plotted points may be estimated by visually drawing a line of best fit among the points, or by calculating the correlation with more precision by **regression analysis**. Although easy to prepare and understand, the results of scatter graph analysis are often treated with caution, owing to the subjectivity involved in estimations of lines of best fit.

schedule

1 An alternative term for **audit schedule**. **2** A document that sets out calculations and information relating to **accounting** and **budgeting**. **3** A plan, timetable, or list.

scenario planning

An assessment of the outcomes of alternative courses of action in a range of potential settings or circumstances. Scenario planning is a means of assessing possible actions in decision-making processes, organizational planning, and **risk assessment**. The range of risk scenarios that a **multinational corporation**

may consider when deciding to establish a remote, overseas **branch** may include
(i) **market** risks, (ii) cultural risks, (iii) political risks, (iv) economic risks, and
even (v) the impact of quirks in local **Generally Accepted Accounting Principles (GAAP)**. For each scenario, a review of potential risks and **rewards** could
lead to either **quantitative** or **qualitative** risk assessments (or a combination
of both) used to determine corporate strategies. Successful scenario planning
requires broad and imaginative thinking, and **brainstorming** activities are frequently employed to tease a wide range of ideas from participants in the process.

scope limitation
A restriction on the performance of an audit. The term is usually used in the
context of **financial auditing**, when restrictions of audit **evidence** or **adversarial** auditee behavior prevent an auditor from offering an **unqualified opinion**
on financial statements. **Disclaimers** are common in such circumstances.

scrap
A residue with little or no value from a manufacturing process.

seasonal
Characteristic of (or fluctuating with) specific time periods. Climate patterns,
popular vacation periods, and the timing of religious festivals are typical causes
of seasonal behavior. Example: sales of sunglasses tend to be seasonally related
to sunny weather, and sales of Christmas cards are seasonally related to the
Christmas period.

secured loan
A loan guaranteed against **default (senses 1** and **2)** through the pledge of an
asset. See **mortgage** and **unsecured loan.**

Securities Act (1933)
Legislation in the United States covering the issuance of **securities**, with a
focus on the **disclosure** of information to **investors** in **prospectuses**. The legislation dates from a turbulent era in the US economy, five years after the 1929
stock market crash and during the subsequent Great Depression. It is not to
be confused with the *Securities Exchange Act* of 1934, which dealt with the

secondary trading of securities. The 1933 act made **financial auditors** liable to third parties under civil law for **negligence** related to material **misstatements** in a prospectus and related registration documents. It also provided for criminal penalties for **fraudulent** behavior by auditors (O'Reilly et al. 1998, 5-17, 5-22). See the *Escott v. BarChris Construction Corp.* **case (1968)**.

Securities Exchange Act (1934)

Legislation in the United States covering secondary markets for the trading of **securities**. The legislation was passed a year after the *Securities Act* **(1933)**, which focused on the issuance of securities. It established the Securities and Exchange Commission to oversee and enforce laws on securities. Its importance for **financial auditing** in the United States has been significant; it has required all listed corporations to file audited financial statements, and it has provided for civil remedies and criminal consequences for auditor **negligence** and **fraud.**

security

1 A **financial instrument** traded on a **stock exchange** or similar market. A security may or may not confer a share of ownership in an organization. Examples include **common stock** and some types of **bonds.** **2** **Collateral** for a debt or loan in case of **default (sense 1)** in repayment. **3** The condition of safety from danger or theft.

segment(al) reporting

In the notes to **financial statements**, analyses of activities, assets, or employees by geographical or operation criteria. Segmental reporting is associated primarily with **diversified (sense 2)**, **multinational** corporations.

segregation of duties / segregation of responsibilities

A division of tasks to enhance **internal controls.** Segregations of responsibilities in an organization act as a **preventive** internal control, and often involve a separation of the administering of transactions or the custody of assets from responsibilities for recording the related accounting **transactions**. Example: the practice of **lapping** (concealing the theft of cash by shifting **cash** between **accounts receivable** balances) can be made more difficult by segregating the tasks of (i) handling cash receipts from customers, (ii) recording cash receipts in accounts receivable balances, and (iii) preparation of the accounts receivable ledger. In small organizations, limited numbers of personnel can complicate the achievement of satisfactory segregations of duties. In such cases, close **supervision** can mitigate some of the risks arising from limited segregations of duties. In organizations of all sizes, **collusion** is a significant threat to the integrity of segregations of responsibilities.

self-financing
Capable of generating **money** without the need for external **funding** or **subsidies**.

semifixed costs / semivariable costs
Items of expenditures that have elements of both **fixed** and **variable costs**. Example: the cost of water supplies tends to constitute a fixed charge, irrespective of the level of usage, and a variable element linked to the level of **consumption**.

service
1 [*Noun*] An activity of economic or social value that involves the use of **labor** rather than tangible **goods** or **commodities (sense 1)**. Examples range from providing haircuts to performing audits. **2** [*Noun*] Employment in an organization or involvement in an activity. Example: "His years of dedicated service to the disarmament movement was widely recognized." **3** [*Verb*] To **settle** on time the **installment** payments (including **interest** charges) arising from a **loan**.

service level agreement (SLA)
Formal performance standards agreed on between two or more parties. An SLA normally involves the use of metrics to monitor performance. Example: an information technology support function may include among its objectives the target of resolving requests for assistance within 24 hours. The use of SLAs may be internal to an organization or between separate organizations.

settlement
1 The payment of a sum of **money** to extinguish a **liability**. The term is frequently used in the context of the purchase of **securities**. **2** An agreement to resolve a dispute or problem.

set-up costs
1 The costs of establishing a new activity. **2** See **fixed charge (sense 2)**.

shadow economy
An alternative term for the **underground economy**.

share
1 A unit of ownership in a corporation. See also **common stock** and **equity (sense 1)**. **2** Part of an asset or activity for which ownership or responsibility is divided, or to which various parties have contributed.

shareholder
A British term for **stockholder**.

short-term
1 Relating to a period of less than one year. **2** For some categories of **liability**, such as loans and debts, the short term may be envisioned as a period of three to five years.

short-termism
An attitude that prioritizes short-term over **long-term** rewards. The term tends to be pejorative. The leadership of a corporation may be tempted to enhance short-term **earnings** to impress investors (and to boost its **remuneration**), yet its decisions could cause long-term damage to the corporation's financial health. Example: reductions in **research-and-development** expenditures may boost **net income** in the short term from immediately lower costs, but the reductions may lead to falling revenues in the long term as a result of increasing product **obsolescence**.

shrinkage
A loss of **inventory** (or other **short-term**, **tangible** assets) through damage, theft, or unexplained reasons.

significant [*Adj.*]
1 Large. In auditing, **judgments** on significance may encompass both **quantitative** and **qualitative** considerations. See also **materiality**. **2** Meaningful,

important. Example: "The results of the **inventory** counts showed modest **variances**, but these differences were significant in that they drew attention to a long-running problem of theft in the warehouse."

simple interest

The calculation of **interest** on a sum of **money** by applying an **interest rate** to the original sum of money alone (and not to any accumulated interest). Contrast **compound interest**.

single-tier board

See **board of directors**.

Six Es

An expansion of the traditional **Three Es** of **economy**, **efficiency**, and **effectiveness** in **operational** or **value-for-money** auditing, to include (i) **equity (senses 3** and **6)**, (ii) environmental concerns, and (iii) **ethics**. Despite this use of Six Es by some commentators, the term "Five Es" is also commonly encountered; the five Es are derived by combining equity and ethics into one category.

skepticism

A frame of mind that avoids naive credulity and demands rigorous **evidence** to support conclusions. An auditor's excessive skepticism would lead to undesirable consequences; audits would grind to a halt if auditors were highly suspicious of most of the evidence they encountered. Skeptical challenges to evidence must therefore be based on sound reasons, to avoid an exaggerated reluctance to accept evidential material. It has been noted that a healthy skepticism can reduce the incidence of cognitive bias (Koch, Köhler, and Yankova 2016). See also **anchoring and adjustment bias**, **availability bias**, **conservatism**, **logic in auditing**, and **Occam's Razor**.

skewed [*Adj.*]

Asymmetrical, distorted, or containing bias. Example: a skewed **sample** does not represent the distribution of items in the **population** from which it was extracted. See **sampling risk**.

slippery slope reasoning

A method of reasoning, often fallacious, that assigns attributes to a whole or larger entity on the basis of the attributes of a part of the entity. Example: an auditor may discover the breach of a minor **internal control** in relation to an organization's **petty cash** disbursements, and assume that this minor matter is bound to lead to unacceptable outcomes in other areas. The auditor may thereby reason that organizational toleration of slack controls over petty cash might imply future internal control breaches of increasing severity, perhaps culminating in the organization's **bankruptcy**, unless the descent down the slippery road is halted. Such reasoning tends to be fallacious; the extrapolation of the impact of a relatively innocuous matter to a chain of events of increasing seriousness tends to be based on prancing leaps of faulty logic and on exaggeratedly speculative fears. However, more restrained expressions of slippery slope reasoning, based on **intuition** and kept within reasonable bounds, may have a place in the auditor's tool kit of judgmental assessment methods, as they permit explorations of possible causal links. See also **analogical reasoning**.

smart [*Adj.*]

1 [*Of an individual*] Intelligent, witty. **2** [*Of a device*] Capable of handling simultaneous, sophisticated tasks. **3** [*As an acronym*] Specific, Measurable, Achievable, Realistic, and Time-bound. The SMART acronym summarizes desirable attributes often applied to audit **recommendations** as a measure of their effectiveness. The term, in a slightly different version, dates from 1981, and it has been applied to a range of organizational processes and activities.

smoothing effect

The recording of an **accounting** item over two or more time periods in a manner that avoids sudden variations. Smoothing is often undertaken for simplicity in accounting. However, financial auditors tend to be alert to risks that the "smoothing" of transactions may involve **allocations** of revenues and expenses that contravene the **accruals basis** of accounting.

smuggling

Illegal international trading in goods and services. Smuggling is often a feature of **underground economies**.

social and environmental reporting (SAR)

The reporting by organizations of information relevant to **corporate social responsibility**. SAR covers two distinct areas: the social context of human interactions and environmental concerns. See **Environmental, Social, and Governance**.

social audit

An audit of the impact on society of an activity or organization. Flint describes social auditing as "monitoring the way in which an organisation conducts itself in its various relationships with society—as employer, manufacturer, supplier, member of the community, etc." (Flint 1988, 175n7). The term is also used (especially in Scandinavia and India) to cover the auditing of citizens' rights in the context of the social and ethical responsibilities of the state and its institutions.

soft asset

An alternative term for **intangible asset.**

soft control

An **internal control** based on intangible factors like organizational culture and behavioral patterns. Soft controls focus on topics such as the loyalty, honesty, and ethical values of employees.

soft currency

A **currency** not widely accepted throughout the world. In contrast to a **hard currency**, a soft currency is not freely convertible.

soft loan

A **loan** at a very low **interest rate**, or with concessions to the borrower like slow repayment conditions or interest **holidays.**

solvency

The condition of being able to settle liabilities and debts. Contrast **insolvency.**

sorting

1 [*Of data*] Arrangement in a systematic or logical manner. **2** [*Of a problem; especially British*] Resolution.

source document
1 In auditing, a document that provides **evidence**. **2** An original document that records a **transaction**.

South, the [Global]
A collective term for economically **developing countries**. This term—often rendered in full as "the Global South"—derives from the location of most of the world's developing countries (e.g., in South America and Sub-Saharan Africa) in the Southern Hemisphere. See also the (Global) **North** and the **Third World**.

spam
Unsolicited messages transmitted over the Internet. See also **junk mail.**

special assignment
1 Work undertaken by an auditor that is either an audit of unusually narrow scope or not strictly of an auditing nature. Example: the performance of **due diligence** and other corporate **acquisition** support work. In recent years, definitions of auditing (and, in particular, of **internal auditing**) have become so wide as to blur traditional distinctions between audit and nonaudit work. See also **management advisory services** in the context of financial auditing. **2** An unplanned audit assignment undertaken at short notice or as a matter of urgency.

speculation
1 High-**risk**, **short-term** investing in anticipation of generous returns. The term often has pejorative undertones; critics of speculation view it as an unproductive or parasitical practice that promotes market instability. In contrast, defenders of speculation claim that the exploitation of short-term price differentials is an essential smoothing mechanism to establish equilibrium prices. **2** A conjecture without firm evidence.

splitting
The division of transactions into smaller amounts to avoid internal control **thresholds**. Example: "He split the payment of $11,000 into two smaller amounts

of $9,000 and $2,000 to avoid a stringent **authorization** process for disbursements over $10,000."

spoilage
Waste, evaporation, and defective items arising from a manufacturing process.
Spoilage is not necessarily without value, because waste or **by-products** can
sometimes be reworked or sold for **scrap** value. A certain amount of spoilage,
referred to as **normal spoilage**, is viewed as inevitable in most manufacturing
processes. In contrast, wastage above anticipated or inherent levels is called
abnormal spoilage and is usually expensed as a cost **variance** as incurred.

spot market
A trading system in which items—typically, **commodities (sense 1)** and **currencies**—are purchased for immediate or near-immediate delivery at current
market prices.

spreadsheet
A computer program that permits the **quantitative** analysis of **data**. Spreadsheet data are arranged in a tabular format, with a grid of **cells** that contain
numbers, mathematical formulas, or text. Auditors and accountants often use
spreadsheets to analyze accounting and other information, owing to their ease
and flexibility of use. Spreadsheets are also commonly used in **what-if analysis**;
to support decision-making, the formulas in individual spreadsheet cells are
altered to present alternative outcomes.

square [*Verb*]
1 To multiply a number by itself. Example: 5 squared = 25. **2** To **reconcile**.
Example: "I'm struggling to square these two accounts." **3** To **settle** a **liability**
in full. Example: "She squared the hotel bill."

stagflation
The simultaneous and persistent occurrence of high levels of **inflation** and
unemployment. The term originated in the 1970s from an abbreviated combination of the words "**stag**nation" and "in**flation**."

stakeholder

An individual or institution with a direct or indirect interest in an organization's activities. Depending on the nature of the organization, stakeholders
may include (i) **stockholders**, (ii) **debenture holders**, (iii) **creditors**, (iv) **customers**, (v) **regulatory** authorities, (vi) employees, (vii) local communities
(especially where an organization is a dominant local employer or a potential
polluter), (viii) the government, and (ix) the wider public (especially when
the organization supplies **public goods**, e.g., transportation and health care).
Stakeholder theory contends that an organization's network of rights and
responsibilities stretches wider than the restricted notions captured by **agency
theory**. See also **corporate social responsibility** and **Environmental, Social,
and Governance**.

standard

1 A rule or guideline. Example: **accounting standards**. **2** A defined level of
attainment, proficiency, or quality. International conformity assessment criteria
for an activity or industry sector define standards to be applied consistently in,
among other things, (i) the manufacture and supply of products, (ii) the classification of materials, (iii) the use of terminology, (iv) the provision of services,
and (v) testing and analysis. **3** A mechanism or practice that serves as a quantifiable performance target or as a means of simplifying record keeping. **Standard
costs**, for example, are used both for **budgetary** purposes and to simplify **cost
accounting** procedures. See also **uniform**.

standard audit program

An **audit program** used as a model, **template (sense 2)**, or framework for
undertaking auditing activity. To enhance the efficiency of **audit planning**,
auditors often use standard audit programs that address broad topics, adapting
them to the circumstances of particular audits. The use of standardized audit
programs also encourages a common auditing approach over time and distance.

standard costs

Predetermined costs established for **budgetary** or motivational purposes. **Variances** from standard costs are classified as either **favorable** or **unfavorable**.

standard deviation

In a mathematical **probability** distribution, a measure of data variability or dispersion. See **normal distribution**. A low standard deviation indicates a small spread of data from the mean, while a high standard deviation indicates a wider data spread.

standard opinion

In financial auditing, an alternative term for an **unmodified** or **unqualified** opinion.

standing data

Information that changes infrequently. Standing data can refer to both computerized and manual records. Example: the recording of customer addresses, trading terms, and **credit limits** in an **accounts receivable** system are viewed as standing data.

State Audit Institution (SAI)

An alternative term for **Supreme Audit Institution.**

statement

1 A formal, written declaration. Example: "The corporation issued a press statement to clarify its position." **2** An abbreviated term for **bank statement** or **statement of account.**

statement of account

A summary of the status of accumulated **transactions** between a **creditor** and a **debtor.** Trading organizations tend to issue periodic statements of account to their customers, and banks usually summarize their customer's credit card transactions in the form of periodic statements.

static budget

A **budget** that is not amended irrespective of changes in activity levels. In contrast to a **flexible budget**, a static budget is not adapted to changes in operational circumstances.

statistical sampling

The selection of a representative **sample** of **data** from a **population**. **Probability** theory and random selection techniques are commonly used in statistical sampling, as are margins of error and **sample risk**. Auditors often use statistical sampling techniques to reach conclusions about larger populations of items. Compare **judgmental sampling** and **stratified sampling**. Power has traced the gradual evolution of sampling by financial auditors in the twentieth century—in the 1930s, British auditing textbooks referred to the concept of the "representative sample," but by the late 1960s the emphasis had switched to explicitly statistical sampling (Power 1997, 73). See also **monetary unit sampling**.

statute

1 A written law passed by a legislative body. **2** An organizational rule.

statutory audit

A **financial audit** required by **legislation**. In most countries, corporations and other institutions above a defined size are required to have an annual, financial audit.

step costs

Costs that are fixed (or are only slightly variable) over defined ranges of activity, but that increase at intervals by significant amounts. Example: a manufacturing process may require additional floor space at various levels of production volume, with rental costs increasing significantly as each of the critical production points is exceeded. When plotted graphically, such activity resembles a series of steps. Owing to the step pattern, step costs tend to be stable over short activity ranges and variable over long activity ranges. Compare **semifixed costs**.

sterling

1 [*Noun*] See **pound sterling**. **2** [*Adj.*] Excellent. Example: "He gave ten years of sterling service to the corporation." **3** [*Adj.*] A measure (92.5 percent) of silver purity in a metal alloy.

stewardship

The act of exercising responsibility for the supervision or management of an asset, activity, or organization. In **agency theory**, a steward acts as an **agent**. See also **accountability** and **authority**.

stock

1 An investment in a share of a corporation's capital. See **security**, **common stock**, and **preferred stock**. **2** An alternative (especially British) term for **inventory (sense 1)**.

stockcount

A British term for **physical inventory (sense 1)**.

stockholder

An investor who holds a share of a corporation's **common stock**.

stock option

A **right** to purchase a specified quantity of a corporation's **common stock** within a defined time period at a specified **price**.

stockout costs

Costs that result from the absence of an item from **inventory (sense 1)**. Stock-out costs may include the loss of a **sale** and the costs of disruption to a **manu-facturing** process, depending on the nature of the absent item.

stock warrant

An option to purchase shares at a specified price for a defined time period. Unlike **put options**, stock warrants may have very long **maturity** dates.

straddle [*Verb*]

To extend over both sides of a physical divide or a point in time. The **cutoff** of **accounting** transactions is complicated when the transactions straddle two or more **financial reporting periods**.

straight-line basis

A cost or revenue **allocation** method that provides for equal amounts in each time period. The rationale for using a straight-line basis is that the economic activity of the underlying assets, liabilities or circumstances occurs at a constant rate or pace over time. Example: under straight-line **amortization**, the cost of a fixed asset is expensed in equal annualized amounts over the asset's **useful economic life**, when circumstances suggest that the asset provides constant economic benefits over the relevant period. Contrast the **accelerated method.**

strategy

Actions planned or undertaken to achieve an objective. Strategies are often differentiated from **tactics**, the latter addressing shorter-aim objectives within an overall strategy. However, the two terms are often used interchangeably.

stratified sampling

The selection of **samples** of **data** from a **population** that have been arranged into groups according to defined traits or attributes. See also **judgmental sampling, random sampling**, and **statistical sampling.**

subledger

An abbreviated form of **subsidiary ledger.**

subscription

1 An agreement for the purchase of items at regular intervals, usually through periodic advance payments. Example: "I purchased a subscription to a monthly auditing magazine." **2** A commitment to contribute money to, or to participate in, an activity or cause. **3** A commitment to purchase newly issued **securities. 4** [*Archaic*] A signature on a legal document.

subsequent event

An alternative term for **event after the balance sheet date.**

subsidiary
An organization whose management, operating policies, or **common stock** voting rights are controlled by a **holding company** or **parent organization**. Subsidiaries are **consolidated** into the **financial statements** of parent organizations. See also **sub-subsidiary**.

subsidiary ledger
A group of related **accounts** used to support a main **general ledger** account. Typically, **transaction**-intensive accounts like **accounts receivable**, **accounts payable**, and **petty cash** are recorded in subsidiary ledgers, the totals of which are transferred to general ledger **control accounts**. See also **journal**.

subsidy
A sum of **money** used to support an organization or activity. The term is often used in the context of financial support given by a government to maintain an economic sector or to reduce the sales **prices** of **public goods**. See also **grant**.

substance over form
The notion that the economic substance of a **transaction**, **asset**, or **liability** takes precedence over its legal or technical form. The exploitation of narrow legal and technical interpretations of items is a typical **creative accounting** mechanism to overstate earnings and understate liabilities (e.g., through **off-balance-sheet liabilities**). Consequently, systems of **Generally Accepted Accounting Principles (GAAP)** around the world are increasingly emphasizing the importance of economic reality over legal form.

substantive testing
Auditing procedures that evaluate the accuracy, completeness, and existence of amounts stated in **general ledger** accounts and **financial statements**. Substantive testing involves the auditing of quantifiable amounts, for individual **transactions** as well as accumulated amounts. The substantive testing of the purchase of a **fixed asset**, for example, may include (i) **physical inspection** of the asset, (ii) verification of cost to a **vendor**'s invoice, (iii) verification of delivery documentation, (iv) the matching of invoiced amounts to related

disbursements, and (v) ascertaining that the asset is recorded in an appropriate general ledger account. Substantive testing also includes **analytical review** procedures, in which the auditor evaluates general ledger or financial statement items for reasonableness and assesses the logical nature of their interrelations over time.

Analytical review procedures apart, detailed substantive testing can be time-consuming, and for most audits only a sample of items in a data **population** can usually be tested. Auditors therefore tend to rely on sampling techniques, both **statistical** and **judgmental**, extrapolating the findings from samples to data populations as a whole.

Auditors undertake the **compliance testing** of **internal controls**, on the assumption that satisfactory controls give assurance on the reliability of transactions, and therefore reduce the risks of incorrectly extrapolating the findings of sample tests. In practice, therefore, auditing often comprises a combination of substantive and compliance testing; the balance between the two types of testing is determined by the volume of transactions to be tested and the sophistication and reliability of an entity's internal controls.

sub-subsidiary
A **subsidiary** organization whose **parent organization** is in turn a subsidiary of another entity.

subvention
An alternative term for **subsidy**.

sufficiency
See **evidence**.

sum-of-the-digits
A method of **allocating** costs to time periods based on the formula $n(n+1)/2$, where n represents the number of years to which the cost is to be allocated. Among **amortization** methodologies, the sum-of-the-digits approach results in an **accelerated method** that amortizes the costs of a **long-term** asset more heavily in the early years of its **useful economic life**. Example: for an asset with

a useful economic life of 5 years, the sum of the digits is 15. This is calculated as 5(5 + 1)/2. In the first year, the costs of the asset are amortized by 5/15, in the second year by 4/15, and so on, until the final year's amortization of 1/15.

sunk costs
Unavoidable items of **expenditure** incurred because of a past decision. In contrast to **avoidable costs**, sunk costs cannot be changed. Example: an organization that has committed to a binding agreement for the **long-term** rental of warehousing space incurs the rental expense as a sunk cost for the duration of the rental agreement. Sunk costs are usually excluded from decision-making because future incremental cash flows are considered to be of greater relevance than historical costs. See also **unavoidable costs**.

supervision
The review or monitoring of an activity. In auditing, the supervision of subordinates' work allows for second opinions on audit **judgments** by more experienced auditors. Supervision is a fundamental control over **audit quality**: "Failure to comply with accepted standards by any [audit] staff member can jeopardize the credibility of the entire audit effort" (Lee 1993, 120).

supplier
An alternative (mainly British) term for **vendor**.

supply
The amount of a good or service available to **consumers** in a market. In unregulated markets, **prices** are (in theory) established by the "invisible hand" of the interactions of large numbers of buyer and seller decisions on matters of supply and demand.

supply chain
The interdependent activities, organizations, and individuals participating in the **supply** of an item to its end user. Supply chain management is a means of enhancing the **Three Es** of collaboration between parts of the "chain" of activities. Supply chain disruption can arise from political, economic, weather, and

public health risks. Example: in 2022, as the COVID-19 pandemic receded, supply chain problems resulted in shortages of foodstuffs and **consumer goods** in North America owing to labor disputes, disruptions to transportation systems, and localized, lingering public health restrictions.

Supreme Audit Institution (SAI)
A country's main body for **public-sector auditing.**

surplus
1 An excess of **income (sense 1)** over a level required to pay expenses or satisfy **investor** expectations. **2** An alternative term for **retained earnings.**
3 In **not-for-profit** organizations, an alternative term for **net income** or profit.

suspense account
A **general ledger** account used for the temporary recording of **transactions.** By nature, a suspense account should be regularly cleared of its contents, as it is merely a location for items awaiting analysis, identification, or investigation. Compare **transit account.**

sustainability
The pursuit of economic growth without excessive degradation of the physical and social environment. Sustainability aims at an ecological and social balance to protect resources so that they can extend as far as possible into the future. Example: restrained fishing practices are undertaken to avoid a dangerous depletion of fish stocks and to protect the livelihoods of traditional fishing communities. See also **corporate social responsibility** and **Environmental, Social, and Governance.**

Sutton Rule, the [*Humorous*]
The notion that the most obvious response is likely to be the most accurate. When asked why he robbed banks, Willie Sutton (1901–80), a career criminal, is reported to have responded: "Because that's where the money is." Although Sutton probably never used the phrase, it has been absorbed into business and management folklore. The "rule" emphasizes the importance of perceiving the

big picture of a situation, and of focusing on the most pressing and evident problems. However, it also runs the danger of accepting oversimplified answers to complex situations. See also **Occam's Razor** for a similar concept, expressed more formally.

sweatshop
A working environment characterized by poor working conditions, low wages, and the exploitation and intimidation of employees. Example: in 2020, the British media reported that sweatshop working conditions involving long hours and **compensation** below the official minimum wage were widespread in garment factories in the city of Leicester, England, involving mainly migrant workers from South Asia as both victims and victimizers.

SWOT (strengths, weaknesses, opportunities, and threats) analysis
An approach to **risk assessment** and organizational planning that aims to identify the strong and weak aspects (actual and potential) of an activity or organization. SWOT analysis is often used as a starting point for discussion.

syndicate
A group of individuals or organizations working in combination for a common purpose. Examples: (i) investment bankers create temporary syndicates to promote the sale of **securities**; (ii) pharmaceutical corporations create syndicates to combine their **research-and-development** resources in the creation of new medicines; and (iii) property development and real estate corporations form syndicates to administer and market large property developments. The term is also used in relation to criminal gangs.

system
1 An aggregation of interconnected elements aiming at a common objective.
2 A systematic set of principles for the achievement of an objective.

systematic risk
The part of **risk** that cannot be eliminated through **diversification**. This type of risk is inherent to a particular sector. Contrast **unsystematic risk**.

systemic risk

The **risk** of catastrophic damage to an entire market, sector, or system arising from a relatively minor event. This type of risk is caused and exacerbated by interdependencies and common risk exposures that cause a failure affecting one part of a system to destabilize the system as a whole. The risk of market failure and infrastructure breakdown arising from systemic risk is often reflected in phrases like "too big to fail" and "too connected to fail."

T-account

In **double entry bookkeeping**, a diagrammatic depiction of a general ledger **account** in the form of the letter "T." The T-shape is created by attaching to a horizontal line a vertical line that extends down the page. The left side of the diagram records **debit entries**, and the right side **credit entries**.

tactic

Actions planned or undertaken to achieve objectives within an overall **strategy**. Although tactics are often differentiated from strategies, the two terms are frequently used synonymously.

takeover

An alternative term for **acquisition (sense 2)**.

tangible asset

A **long-term** asset that possesses physical substance. Examples include **property, plant, and equipment**. Contrast **intangible asset**.

tariff

A **customs** duty levied on the **exportation** or **importation** of goods and services. A tariff may be imposed by a government purely for revenue-generating **taxation** purposes, or it can serve political ends. Examples of the latter include (i) trade **protectionism**, (ii) **barriers to entry** to a **market**, (iii) anti**dumping** measures, (iv) retaliation against the tariffs of another country, and

(v) protection of a nation's cultural heritage (by discouraging the export of works of art and items of national treasure).

tax

1 An abbreviated term for **taxation**. **2** An individual category of taxation. Examples: **sales tax** and **value-added tax**.

taxation

The levying of compulsory contributions to state finances. Taxation falls on both individuals and organizations, and it is used (i) to fund **public-sector** expenditures, and (ii) to pursue political policies (like the redistribution of wealth). See also *ad valorem* **tax**, **consumption tax**, **direct taxation**, **indirect taxation**, **progressive tax**, **regressive tax**, **sales tax**, **value-added tax**, and **windfall tax**.

tax avoidance

The legal minimization of **taxation** liabilities. Contrast **tax evasion**.

tax break

A **taxation** concession or exemption given by a government to an individual or organization.

tax effect

The **taxation** consequences of an event or course of action. The term is often used to differentiate between the treatment of an accounting **transaction** under **Generally Accepted Accounting Principles (GAAP)** and its comparative treatment under tax rules.

tax evasion

The illegal avoidance or underpayment of **taxation** liabilities. Contrast **tax avoidance**.

tax haven

A country or territory that offers low **tax rates** or **tax avoidance** benefits to individuals or organizations. The economic impact of tax havens tends to be disproportionate to their size; tax havens are often small island nations or tiny territories at the geographical fringes of major economies.

tax holiday
A period of time during which, by agreement with the relevant authorities, no **taxation** is paid.

tax rate
Taxation applied as a percentage of (i) the income of an individual or organization or (ii) the value of other resources or goods. See **progressive** and **regressive** tax rates.

tax return
A document used to declare information to **taxation** authorities.

tax shelter
An **investment** mechanism that legally offers low **taxation** liabilities. See **tax avoidance**, **tax haven**.

teeming and lading
A British term for **lapping**.

telegraphic transfer [*Archaic*]
An alternative term for **wire transfer**.

template
1 A shaped or patterned item used as an aid in drawing, designing, cutting, and similar activities. Templates are often used in the manual preparation of **flowcharts**. **2** An item that serves as a **standard (sense 2)** or model. **3** A pre-prepared document or computer program used for the periodic recording of **data** of a recurring nature. Example: "He's developed a **spreadsheet** template for the monthly budgetary analysis."

temporary difference
A transitory difference between **income (sense 2)** calculated under **Generally Accepted Accounting Principles (GAAP)** and income calculated according to **taxation** rules. Temporary differences originate in one **fiscal year** and reverse in another. Contrast **permanent difference**.

tender
1 A formal communication or presentation. Example: "He tendered his resignation last week." **2** A competitive process of bidding for a **contract** in order to perform work or to supply goods or services at a defined **price**. Example: "The corporation invited tenders for its annual financial audit."

tenure of financial auditors
See **auditor rotation.**

test
See **audit test.**

test data
1 A **sample** of information used in an **audit test.** **2** Simulated data and transactions used in the **compliance testing** of computerized **application controls.** See also **computer-assisted auditing techniques.**

test of controls
An alternative term for **compliance testing.**

test of design
An **audit test** undertaken to assess the extent to which **internal controls** have been established and are operating. Compare **test of (operating) effectiveness.**

test of detail
An alternative term for **substantive testing**, or for the elements of substantive testing that exclude **analytical review** procedures.

test of (operating) effectiveness
An **audit test** undertaken to assess the extent to which **internal controls** have been operating consistently over time. Compare **test of design.**

thinking outside the box
The generation of fresh, innovative, creative, or unconventional ideas. See the comments on abductive logic under **logic in auditing.**

third party

1 An individual or organization not directly involved in a contract, transaction, or dispute. **2** An individual or organization separate from an auditor or auditee. Audit **evidence** gathered from third parties (e.g., through the **circularization** of an auditee's banks or customers) is generally considered to be strong evidence.

Third World [*Archaic*]

An alternative, rather archaic term for **developing** countries. The term was coined during the Cold War as part of the classification of the world's nations into three groups: (i) communist countries, (ii) economically advanced capitalist countries, and (iii) economically underdeveloped nations that did not fall into either of the preceding categories. The term entered English by translation from the French *tiers monde* but, after the collapse of the Soviet Bloc in the late twentieth century, the notion of the threefold division of nations lost much of its significance. The term has an antiquated ring today.

Three Es

A term used in auditing to denote the **economy**, **efficiency**, and **effectiveness** of operations. **Operational audits** and **value-for-money** audits frequently use these three criteria, which have been summarized succinctly by Sawyer and Vinten (1996, 66–67):

- "Economy is doing things cheap
- Efficiency is doing them right
- Effectiveness is doing the right things."

In recent years, some commentators have expanded the list of criteria from three to six, to create the **Six Es**.

Three Lines Model / three lines of assurance (or defense)

A concept based on military and sporting analogies that envisions concentric layers of **risk management** activities and **risk-mitigating** internal controls to protect an organization. The first and second lines are both the responsibility of management; the first line relates to the operation of day-to-day **internal controls**, and the second to managerial monitoring and **compliance** activities. The third line is the **assurance** provided by **internal auditors**. In other words, the first line refers to managerial functions that own risks; the second to managerial functions that oversee risks; and the third to the internal auditors who review and advise on risks.

The Three Lines Model clearly separates managerial responsibilities from internal auditing. Organizations design, maintain, and monitor systems of risk management and internal control, and the role of internal auditing is to provide opinions on the **effectiveness** and **efficiency** of the managerial systems. Organizations seek to coordinate the three lines to encourage a comprehensive coverage of risks, while eliminating duplications and overlaps in coverage.

The model was developed by the Institute of Internal Auditors (IIA) in 2013, and in July 2020 the IIA dropped reference to the word "defense," to avoid an excessive focus on **risk aversion**. Subsequently, although the word "assurance" has often substituted for "defense," the phrase "three lines of defense" nonetheless remains in common use. Some commentators have added a fourth line of **financial auditing** and regulation to create a **Four Lines Model**.

threshold

1 A **quantifiable** limit beyond which the nature or treatment of an item changes. Example: a **taxation** threshold is a point at which a **tax rate** changes.
2 A quantifiable limit used in the establishment of **internal controls** for **authorization** procedures. Example: the authorization of **disbursements** in an organization may require written approval for transactions over $100. Disbursement thresholds typically define individual employees' authorization rights in line with their organizational responsibilities and status. The splitting of disbursements into smaller amounts is a common means of attempting to circumvent the use of thresholds as an internal control.

ticking

The making of small pencil or ink marks on physical documents to indicate the performance of an **audit test**. Tick marks are traditionally associated with manual audit **work papers**. Different marks may represent different aspects of testing, and the interpretation of the tick marks is usually facilitated by a glossary or key to the audit work performed. Compare **box-ticking** approach.

time-and-motion study [*Archaic*]
A formal **evaluation** of the **efficiency** and **effectiveness** of operational performance in an organization. Time-and-motion studies typically look at the
physical procedures and time taken to perform defined activities, with a view to
simplifying and speeding up the activities reviewed.

time value of money
The notion that a unit of **money** is worth more at the present time than in the
future, owing to the erosion of its future value by **inflation**. The concept is central to **discounted cash flow analysis**.

timing difference
1 An inconsistency between the timing of the recording of an **accounting**
item and the timing of its underlying circumstances. **2** A different treatment of
an **accounting** item between **Generally Accepted Accounting Principles (GAAP)**
and **taxation** rules. See also **permanent difference** and **temporary difference**.

token
1 [*Adj.*] Small, insignificant. Example: "They were offered token payments as
compensation." **2** [*Adj.*] Representative or symbolic. Example: "Please except
this award as a token of our esteem." **3** [*Noun*] A **coupon** or **voucher** that can
be exchanged for a good or service. Example: "She gave him a book token as a
birthday gift."

tolerable rate
1 In financial auditing, a measure of the extent to which the **misstatement** of
an accounting balance does not **materially** misstate the overall **financial statements** of which it forms a part. **2** In **budgeting**, an acceptable divergence of
actual from budgeted results.

tone at the top
The attitudes of an organization's leadership toward **corporate governance,
ethics, risk management**, and **internal controls**. The tone at the top influences the culture of the entire organization; the acceptance by a **board of**

directors of good ethical and governance standards is therefore deemed to be a prerequisite for good corporate governance throughout the organization as a whole. It has been suggested that boards of directors "have the dual role of framing codes of conduct and of living by them" (Cadbury 2002, 38).

Major corporate scandals and misconduct have often derived from a weak governance culture at an organization's highest echelons. "A fish rots from head," as an old proverb says. The term "tone at the top" entered widespread use after the issuance of the 1987 report of the **National Commission on Fraudulent Financial Reporting (the Treadway Commission)**, in which it was used prominently to describe top table attitudes toward internal control.

top-down system
A **hierarchy** in which **authority** and decisions cascade downward in a **chain of command**. See **delegation**.

top table
A slightly informal term for a corporation's main **board of directors** or an organization's similar governing body.

total quality management (TQM)
A management philosophy that stresses the responsibilities of all employees in an organization to contribute to improvements and **efficiencies** in the achievement of organizational objectives. Originally an engineering concept and extended over time to encompass a more holistic range of activities, TQM emphasizes the quality of output and is characterized by a rigorous attention to operational detail. It exhibits some or all of these characteristics: (i) a commitment to **continuous improvement**, (ii) the minimization or elimination of waste and error, (iii) the minimization or elimination of defects in products or services, (iv) a commitment to satisfying (or exceeding) customer expectations, and (v) an ambitious, ongoing search for perfection rather than remaining satisfied with a modest range of acceptable quality. See **quality auditing**.

trace [*Verb*]
1 To uncover something, or the origin of something, through analysis or **investigation**. Example: "He traced the source of the pollution to a production

fault." **2** To describe something in outline form. Example: "At the **audit committee**'s request, he briefly traced an outline of how the fraud was perpetrated." **3** In financial auditing, an **audit test** in which the auditor follows documentary evidence on the details of a transaction or the contents of general ledger accounts. Contrast **vouch.**

traceable costs
Costs that can be related directly to a particular activity or item. Example: the costs of a manufactured product can be traced to **cost centers** or to purchases of specific **raw materials**, and the costs of a business journey can be traced to supporting invoices and receipts.

trade
1 The activity of buying and selling goods and services. **2** A defined sector of economic activity. Example: "She was well known in the furniture trade." **3** Work or related activity that requires skills and training, but which does not enjoy the elite social status of a **profession.**

trade barrier
An impediment to a **free market**. See also **protectionism** and **tariff.**

trade creditors
A British term for **accounts payable.**

trade debtors
A British term for **accounts receivable.**

trademark
1 A registered name, design, or logo that provides legal protection over the use of related goods or activities. See also **patent. 2** A characteristic or distinctive aspect of an individual, item, or activity. Example: "He performed the audit with his trademark charm and eloquence."

trade receivables
A British term for **accounts receivable.**

trade union
A British term for **labor union.**

trafficking
Illegal trading. Trafficking can encompass goods like cigarettes as well as the trading of human individuals.

trail
See **audit trail.**

***tranche* [*French*]**
An installment or portion of **money.** The word is taken from the French noun meaning "slice." Example: "The first *tranche* of the loan will be paid next month."

transaction
An event or interaction between individuals or organizations that has economic or legal consequences. A common example of a transaction is the buying or selling of a good or service.

transfer price
The price of a good or service in **transactions** between parts of a decentralized organization or between **related parties.** Transfer pricing arrangements of **multinational corporations** may be used to shift taxable **income (sense 1)** to low-tax countries, but regulatory authorities closely monitor international transfer pricing practices.

transit account
An alternative term for **suspense account.** However, the terms transit account and suspense account are sometimes differentiated as follows: (i) a suspense account is used for items awaiting analysis or investigation; (ii) a transit account is used for items whose proper **general ledger** classification is subject to an underlying time restriction (e.g., the receipt of a customer **statement of account**).

translation
1 The process of converting financial data between **currencies**. **2** The process of converting written text between languages.

transnational corporation (TNC)
An alternative term for **multinational corporation**.

transparency
The condition of being open to scrutiny. Transparency is widely considered central to best practice in **corporate governance**; but in practice, it is balanced against the confidentiality of information.

traveling auditor
An auditor whose duties are not fixed to a specific location within a **decentralized** organization. See **field auditor**.

Treadway Commission / *Treadway Commission Report*
See the **National Commission on Fraudulent Financial Reporting**.

treasury
1 The administration of the financial assets of an organization, including relationships with financial markets. In modern corporations the responsibilities of treasury functions encompass, among other things, (i) banking, (ii) investments, and (iii) foreign exchange. **2** The finances of a country. **3** [*Archaic*] A physical location at which tangible items of wealth are stored.

Treasury bill (T-bill)
A **short-term**, federal government debt instrument in the United States. T-bills are considered to be virtually **risk-free**, and they tend to carry low **yields**. Compare **Treasury bond (sense 1)**.

Treasury bond
1 [*Upper case initial letter*] A long-term, federal government bond in the United States. Treasury bonds are viewed as safe, low-yield investments, with a

low risk of default (sense 2) and correspondingly low returns. Compare treasury bill. **2** [*Lower case initial letter*] A bond issued by a corporation and subsequently repurchased. See also **treasury stock**.

treasury stock
1 **Common stock** issued by a corporation and subsequently repurchased. See also **treasury bond** (sense 2). **2** The British equivalent of a **Treasury bond** (sense 1).

trend analysis
An alternative term for **horizontal analysis**.

trial balance (TB)
A list of all **account** balances in a **general ledger**. Under the conventions of **double entry bookkeeping**, **transactions** are recorded through corresponding **debit** and **credit entries** of equal value. A trial balance establishes the arithmetic accuracy of the **accounting equation**, under which the total of debit entries equals the total of credit entries. Although a trial balance demonstrates the arithmetical balancing of the general ledger's debit and credit entries, it does not confirm that individual accounting entries have been recorded in the correct accounts. An **extended trial balance** records adjustments and reclassifications made to a basic trial balance in the preparation of **financial statements**.

true and fair view
The traditional British term for the **fair presentation** of **financial statements**. The first element of the phrase—"true"—refers to the existence of financial statement items. The second element—"fair"—refers to the integrity of their measurement and manner of presentation and **disclosure**. In the United Kingdom, expressions used before the adoption of the phrase "true and fair" included (i) "full and fair" and (ii) "true and correct." See *Companies Act* (1948) and the *Royal Mail Steam Packet Co.* case (1931).

trust
1 A legal agreement for a **trustee** to hold or manage assets on behalf of a beneficiary. Trusts involve a distinction in the title to property between trustees

and beneficiaries; the beneficiary is the true owner of the trust's assets, while the trustee holds formal legal title. Trusts are encountered most commonly in legal traditions influenced by the English common law. See also **fiduciary**. **2** [*Archaic*] A somewhat outdated term for a group of corporations with the characteristics of a **monopoly**. See **antitrust** laws. **3** Confidence in the character, reliability, or truth of someone or something.

trustee
A party to a **trust (sense 1)** who holds legal title to the trust's assets and manages the assets on behalf of a beneficiary.

turnover
1 The frequency with which an **asset** is used or replaced during a defined time period. Example: **inventory** turnover is calculated as the total value of the throughput of inventory in a defined period divided by the average value of inventory held. The term is also used to designate the frequency of employee changes in an organization. **2** A British term for **sales (sense 1)**.

two-bin inventory procedure
An **inventory** control procedure in which two locations (bins) store quantities of a **raw material** or product. The first bin is used for day-to-day use, and the second bin serves as a backup buffer of safety stock to avoid **stockouts** while the first bin awaits replenishment.

two-tier board
See **board of directors**.

ultra vires [Latin]
Literally "beyond the powers." This term is used to refer to actions of an individual or organization that exceed the scope of defined legal or organizational **authority**.

unadjusted trial balance
A **trial balance** that lists all **account balances** in a **general ledger** before
the application of adjustments and reclassifications. Compare **extended trial
balance**.

unaudited
Not (yet) subjected to an audit.

unavoidable costs
Items of expenditures incurred irrespective of the discretion of an individual or
organization. Compare **avoidable costs**, **controllable costs**, and **sunk costs**.

uncertainty
The condition of being unknown or incompletely known. In auditing and **corporate governance**, uncertainty is sometimes distinguished from **risk** on this
basis: (i) uncertainty is a situation in which the outcomes of various courses of
action are either unknown or cannot be estimated, while (ii) risk is a situation
where outcomes can be estimated using **probability** theory. This differentiation
of uncertainty and risk appears to have originated more than a century ago,
with the writings of the economist Frank Knight (1885–1972). Knight portrayed
risk as measurable, and therefore as amenable to quantification and attempts to
control it, in contrast to uncertainty, which was not measurable and therefore
demanded qualitative responses (Knight 1921). Contrast **certainty**.

unconsolidated
Not yet subjected to **consolidation accounting**.

uncontrollable risk
A **risk** that cannot be mitigated, transferred, or eliminated. Contrast **controllable risk**.

underground economy
Economic activity undertaken outside official channels. **Transactions** in the
informal economy are often designed to circumvent laws, **regulations**, and **taxation**. They also tend to be settled in cash to reduce **traceability**. Activities in an

underground economy are normally excluded from a country's **gross domestic product** statistics, unless such activities are large in comparison with the formal economy.

understandability

The comprehensibility of a matter. Understandability is central to auditing and **auditability** in two senses: (i) Auditors are unable to perform satisfactory auditing duties if the subject matter of an audit is beyond their comprehension; see also **outside expertise**. (ii) The reliability of audit **evidence** should allow for consistent interpretation by different auditors in replicated tests. In addition, understandability is central to the **fair presentation** of **financial statements**.

understatement

The inadequate **quantification** or description of an item. The term is often used in the context of incorrectly measured items in **financial statements**. Contrast **overstatement**.

undertaking

1 An **enterprise** or activity. **2** A commitment or promise to perform an action.

underwriting

1 The process of accepting the **risks** and potential **liabilities** arising from an **insurance policy** or **guarantee**. Underwriters are compensated for their risks by the payment of **premiums (sense 1)**. **2** An agreement to purchase all unsold **securities** arising from a new issuance of securities.

undue professional care

See **due professional care**.

unearned income / unearned revenue

Revenue not yet earned in a **financial reporting period**, but for which the related cash has already been received. In line with the **accruals basis** of accounting, unearned revenue is recorded in **current** or **long-term** deferred revenue accounts (classified among **liabilities**) in the **balance sheet**, and is released to the **income statement** in the accounting periods to which it relates.

Typical examples of unearned revenue are income from **rents (sense 1)** and **subscriptions**.

unemployment
The condition of individuals who are available for work yet unable or unwilling to obtain fixed employment.

unfavorable variance
In **budgeting**, the incurring of larger-than-anticipated costs or the earning of lower-than-anticipated revenues. An unfavorable **variance** indicates that performance is worse than expected. Contrast **favorable variance**.

unfunded [*Adj.*]
Without **money** needed to achieve a defined purpose.

uniformity
The condition of having minimal or no variations. Both **Generally Accepted Accounting Principles (GAAP)** and **Generally Accepted Auditing Standards (GAAS)** encourage uniform bases for the preparation of **financial statements**. This uniformity is sought between organizations and between **financial reporting periods** for a specific organization.

unit
A defined magnitude of quantity that is undivided into smaller elements for analytical or operational purposes. Example: in production processes, manufactured items are often identified as units (which typically represent a finished **consumer good**), and production unit volumes drive **absorption costing** methodologies. In auditing, an **audit universe** is analyzed into **auditable** units for **risk assessment** and planning purposes.

unitary board
See **board of directors**.

unit cost
Total production costs attributable to individual **units** of **production** output. See **absorption costing**.

United States v. Arthur Young & Co. et al. case (1984)

A legal case noted for its strong affirmation of the financial auditor's responsibilities for the **public good**. The case dealt with the demand of tax authorities for access to a financial auditor's **work papers**. The judicial reasoning emphasized the widest possible conception of the public interest in the outcomes of a financial audit: the financial auditor "assumes a public responsibility transcending any . . . relationship with the client, . . . [and financial auditing] owes fidelity to the public trust" (cited by Chambers 1995, 944–45).

United States v. Simon case (1969)

A legal case in the United States significant for its finding that a **financial auditor**'s **professional** duty of care may, in some circumstances, exceed the formal requirements of **Generally Accepted Auditing Standards (GAAS)**. The case centered on an auditor's limited inquiries into loan transactions between an **auditee** and a corporation affiliated with the auditee. The auditors defended their actions on the grounds of adherence to GAAS, but the court found that the circumstances had warranted more extensive inquiries than are usually required under GAAS into the recoverability of the loan transactions with the affiliate corporation.

unmodified opinion

In **financial auditing**, an alternative term for an **unqualified opinion**. Contrast **modified opinion**.

unqualified opinion

A **financial auditor**'s **opinion** that an entity's **financial statements** conform with **Generally Accepted Accounting Principles (GAAP)** and offer a **fair representation** of the entity's financial position, the results of its operations, and changes in cash flows. The unqualified opinion is often described as a "clean opinion." Compare **qualified opinion**, **adverse opinion**, and **disclaimer**.

unrealized gain or loss

The increase (gain) or decrease (loss) in the value of an owned **asset**. Once the asset in question is sold, the gain becomes realized. See **paper profit** and contrast **realized gain or loss**.

unsecured loan

A loan that is not guaranteed against **default (senses 1** and **2)** through the pledge of an asset. Contrast **secured loan**.

unsystematic risk

Risk associated with a specific organization or financial instrument. Unsystematic risk may be mitigated by **diversification**. Contrast **systematic risk**.

useful economic life

A period of time over which an asset provides economic benefits to its owner. The costs of **long-term** assets are **amortized** over their useful lives. See also **wasting asset**.

utility

1 The benefit, pleasure, or satisfaction obtained by consuming a product or enjoying a service. See also **diminishing returns** and **value (sense 1)**. **2** The usefulness of an item. **3** An abbreviation for **public utility**.

validity

1 The state of being accurate and relevant. Audit **evidence** is valid only if it relates directly to the supporting or refuting of an audit **objective**. **2** [*Of a contract*] The condition of being legally binding.

value

1 The monetary worth of an item. See **book value**, **market value**, **price**, and **wealth**. **2** The **qualitative** worth of an item, activity, or individual. Example: "Her experience has made her of great value to the audit department." **3** An ethical principle or standard of behavior. Example: "She has impeccable values."

value-added tax (VAT)

An **indirect tax** on goods or services collected at incremental stages of **production**, distribution, performance, and consumption. The burden of the VAT falls on the final consumer as part of the selling price of the good or service, and it is often characterized as a **regressive** form of taxation. See also **consumption tax** and **sales tax.**

value-at-risk (VAR)
A measure used by financial institutions to assess the extent of possible financial losses over a defined time period. VAR focuses on market and credit risks.

value-for-money (VFM) auditing
An alternative term for **operational auditing** or **performance auditing**. The term is frequently used in the United Kingdom, in the **public-sector** context, for audits that assess the **Three Es** of **economy**, **efficiency**, and **effectiveness**. Power (1997, 44) has attributed a politicized and rhetorical use to notions of VFM, describing VFM as comprising the Three Es, "in conjunction with . . . populist appeals to notions of empowerment and service quality" (Power 1997, 44).

value in use
The **present value** of an asset's economic benefits. Value in use is calculated by discounting future cash flows attributable to the use of the asset, including the asset's estimated disposal proceeds.

variable budget
An alternative term for **flexible budget.**

variable costs
Items of expenditures that are linked closely to levels of activity. Example: the costs of **raw materials** in the manufacture of a product tend to be related closely to production levels. Contrast **fixed costs.**

variance
1 In **budgeting** and **standard costing**, the difference between actual and anticipated costs or revenues. Variances are often categorized as positive or negative, or **favorable** or **unfavorable**. **2** A measure of the dispersion of a **probability** distribution, calculated by squaring the **standard deviation.**

vendor
A **supplier** of goods or services. Organizations manage their **credit** transactions with vendors through **accounts payable** records.

venture capital
Sources of finance for new business enterprises that carry high **risks** and potentially high **rewards (sense 1)**.

verification
An **inspection** of an activity or item to obtain **evidence** of its existence and condition. Verification is an important **substantive audit test**: "depending on the . . . circumstances, verification takes place intuitively or by instruction; instantly or over time; expertly or crudely; explicitly or implicitly; and formal[ly] or informal[ly]. Whatever the mechanism, however, verification . . . is conducted with the objective of establishing the degree of correspondence between [an] object of doubt and some acceptable criteria by which it can be judged" (Lee 1993, 20). The condition of being capable of verification in an audit implies that different auditors would likely reach similar conclusions on the basis of the same evidence in replicated testing. See also **physical verification.**

Verification is a vital component of auditing but it is not synonymous with auditing, because many users of the term "verification" take it to mean absolute or near-absolute **assurance** (or "proof beyond all doubt," in the words of Mautz and Sharaf 1961, 50). Auditing, in contrast, seeks only **reasonable** assurance; an auditor may, for example, verify only through sample testing the existence of a large number of assets. Verification is therefore best understood as one category of auditing technique. In addition, although the term "verification" has also frequently been used synonymously with "examination" in an auditing context, there have been attempts to differentiate the terms—as outlined in the entry for **examination (sense 1).**

vertical analysis
The use of one **financial statement** item as a basis for comparative purposes. Example: if the value of **gross sales** in an **income statement** is set at 100 percent, the various expenses within the income statement can be expressed as a percentage of gross sales. Compare **horizontal analysis.**

vertical integration
A **business combination** of an organization with its suppliers or its customers. Example: a corporation might acquire its suppliers of **raw materials** and components to control and reduce **risks** in **supply chains**.

virus
1 An organism, typically made up of nucleic acid coated in protein, that causes infection or disease. The spread of viruses can present a serious operational **risk** to organizations. Example: starting in late 2019, the COVID-19 pandemic resulted in severe damage to social and economic life around the world and led to a significant death toll. **2** A program defect or code that corrupts computer software programs. The potentially devastating risks of computer viruses can be prevented through antivirus software programs, and mitigated through the adequate **backup** of data.

visible asset
An alternative term for **tangible asset**.

volatility
The condition of being prone to rapid and unpredictable changes, with resulting high **risks**. Example: "The volatility of the oil markets is legendary." See **Black Swan event**.

volume
1 The quantity of an item, or the amount of space occupied by an item. **2** The loudness of a noise. **3** [*Of books and magazines*] A collection of publications within a larger series or sequence.

vouch [*Verb*]
In financial auditing, an **audit test** in which the auditor seeks documentary evidence to support the contents of general ledger accounts. Contrast **trace (sense 3)**.

voucher
1 A document that confers an economic benefit. Example: a retail organization may give customers vouchers that entitle them to **discounts (sense 1)**. See

also **coupon** and **token (sense 3)**. **2** A **hard copy** document used as part of an **internal control** system. Example: an organization may control its **disbursements** by linking to every vendor **invoice** a sequentially numbered voucher that records written authorization of the payment. **3** An alternative term for **receipt (sense 1)**.

wage
Remuneration paid to an employee. Wages are differentiated from **salaries** in several ways: (i) wages often vary in accordance with the amount of time worked, or a measure of output, while salaries tend to be fixed amounts; (ii) more often than is the case with salaries, wages are frequently paid in cash rather than by **check** or **wire transfer**; and (iii) wages are sometimes paid daily or weekly, in contrast to monthly salaries. However, the terms are frequently used interchangeably.

walk-through test
In auditing, a **compliance** test of operational **internal controls** and processes. Walk-through tests involve the **tracing** of a **transaction** (or a **sample** of transactions) through sequential accounting and operational processes. Through analysis of the **audit trail** in the walk-through test, the auditor seeks to obtain **evidence** of the reliability of internal controls and operational procedures.

warehouse
A storage facility for **inventory**.

warrant
1 An abbreviated term for **stock warrant**. **2** A document that authorizes police or other law enforcement agents to arrest an individual, search a building, or seize assets. **3** A legally binding **guarantee** to support an activity or **transaction**. **4** In some **public-sector** organizations, an instruction that authorizes a **disbursement**.

warranty

An undertaking or guarantee made by the seller of a good or service to compensate a customer for any deficiencies in the integrity of the good or service within a defined time period.

waste

1 An alternative term for **spoilage** arising from production processes. The term is sometimes restricted to spoilage with no resale value, but the terms spoilage and waste are often used synonymously. See **scrap**. **2** An alternative term for **shrinkage**.

wasting asset

A **fixed asset** with a limited **useful economic life**. Wasting assets are normally subjected to **amortization** charges.

watchdog, auditor as

The notion that **financial auditing** is an independent yet cooperative search for assurance rather than an **investigative** activity. Contrast **bloodhound**. The metaphor of a watchdog emphasizes the auditor's activity as being characterized by surveillance and the safeguarding of the public interest in financial reporting. The terms "bloodhound" and "watchdog" are associated with the *Kingston Cotton Mill Company* case.

wealth

1 The possession of items of **value (sense 1)**. Wealth covers **money** and **tangible assets**, as well as **intangible** assets like **intellectual capital**. **2** An abundant or generous amount of something. Example: "She has a wealth of experience in internal auditing."

wear and tear

A reduction in the value of a **fixed asset** owing to damage and depletion experienced through its normal use. Wear and tear is a major contributory factor in **amortization**. See also **impairment (senses 1 and 2)**.

weighted average

The **mean** of a number of items that has been calculated to reflect the individual items' relative importance. For example, a corporation that purchases **inventory** of the same **raw material** on two separate dates, with 100 units at $10 per unit and 50 units at $5 per unit, calculates the weighted average of the inventory as $8.33. This represents $[(100 \times 10) + (50 \times 5)]/150$.

weighted average cost of capital (WACC)

A corporation's **cost of capital** derived from—and **weighted** in proportion to—the capital structure of its **equity** and **debt finance**.

weighting

1 The calculation of amounts of various items in proportion to their importance. See **weighted average**. **2** To regard or treat with importance or preference. Example: "The organization weighted its purchases toward European suppliers."

what-if analysis

A form of **quantitative** analysis in which assumptions are flexed and the resulting outcomes compared. Example: an analysis of the potential profitability of a manufactured product may be analyzed for a range of sales levels to illustrate the resulting effects on **income (sense 1)**. What-if analysis is a common decision-making tool, and it has been facilitated by the increasing sophistication of **spreadsheets**.

whistle-blower

An individual who publicly exposes improper or illegal activities in an organization. The coining of the term is often attributed to the US consumer protection campaigner Ralph Nader (b. 1934) in the 1970s, as an alternative to pejorative terms like spy, mole, informer, and traitor. However, it seems to have been first used in the nineteenth century, and is based on the police practice of those times of blowing a whistle to bring attention to the commissioning of a potential crime or to the presence of a criminal.

Whistle-blowers sometimes face ambiguities and moral dilemmas; they are often praised for identifying matters of public interest, including misconduct and illegality, but they are often accused of organizational disloyalty and breaching institutional confidentiality. In our age of the so-called **organization man or woman**, to blow the whistle on improper activities can be a brave act. Social ostracism or even dismissal can be the consequences. Example: the whistle-blowing actions of internal auditor Cynthia Cooper at WorldCom Corporation at the beginning of the twenty-first century were celebrated in the popular media (Carozza 2008).

white-collar [*Adj.*]
Relating to office work, as distinct from manual work. Contrast **blue-collar**.

white-collar crime
The undertaking of **fraudulent** or other illegal activity by individuals engaged in clerical or other nonmanual occupations. The term is often used in the context of nonviolent yet serious financial crime like (i) **false accounting**, (ii) **tax evasion**, (iii) **insurance** fraud, and (iii) **money laundering**.

wholesaling
The arrangement of selling large volumes of goods to businesses for resale to the final consumer. Compare **retailing**.

widget [*Humorous*]
A standardized gadget or manufactured product of small size and low value. Example: "She made a fortune from manufacturing and selling millions of widgets."

Willie Sutton Rule, the
See **Sutton Rule**.

windfall profit
Large-scale **income (sense 2)** of an unexpected, exceptional, or sudden nature.

windfall tax

A one-off **taxation** charge on the profits of a corporation or economic sector, often justified on the grounds of unusual or exceptional circumstances. Example: the *Crude Oil Windfall Profit Tax Act* of 1980 in the United States was enacted after oil producers profited from a period of unusually high oil prices in the 1970s. The term carries pejorative overtones, suggesting political and economic opportunism in fiscal governance, and politicians increasingly tend to avoid the term. Example: in 2022, the British government announced a 25 percent **levy** on the "extraordinary" profits of oil and gas corporations in the United Kingdom, choosing to avoid the phrase "windfall tax" in favor of the somewhat euphemistic **levy.**

winding up

The closure of an organization or completion of an activity. See also **liquidation.**

window dressing

A **creative accounting** technique that manipulates transactions around a **cutoff date** to improve the appearance of a **balance sheet**. Example: an organization may delay payments until after a sensitive financial reporting date to boost cash balances and **liquidity** ratios at that date. Around the world, systems of **Generally Accepted Accounting Principles (GAAP)** aim to reduce the scope for window-dressing techniques. See **channel stuffing.**

wire transfer

An electronic transfer of **money** directly from one bank account to another, without recourse to the physical handling of **cash** or **checks.**

Wirtschaftprüfer [German]

A term—used in Germany, Austria, and Switzerland—that approximates to **Certified Public Accountant** or **Chartered Accountant.**

withholding tax

1 Deductions of **taxation** made by an employer from an employee's **salary** or **wage** and paid directly to taxation authorities. **2** Deductions of taxation from **dividend** and **interest** income paid to a country's nonresidents.

working capital
Short-term assets that finance an organization's day-to-day operations. Working capital comprises **cash**, **accounts receivable**, **inventory**, and **prepaid expense**s.

working papers
1 An alternative term for **work papers**. **2** A document that shows detailed calculations to support a **general ledger** balance or similar item.

work-in-process (WIP)
1 The partially completed outputs of a **manufacturing** process. Contrast **raw materials** and **finished goods**. **2** A partially completed, **long-term** contract.

work-in-progress (WIP)
A British term for **work-in-process**.

work papers
Records that document audit **evidence** and **audit tests**. Work papers are evidence to support the conduct and conclusions of an audit—in **financial auditing**, they may be reviewed in court in cases of claims of **negligent** or unsatisfactory audit work. In internal auditing, the Professional Practices Framework of the Institute of Internal Auditors requires adequate documentation of auditing work. See also **ticking**.

worksheet
See **spreadsheet**.

write-down
A reduction of the **book value** of an **asset** owing to a decrease in its quality or economic worth. Contrast **write-off** and **write-up**.

write-off
The elimination of a **balance sheet** item by direct transfer to an **income statement**. Example: an irrecoverable **accounts receivable** balance owed by a **bankrupt** customer is normally eliminated by writing off the item. (In contrast, the

existence of a customer receivable balance of doubtful yet possible recovery is normally reflected in the creation of an **allowance for doubtful debts**.)

write-up
An increase in the **book value** of an **asset**. This may occur when, for example, the discovery of a valuable natural resource increases the value of land. Contrast **write-down** and **write-off**.

yardstick
A comparative measurement used to assess an organization or activity. Example: an industry average of employee costs as a proportion of sales may be used as a yardstick to measure the reasonableness of an organization's payroll expenditures. See also **benchmarking**.

year end
1 The end of the calendar year—that is, December 31. **2** The end of a **financial reporting period** of twelve months' duration, whether or not it coincides with the calendar year's end.

Yellow Book, the
A common name for **Government Auditing Standards** in the United States.

yield
1 The **return (sense 1)** from an investment, expressed as a percentage of the investment's original or nominal value. Yields may be calculated on a nominal basis or adjusted for **interest rate**s and **inflation**. **2** The output from an agricultural or industrial process.

Zeitgeist [German]
The prevailing conventional wisdom or the mood of the times. In German, the term literally translates as "the spirit of the times." It can describe a vast range of matters, ranging from catwalk fashion trends to social attitudes to auditing.

The first letter of the word is often in upper case, to reflect the spelling convention for all German nouns.

zero-base budgeting (ZBB)
A **budgeting** methodology based on the fresh recalculation of costs for each budgetary period. In contrast to traditional budgeting, which is based on historical assumptions and incremental changes over the years, ZBB requires new cost estimates for each budgeting period, irrespective of historical performance. ZBB also frequently uses **cost-benefit analysis** to determine optimal resource allocations in an organization.

zero-sum game
A branch of **game theory** for the systematic analysis of competitive strategies for the optimal selection of alternative courses of action, in which the participants have conflicting interests. In a zero-sum game, one participant's gain is another participant's loss, and there is no basis or rationale for cooperation. The division of an organization's fixed **budget** among competing participants is an example of a zero-sum game.

Appendix A: Abbreviations and Acronyms

The abbreviations and acronyms listed here cover individual entries in the text. The list follows the format of the entries—for example, in the italicization of non-English words. The alphabetical order of the list does not always follow the sequence of the underlying entries; for example, "BCP" precedes "BOM," despite "business continuity planning" coming after "bill of materials."

AA	Arthur Andersen
AG	Auditor General
BCP	business continuity planning
BOM	bill of materials
BPO	business process outsourcing
BPR	business process reengineering
CA	chartered accountant
CAE	Chief Audit Executive
CAPM	capital asset pricing model
CAATs	computer assisted audit techniques
CEAVOP	[*assertions in financial statements*] completeness, existence, accuracy, valuation, ownership, and presentation
CEO	Chief Executive Officer
CFO	Chief Financial Officer
CFPOA	Corruption of Foreign Public Officials Act
CI	continuous improvement
CIA	Certified Internal Auditor
	also Chief Internal Auditor
COGS	cost of goods sold
COS	cost of sales
COSO	Committee of Sponsoring Organizations (of the Treadway Commission)
CPA	Certified Public Accountant
	also critical path analysis
CRSA	Control Risk Self-Assessment

CSA	Control Self-Assessment
CSR	corporate social reporting
	also corporate social responsibility
CV	*curriculum vitae*
DBMS	database management system
DCF	discounted cash flow analysis
DUS	dollar unit sampling
EMH	efficient markets hypothesis
EOQ	economic order quantity
EPS	earnings per share
ERM	enterprise risk management
ESG	Environmental, Social, and Governance [assurance]
EV	expected value
FCPA	Foreign Corrupt Practices Act
FIFO	first-in first-out
FMCG	fast-moving consumer goods
FV	future value
FY	fiscal year
	also financial year
GAAP	Generally Accepted Accounting Principles
GAAS	Generally Accepted Auditing Standards
GAGAS	Generally Accepted Government Auditing Standards
GAS	Government Auditing Standards
GDP	gross domestic product
GL	general ledger
	also grand livre
HP	hire purchase
IRR	internal rate of return
ISA	International Standards on Auditing
JIT	just-in-time
J-SOX	Financial Instruments and Exchange Act (2006)
KPI	key performance indicator
L/C	letter of credit
LDC	less-developed country
LIFO	last-in first-out

MAS	management advisory services
MNC	multinational corporation
MUS	monetary unit sampling
NAS	nonaudit services
NED	nonexecutive director
NIFO	next-in first-out
NGO	nongovernmental organization
NPV	net present value
NRV	net realizable value
OBS	off-balance-sheet
PCG	*plan comptable général*
P/E ratio	price/earnings ratio
PI	perpetual inventory
POS	point of sale
R&D	research and development
RBA	risk-based auditing
SAI	state audit institution
	also Supreme Audit Institution
SAR	social and environmental reporting
SDG	Sustainable Development Goals
SLA	service level agreement
SMART	Specific, Measurable, Achievable, Realistic, and Time-bound
SOX	*Sarbanes-Oxley Act* (2002)
SWOT	strengths, weaknesses, opportunities, and threats
TB	trial balance
T-bill	Treasury bill
TNC	transnational corporation
TQM	total quality management
VAT	value-added tax
VAR	value-at-risk
VFM	value for money
WACC	weighted average cost of capital
WIP	work-in-process / work-in-progress
ZBB	zero-base budgeting

Appendix B: Auditing and the Law

Legislation

Bribery Act [UK, 2010]

Companies Act 1948 [UK, 1948]

Companies Act 2013 [India, 2013]

Corruption of Foreign Public Officials Act (CFPOA) [Canada, 1999]

Financial Instruments and Exchange Act (J-SOX) [Japan, 2006]

Foreign Corrupt Practices Act (FCPA) [US, 1977]

Sarbanes-Oxley Act (SOX) [US, 2002]

Securities Act [US, 1933]

Securities Exchange Act [US, 1934]

Case Law

Allied Crude Vegetable Oil Refining Corporation [US, 1963]

Escott v. BarChris Construction Corp. [US, 1968]

Irish Woollen Company Ltd v. Tyson and Others [UK, 1900]

Kingston Cotton Mill Company [UK, 1896]

Leeds Estate Building and Investment Company [UK, 1877]

London and General Bank case [UK, 1895]

McKesson and Robbins [US, 1939]

Royal Mail Steam Packet Co. [UK, 1931]

United States v. Arthur Young & Co. et al. [US, 1984]

United States v. Simon [US, 1969]

Appendix C: Non-English Terms

The non-Englsh terms listed here appear as entries in the dictionary. Although some of the terms have been acclimatized to a degree into English, all recognizably non-English words have been included here for the sake of completeness. In accord with the format of the entries, non-English terms and names of languages are in italics.

ad hoc [*Latin*] spontaneous, one-off

ad valorem [*Latin*] in proportion to the value

caveat [*Latin*] warning, limitation, caution

caveat emptor [*Latin*] let the buyer beware

challan [*Hindi*] voucher, form, document

comptroller [*French*] financial controller

crore [*Hindi*] ten million

curriculum vitae [*Latin*] a summary of an individual's work experience, abilities, educational achievements, and professional qualifications, used typically for job applications

de facto [*Latin*] in practice

de jure [*Latin*] in law

dottore commercialista [*Italian*], similar to Certified Public Accountant

ex ante [*Latin*] before an event

ex gratia [*Latin*] discretionary

expert-comptable [*French*], similar to Certified Public Accountant

ex post [*Latin*] after an event

grand livre [*French*] general ledger

gratis [*Latin*] free of charge

inter alia [*Latin*] among other things

kaizen [*Japanese*] continuous improvement

kanban [*Japanese*] ticket, card (used to display inventory in lean manufacturing systems)

lakh [*Hindi*] one hundred thousand

lex [*Latin*] law

modus operandi [*Latin*] manner of operating

pari passu [*Latin*] in proportion, at an equal rate of progress

per annum [*Latin*] annually

per capita [*Latin*] by head of population

per diem [*Latin*] daily

plan comptable général [*French*] chart of accounts

prima facie [*Latin*] at first sight

pro forma [*Latin*] for form's sake, as a matter of form

pro rata [*Latin*] on a proportionate basis

quasi- [*Latin*] almost, similar to—a prefix

quid pro quo [*Latin*] something for something, an exchange of favors

Registeraccountant [*Dutch*], similar to Certified Public Accountant

résumé [*French*] a summary of an individual's work experience, abilities, educational achievements, and professional qualifications, typically used in job applications

savoir-faire [*French*] know-how

tranche [*French*] slice, installment

ultra vires [*Latin*] beyond one's power or authority

Wirtschaftprüfer [*German*] similar to Certified Public Accountant

Zeitgeist [*German*] the mood of the times

References

Abbott, Andrew. 1988. *The System of the Professions: An Essay on the Division of Expert Labor*. Chicago: University of Chicago Press.

Akpanuko, Essien, and Ntiedo Umoren. 2018. "The Influence of Creative Accounting on the Credibility of Accounting Reports." *Journal of Financial Reporting and Accounting* 16, no. 3.

American Accounting Association. 1973. *A Statement of Basic Accounting Concepts*. Sarasota: American Accounting Association.

Applebaum, Deniz, and Robert A. Nehmer. 2017. "Using Drones in Internal and External Audits: An Exploratory Framework." *Journal of Emerging Technologies in Accounting* 14, no. 1: 99–113.

Baxter, William T. 1996. *Accounting Theory*. New York: Garland.

Beasley, M. S., J. V. Carcello, and D. R. Hermanson. 1999. *Fraudulent Financial Reporting: 1987-1997—An Analysis of US Public Companies*. New York: Committee of Sponsoring Organizations of the Treadway Commission.

Black, Robert A. 2019. "Accounting and the Auditing Function in Economic History: Transaction Costs, Trust, and Economic Progress." *Journal of Markets & Morality* 22, no. 1: 41–65.

Blix, Hans. 2004. *Disarming Iraq*. New York: Pantheon.

Brink, Victor Z. 1977. *Foundations for Unlimited Horizons: The Institute of Internal Auditors 1941-1976*. Altamonte Springs, FL: Institute of Internal Auditors.

Bryce, Robert. 2002. *Pipe Dreams: Greed, Ego, and the Death of Enron*. New York: PublicAffairs.

Cadbury, Adrian. 2002. *Corporate Governance and Chairmanship: A Personal View*. Oxford: Oxford University Press.

Carozza, Dick. 2008. "Extraordinary Circumstances: An Interview with Cynthia Cooper." *Fraud Magazine*, March–April.

Chakrabarti, Kisor Kumar. 1995. *Definition and Induction: A Historical and Comparative Study*. Monographs of the Society for Asian and Comparative Philosophy, 13. Honolulu: University of Hawaii Press.

Chambers, Raymond John. 1995. *An Accounting Thesaurus: 500 Years of Accounting*. Oxford: Pergamon.

Chin, Angelina. 2022. *Recognizing and Mitigating Cognitive Biases: A Threat to Objectivity*. Lake Mary, FL: Internal Audit Foundation.

Cohen Commission Report [*Report, Conclusions, and Recommendations of the Commission on Auditors' Responsibilities*]. 1978. New York: American Institute of Certified Public Accountants.

Deepal, Aluthgama Guruge, and Ariyarathna Jayamaha. 2022. "Audit Expectation Gap: A Comprehensive Literature Review." *Asian Journal of Accounting Research* 7, no. 3.

Dennis, Ian. 2015. *Auditing Theory*. Abingdon, UK: Routledge.

Dicksee, Lawrence Robert. 1902. *Auditing: A Practical Manual for Auditors, 5th Edition*. London: Gee.

Dierynck, Bart, and Christian Peters. 2022. "Auditor Task Prioritization: The Effects of Time Pressure and Psychological Ownership." Paper from Social Science Research Network. https://papers.ssrn.com/sol3/papers.cfm?abstract_id=3450363.

Evans, Jonathan St B. T. 2017. *Thinking and Reasoning*. Oxford: Oxford University Press.

Fischer, David Hackett. 1970. *Historians' Fallacies: Toward a Logic of Historical Thought*. New York: Harper & Row.

Flesher, Dale L. 1991. *50 Years of Progress Through Sharing*. Altamonte Springs, FL: Institute of Internal Auditors.

Flew, Anthony. 1984. *A Dictionary of Philosophy, 2nd ed*. New York: St. Martin's Press.

Flint, David. 1988. *Philosophy and Principles of Auditing: An Introduction*. Basingstoke, UK: Macmillan.

Fonfeder, Robert, Mark P. Holtzman, and Eugene Maccarrone. 2003. "Internal Controls in the Talmud: The Jerusalem Temple." *Accounting Historians Journal* 30, no. 1: 73–93.

Fox, Loren. 2003. *Enron: The Rise and Fall*. Hoboken, NJ: Wiley.

Friedman, Milton. 1982. *Capitalism and Freedom*. Chicago: University of Chicago Press.

Gendron, Yves, and Laura F. Spira. 2009. "What Went Wrong? The Downfall of Arthur Andersen and the Construction of Controllability Boundaries Surrounding Financial Auditing." *Contemporary Accounting Research* 26, no. 4: 987–1027.

Giroux, Gary. 2017. *Accounting History and the Rise of Civilization*. Two volumes. New York: Business Expert Press.

Global Compact. 2005. *Who Cares Wins: Connecting Financial Markets to a Changing World*. New York: United Nations Global Compact.

Hay, David. 2020. *The Future of Auditing*. Abingdon, UK: Routledge.

Henrizi, Philipp, Dario Himmelsbach, and Stefan Hunziker. 2020. "Anchoring and Adjustment Effects on Audit Judgments: Experimental Evidence from Switzerland." *Journal of Applied Accounting Research* 22, no. 4, 598–621.

Humphrey, C. 1991. "Audit Expectations." In *Current Issues in Auditing*, edited by M. Sherer and S. Turley, 3–21. London: Paul Chapman.

Institute of Chartered Accountants of India. 2009. *What Is an Internal Audit?* New Delhi: Institute of Chartered Accountants of India.

Jeter, Lynne W. 2003. *Disconnected: Deceit and Betrayal at WorldCom*. Hoboken, NJ: Wiley.

Kahneman, Daniel. 2011. *Thinking, Fast and Slow*. New York: Farrar, Straus & Giroux.

Ketz, J. Edward. 2020. "The Myth of Auditor Independence: Waking Up to Unconscious Bias." *CPA Journal*, February.

Knight, Frank H. 1921. *Risk, Uncertainty, and Profit*. Boston: Houghton Mifflin.

Koch, Christopher, Annette Köhler, and Kristina Yankova. 2016. "Professional Skepticism and Auditor Judgment: Does Trait Skepticism Mitigate the Recency Bias?" http://dx.doi.org/10.2139/ssrn.2880653.

Lee, Tom A. 1993. *Corporate Audit Theory*. London: Chapman and Hall.

———. 2002. "The Shame of Auditing." *International Journal of Auditing* 6, no. 3: 211–14.

Lenz, Rainer, and Florian Hoos. 2023. "The Future Role of the Internal Audit Function: Assure; Build; Consult." *EDPACS: The EDP Audit, Control, and Security Newsletter* 67, no. 3: 39–52.

Maradona, Agus Fredy. 2020. "A Qualitative Exploration of Heuristics and Cognitive Biases in Auditor Judgements." *Accountability* 9, no. 2: 94–112.

Matilal, Bimal Krishna. 1998. *The Character of Logic in India*. Albany: State University of New York Press.

Matthews, Derek, Malcolm Anderson, and John Richard Edwards. 1998. *The Priesthood of Industry: The Rise of the Professional Accountant in British Management*. Oxford: Oxford University Press.

Mautz, Robert Kuhn. 1954. *Fundamentals of Auditing*. New York: Wiley.

Mautz, Robert Kuhn, and Hussein A. Sharaf. 1961. *The Philosophy of Auditing*. Sarasota: American Accounting Association.

McElveen, Mary. 2002. "New Rules, New Challenges." *Internal Auditor*, December, 40–47.

McNamee, David, and Georges M. Selim. 1998. *Risk Management: Changing the Internal Auditor's Paradigm*. Altamonte Springs, FL: Institute of Internal Auditors.

Metcalfe, Lee. 1977. *Improving the Accountability of Publicly Owned Corporations and Their Auditors [The Metcalfe Report]*. Washington, DC: US Government Publishing Office.

Miller, Norman C. 1965. *The Great Salad Oil Swindle*. New York: Coward-McCann.

Moeller, Robert R. 2016. *Brink's Modern Internal Auditing: A Common Body of Knowledge*, 8th ed. Hoboken, NJ: Wiley.

National Commission on Fraudulent Financial Reporting. 1987. *Report of the National Commission on Fraudulent Financial Reporting [Treadway Commission]*. Washington, DC: National Commission on Fraudulent Financial Reporting.

Nelson, Irvine T., Richard L. Ratliff, Gordon Steinhoff, and Graeme J. Mitchell. 2003. "Teaching Logic to Auditing Students: Can Training in Logic Reduce Audit Judgment Errors?" *Journal of Accounting Education* 21, no. 3: 215–37.

Newman, Benjamin. 1964. *Auditing: A CPA Review Text*. New York: Wiley.

Normanton, E. L. 1966. *The Accountability and Audit of Governments: A Comparative Study* Manchester: Manchester University Press.

Olojede, Paul, Olayinka Erin, Osariemen Asiriuwa, and Momoh Usman. 2020. "Audit Expectation Gap: An Empirical Analysis." *Future Business Journal* 6, no. 10.

O'Regan, David. 2004. *Auditor's Dictionary*. Hoboken, NJ: Wiley & Sons.

O'Reilly, Vincent M., Patrick J. McDonnell, Barry N. Winograd, James S. Gerson, and Henry R. Jaenicke. 1998. *Montgomery's Auditing, 12th Edition*. New York, Wiley.

Porter, Brenda. 2018. "The Audit Expectation Gap: A Persistent but Changing Phenomenon." In *The Routledge Companion to Auditing*, edited by David Hay, W. Robert Knechel, and Marleen Willekens. Abingdon, UK: Routledge.

Power, Michael, ed. 1994a. *Accounting and Science: Natural Enquiry and Commercial Reason*. Cambridge: Cambridge University Press.

———. 1994b. *The Audit Explosion*. London: Demos.

———. 1997. *The Audit Society: Rituals of Verification*. Oxford: Oxford University Press.

———. 2000. "The Audit Society—Second Thoughts." *International Journal of Auditing* 4, no. 1: 111–19.

———. 2003. "Auditing and the Production of Legitimacy." *Accounting, Organizations and Society* 28, no. 4: 379–94.

———. 2022. "Afterword: Audit Society 2.0?" *Qualitative Research in Accounting and Management* 19.

Prasad, Krishna, Nandan Prabhu, and K. Sankaran. 2019. "Relationship Between Gray Directors and Executive Compensation in Indian Firms." *European Journal of Management and Business Economics*.

Ratliff, Richard L., and Kurt F. Reding. 2002. *Introduction to Auditing: Logic, Principles, and Techniques*. Altamonte Springs, FL: Institute of Internal Auditors.

Sangster, Alan. 2018. "Pacioli's Lens: God, Humanism, Euclid, and the Rhetoric of Double Entry." *Accounting Review* 93, no. 2: 299–314.

Saputra, Komang, Adi Kurniawan, and Putu Budi Anggiriawan. 2021. "Accounting, Auditing and Corruption in Kautilya's *Arthasastra* Perspective." *South East Asia Journal of Contemporary Business, Economics and Law* 24, no. 2: 67–72.

Sawyer, Laurence B., and Gerald Vinten. 1996. *The Manager and the Internal Auditor: Partners for Profit.* New York: Wiley.

Schandl, Charles W. 1978. *Theory of Auditing: Evaluation, Investigation, and Judgment.* Houston: Scholars Book Company.

Schwartz, Mimi, and Sherron Watkins. 2003. *Power Failure: The Inside Story of the Collapse of Enron.* New York: Doubleday.

Scruton, Roger. 2002. *The West and the Rest: Globalization and the Terrorist Threat.* New York: Continuum.

———. 2007. *Dictionary of Political Thought*, 3rd ed. Basingstoke, UK: Palgrave Macmillan.

Smith, James E. 1975. *An Evaluation of Selected Internal Auditing Terms [IIA Research Report 19].* Altamonte Springs, FL: Institute of Internal Auditors.

Spacek, Leonard. 1989. *The Growth of Arthur Andersen & Co., 1928–1973: An Oral History.* New York: Garland.

Systems and Productivity Improvement Bureau. 2020. *Revised Philippine Government Internal Audit Manual.* Manila: Systems and Productivity Improvement Bureau.

Taleb, Nassim Nicholas. 2007. *Black Swan: The Impact of the Highly Improbable.* New York: Random House.

Toffler, Barbara Ley, and Jennifer Reingold. 2003. *Final Accounting: Ambition, Greed, and the Fall of Arthur Andersen.* New York: Broadway Books.

Turnbull Report [Internal Control: Guidance to Directors on the Combined Code]. 1999. London: Institute of Chartered Accountants in England and Wales.

Whyte, William H. 1956. *The Organization Man.* New York: Simon & Schuster.

Woller, Basil. 2017. *Quality Assessment Manual for the Internal Audit Activity.* Altamonte Springs, FL: Internal Audit Foundation.

Wolnizer, Peter W. 1987. *Auditing as Independent Authentication.* Sydney: Sydney University Press.

About the Author

David J. O'Regan is auditor general of the Pan American Health Organization in Washington and a fellow of the Institute of Chartered Accountants in England and Wales. His previous posts include auditing for the Organisation for the Prohibition of Chemical Weapons in The Hague, and, before entering the United Nations system, serving as head of audit at Oxford University Press. He has written six books on auditing, including *Bribery: Identify Hidden Risks in Your Organization* (Institute of Internal Auditors, 2014). He received his doctorate in accounting and finance from the University of Liverpool.